CRISES AND OPPORTUNITIES

Crises and Opportunities

The Shaping of Modern Finance

YOUSSEF CASSIS

OXFORD
UNIVERSITY PRESS

OXFORD

UNIVERSITY PRESS

Great Clarendon Street, Oxford OX2 6DP,
United Kingdom

Oxford University Press is a department of the University of Oxford.
It furthers the University's objective of excellence in research, scholarship,
and education by publishing worldwide. Oxford is a registered trade mark of
Oxford University Press in the UK and in certain other countries

First Edition published in 2011
First published in paperback 2013

Impression: 1

British Library Cataloguing in Publication Data
Data available

Library of Congress Cataloging in Publication Data
Data available

ISBN 978–0–19–960086–1
ISBN 978–0–19–967243–1 (pbk.)

Printed in Great Britain
on acid-free paper by
MPG Books Group, Bodmin and King's Lynn

Contents

Foreword

One hundred and twenty-five years of history can seem like both a short and a long time. Short when you consider that the history of private banking can be traced back almost four hundred years. Long when you consider that the Pasche group has successfully lived through eight major global financial crises, astutely examined in the pages of this book by Youssef Cassis, Professor and Director of the Department of Economic History at the University of Geneva. Despite some upheavals in its time, the firm has nevertheless managed to draw strength from some of these financial crises. Now, on the strength of its tightly knit global network and its business model founded on international private banking, the Geneva-based bank is enjoying a period of rapid expansion, with excellent prospects of long-term, sustainable growth in the years to come.

The Pasche group has experienced three major phases in its history. These stages are referred to as 'origins', 'transformation', and 'expansion' in what follows; each of these cycles is specific to the international financial situation of the time.

ORIGINS

It all started back in 1885 with the foundation of 'Messieurs Girard Roux & Cie', a foreign-exchange office in Geneva. At the time, the world of finance was about to experience its first-ever truly 'global' crisis as a result of countries defaulting on sovereign debt, in Argentina and Uruguay in particular. Despite this period of international financial instability, the first solid foundations of the group had been laid in Geneva. But it did not yet have the title or go by the name that makes the Banque Pasche group what it is today. These were to come fifty years later with the arrival on the scene of Geneva banker and former representative of Lombard Odier: Albert Pasche. Upon his appointment as an associate of the company in 1935, the new institution first changed its name to 'Girard Pasche & Cie', before opting for the more elegant 'Messieurs Pasche & Cie, agents de change'. As the last part of the name would indicate, the company also offered its management skills as brokers and foreign-exchange agents. Very rapidly, it earned itself a good reputation on the more promising markets of the time, such as those in South America and Russia, by offering its clients shares in bond debt. This phase of growth came to an end in 1957 with a last change of status, which transformed the institution into a joint stock company. It was at this time that the firm started to consolidate its activities from its base in Switzerland. It was also as a result of this most recent transformation that Prince Louis Napoléon (a descendant of Jérôme Bonaparte, the King of Westphalia and youngest brother of Napoléon Bonaparte), Lyonnaise de Banque, and the Italian group Banca Nazionale del Lavoro took a stake in the capital of the new entity. Thus, in 1957, the final building block was put to the edifice of what we know today as Banque Pasche. At the time, the group had all the necessary skills at its disposal to begin to establish itself in the field that has now come to be known as international private banking.

TRANSFORMATION

In 1981, when the Left won the elections in France, Prince Louis Napoléon, sensing that nationalization was on the horizon, sold his stake in the bank to CIC Lyonnaise de Banque. Frightened by this prospect, the French clients who had sought a safe haven in Switzerland were handed over to another private bank in Geneva. Moreover, this fear proved to be well founded as CIC was nationalized by the French government the following year. Despite intimations of a possible privatization by Jacques Chirac (French Prime Minister from 1986 to 1988) several years later, these clients were never to return to the group. In 1988, four years after the death of Albert Pasche, CIC used its new-found freedom resulting from partial privatization to acquire the entire stake held by Banca Nazionale del Lavoro. As a result, it became the majority shareholder in Banque Pasche. It was only later, after several changes in ownership in 1994, that CIC handed over control of the bank, in two phases, to a number of its management staff, itself retaining only a 9 per cent share in the capital.

EXPANSION

When CIC reassumed control of Banque Pasche at the end of 1996 (fully privatized this time), the synergies existing between the two entities were clear to see. In particular, this gave the group the opportunity to regain a foothold in international asset management. Importantly, while the acquisition did require an injection of funds of 75 million francs to be made by CIC, this investment was more than compensated for by the resulting increase in the valuation of Banque Pasche. The acquisition thus proved to be a very profitable operation. At that time, it is also worth recalling that the core activity of CIC was retail banking, while the activity of Banque Pasche was rooted firmly in private banking. CIC's portfolio consisted mainly of clients from the trade and business sector. It was, of course, also serving private customers but essentially with a retail banking profile. In contrast, Banque Pasche could boast a loyal international client base, spread over more than seventy countries, and this is where its strength lies today.

When I joined the bank in 1998, first as Senior Vice-President, before being promoted to the position of President and CEO of the Banque Pasche group in 2000, I embarked upon a programme of sustained expansion with the full support of the shareholders and my teams. We started to deploy a business model, the relevance of which continues to be seen today. This was to mark the start of a period of regular and powerful growth, based on a perfect synergy with our parent company, which has always been exemplary in its support for our ambitious project to embody a bold, new, more straightforward, and transparent vision of private banking.

Today, this desire to extend its activities to all four corners of the globe is something that is clearly at the heart of the group's approach. Starting in 1998 with the inauguration of an office in Monaco, Banque Pasche went on to establish a presence in Nassau the following year. Development beyond the confines of the Geneva marketplace soon put new financial resources at the group's disposal. It was only once this period of drastic restructuring was complete in 2000 that we could allow ourselves to focus on a strategy of external growth, in Europe in particular. We can now safely say that this strategy was the right one. But it took a few years to turn the vision into reality. So, in 2005, with Banque Pasche reaping the rewards of its successful, organic growth, the decision was taken to build on that base by making external acquisitions further to accelerate its development. This led to the acquisition of Swissfirst Bank in Zurich in 2007. Why did we specifically choose that institution? Quite simply because it has a very well-diversified client base, one that is essentially onshore and that we can deploy on the trading market. The fusion of the two banks thus proved to be a profitable initiative, the jewel in the crown being the Swissfirst building in Zurich, a veritable architectural masterpiece. In the same year, the group completed the acquisition of Agefor. Subsequently, the bank also opened a branch office in Montevideo, giving the group excellent access to the asset-management market in Latin America.

This external growth was not to stop there. On the strength of our success, we decided to pursue the policy of external acquisitions further. In 2008, our ongoing expansion was underlined by the takeover of the Liechtenstein bank SFL. This operation led to an increase in managed assets. To some Banque Pasche may have seemed reticent about going ahead with this acquisition.

But nothing could be further from the truth. Most importantly, it is an impeccably run bank on a closely controlled financial market. At the same time, Liechtenstein continues to enjoy a global reputation in the creation of foundations. The client base of SFL is diverse and spread across several continents. This obviated the political risk that has recently been seen with the principality hitting the headlines concerning its relations with its powerful neighbour. Finally, with the main shareholders also bringing business to the table, this acquisition allowed us to benefit from local experience and expertise. This acquisition will soon generate economies of scale in logistics and bring us a new clientele in geographical areas where the development of Banque Pasche has, until recently, been a little lacking. Only time will tell us what real benefits this will bring.

The companies Valeroso and Alternative Gestion also joined the group in that same year. The aim of these acquisitions was further to strengthen the Family Office segment. Further afield, the bank consolidated its international network with the opening of branch offices in Dubai, Shanghai, Sao Paulo, and Rio de Janeiro, four nerve centres of countries with high economic growth potential. This deployment of onshore skills and resources allows us to offer a special level of service close to where our clients are located. This banking network, which is now well established, allows us to maintain an ongoing and fully personalized relationship with each and every one of our clients by offering a range of products and services individually tailored to their needs. This means that Banque Pasche is able to offer clients the same level of attentive service and responsiveness across all its entities and on all continents. We know the meaning of 'made-to-measure'.

BUSINESS MODEL

Our growth has been ongoing since 2005. The strength of our results is living proof that our business model, which places the emphasis firmly on international private banking, is bearing fruit in the long term. By devoting all our skills and resources to our core activity of private banking, we can but further strengthen our expertise. Moreover, the fact that the development model adopted by the bank is founded on building a closely knit international network is of crucial importance precisely because it allows our clients to stay mobile. This means we need to be targeting new, attractive, and innovative areas such as Brazil and Uruguay. In addition to Latin America, we shall also be focusing our attention on developing an onshore client base in countries such as India and China, which are now experiencing booming economic growth. In this way, the mobility that our network is in a position to offer will enable us to make the most of each location for our clients, no matter what challenges are presented by local financial markets and their sometimes far-from-optimal approaches to regulation. Another strength of Banque Pasche lies in its open architecture, which allows it to maintain performance as its absolute priority at all times. This type of organization, which allows the group to offer a totally independent approach, lends genuine credibility to our group, and is the key to us being able to offer our clients the very best financial products available on the market. It is also essential never to neglect the importance of 'points of entry' for new clients. These must be manifold. By offering all the services expected of a traditional bank in conjunction with those provided by the Family Office (through Serficom in particular), we are able to cover all the needs of a demanding, international clientele. Furthermore, our close contact with local partners also gives us the wherewithal to provide the added value of consulting services in a wide variety of areas, including the art, precious stones, and real-estate markets.

Our success is not only founded upon our choice of business model and its structure. It stems also from the ability to anticipate risk. We were able to protect our clients' assets during the subprime crisis by taking preventative measures to drastically limit the extent of our involvement in hedge funds in July 2008, a good three months before the speculative bubble finally burst in October. Our rigorous investment strategy, bound as it is by very strict rules, also meant we avoided buying into the financial vehicles offered by the now-defunct Lehman Brothers and the now, alas somewhat infamous, Mr Madoff. A similar sceptical approach was adopted to the financial products offered by the Icelandic banks, which promised levels of yield that were disproportionate to market conditions.

VISION FOR THE FUTURE

One thing is certain: 2010 is set to be a pivotal year. In order to stimulate external growth abroad, and particularly in the emergent countries falling under the acronym BRIC (Brazil–Russia–India–China), we have the firm intention of opening up the capital of Banque Pasche. To do this, it is essential to be able to work with reliable international financial partners. The reason for this decision to open up the capital to other continents lies in the fact that Europe is today 'polluted' by offshore management.

The other objective is to use the skills at our disposal in asset management to best effect both in Switzerland and on all the other financial markets where we operate. For it should not be forgotten that we are now, after many years of flat calm, witnessing a rapid and irreversible process of the legalization of assets. More than any fears and concerns this may generate, this new situation in fact represents an excellent opportunity for Banque Pasche.

The existence of Banque Pasche has of course been deeply marked by the financial and banking history of the last century. Its development is dependent on advances in banking tools and the stability of the international financial system. But it is also affected by crises. Any group that is celebrating its 125th anniversary must know how to stay on course even when the winds are contrary. While it may be easy to maintain one's course in calm waters, it is only when the big storms hit that you can truly appreciate the skills of a good captain.

This brings us to the deeper purpose of this book. The idea is to offer the reader a historical perspective on banking and to provide clues as to how we may best learn the lessons of the past. This is also why we have asked Youssef Cassis to shed some light on the major global banking crises that have had an impact on Banque Pasche. This recognized specialist in the history of banking, finance, and business has identified eight such crises. We will mention just a few here. The first of them occurred in 1890 with the troubles that hit Barings Bank in Argentina. The world of finance was later shaken by the collapse of trust companies in 1907. Then there was, of course, the Great Depression of the 1930s. This very painful period is, for obvious reasons, the first point of reference in any discussion of the subprime crisis, and this book seeks to highlight both the points in common and the differences between these two periods. Later in its history, the group was faced with the end of the fixed exchange-rate system and the upheavals it entailed that led to the banking crisis of the early 1970s. The international debt crisis of the early 1980s is also not to be forgotten, closely linked as it was to the pouring of petrodollars into the economy, finally giving rise to credit of pharaonic proportions granted to Third World countries, to use a now unfashionable coinage. The triggers for each of these financial upheavals are, of course, different, but in each case it is possible to trace them back to the same underlying origins: a sudden and abrupt loss of confidence in the markets, an extremely poor assessment of the risk, and a slowness to react on the part of the authorities. So there are some similarities between each of these crises.

In this history of the trials and tribulations of the world of finance that you are about to read, Youssef Cassis also looks at the more recent topic of the subprime crisis, even though this period is perhaps still a little fresh in our memories to be studied from a historical point of view. It is important to point out that the historical questions raised in this book are focused particularly on the acute events of 2007–8. In the view of Youssef Cassis, this most recent crisis, with its tsunami-like effect, is comparable, though to a more serious degree, to the crisis of 1982 because of the excessive risk-taking behaviour. Never before has the world of finance been so close to the brink of total implosion. What the global effects of the recovery plans and the massive injections of liquidity into the international financial system made by states will be is something only time will tell. Despite the many relevant historical comparisons drawn in this book, it is still far too early to be able to analyse all the consequences.

This work attempts, in narrative form, to show, in detail, the failures of the international banking system and to identify their causes. We have not sought to adopt a quantitative and statistical approach. Our reasons for not doing so are clear: such a method allows us to gain a deeper insight into the relations that exist between politics, banking, and finance. We hope this book will provide you with keys to analysing the next financial crisis so that it can be better understood—and, most importantly, be overcome.

Christophe Mazurier

President and CEO of the Banque Pasche group
26 January 2010

Preface

This book has been written to mark the 125th anniversary of the Pasche group, now the private banking arm of the French group CM-CIC. To celebrate this anniversary, Banque Pasche has chosen to support an academic work that will be a contribution to banking and financial history. In March 2009, I discussed the topic with Christophe Mazurier. In the face of the magnitude of a shock from which we were just starting to recover, a historical reflection on financial crises was the only conceivable choice. There has been, since then, a huge demand for history—in order to compare the Financial Debacle of 2007–8 with previous ones, especially that of 1929, and to ponder on the direction of things to come in the light of past experiences. In commissioning this book, Banque Pasche has responded to the needs not only of the general public, but also of decision-makers in politics, business, and finance. I am grateful to Christophe Mazurier for giving me the opportunity to write this timely work. I only hope that it will contribute to the better understanding of a momentous event, which will be debated for years to come.

The history of financial crises is a vast subject. One question seems to me particularly relevant as the world's political and economic leaders struggle with the aftermath of the credit crunch: have financial crises in the past presented opportunities to rebuild the financial system? Reflecting upon eight global financial crises since the late nineteenth century, the study enquires into how the financial land-scape—banks, governance, regulation, international cooperation, and balance of power—has been (or has failed to be) reshaped after a systemic shock. The book is the work of a historian and is rooted in a narrative account without, however, neglecting the contribution of financial economics to the analysis of financial crisis. Without the sacrifice of scholarly rigour, the style adopted is not intended primarily for specialists, even though they too should find plenty to appreciate here. I hope that not only academics, particularly historians, economists, and other social scientists, and practitioners of banking and finance, but all those wishing to make sense of the Financial Debacle of 2007–8 by putting it in a historical perspective, will find reading this book worthwhile and enjoyable. It would have been impossible to write it without the contribution and advice of many colleagues and trusted friends. I would like to thank, in particular, Edoardo Altamura, Stefano Battilossi, Mikael Bourqui, Philip Cottrell, Michel Dacorogna, Yann Decorzant, Juan Flores, Mary O'Sullivan, Laure Quennouëlle-Corre, Ileana Racianu, Richard Roberts, Janette Rutterford, Catherine Schenk, Richard Sylla, Jean-Jacques Van Helten, and Patrick Verley. I should also like to thank Sandra Sestito, of Banque Pasche, David Musson, at Oxford University Press, and their teams, for help and support, and for making it possible to produce this book. I am, of course, responsible for any errors that may remain and for the views that are expressed in it.

Youssef Cassis
March 2010

Introduction

The Financial Debacle of 2007–8 has raised many questions, at economic, political, social, and international levels, revolving around its causes and its consequences. How did we get there? Where do we go from here? For years to come, economists, historians, and other social scientists will attempt to answer these questions. While the first one will remain the same, the second will gradually become: where *did* we go from there, and how? It is with this second question that this book is primarily concerned, even though the present tense is still being used. It could be argued that dealing with this issue is rather premature. The answer is: yes and no. Yes, because nobody, least of all historians, can predict the future, so the exercise might be judged futile. No, because history can inform discussions regarding the future: an enquiry into the effects of past financial collapses could be illuminating in the current turmoil, and historians have a unique role to play.

There remains much uncertainty about the outcome of the crisis. Some questions are of a general, others of a more specific order; some are still topical, others already, or in the process of being, outdated. In the early days of the crisis, for example, there was some concern about the future of capitalism.[1] Not so much its survival as a mode of production—as a matter of fact, capitalism has never *really* been under threat during an economic crisis in the last 200 years—as the type, or types, of capitalism most likely to prevail after the downturn. Has the 'Anglo-Saxon' model of market-dominated capitalism had its day? Has the European model of a more regulated and socially conscious capitalism still something to offer? Is there room for the emergence of a new model, possibly influenced by Asian practices? The debate, however, has moved on. In early 2009, the main area of anxiety was about the effects of the financial crisis on the 'real economy' and the risks of what has been labelled the 'Great Recession' turning into a 'Great Depression'.[2] Attention was focused on the discretionary fiscal measures taken by governments in order to prevent such an outcome. As they appeared to have worked, questions were raised about the right exit strategies and the long-term consequences of the deterioration of fiscal balances. By the time this book has been published, new questions will no doubt have arisen.

However, given the violence of the shock and the direct responsibility of financial institutions for the outbreak of the crisis, many questions have unabatedly revolved around the financial sector itself. Have banks become 'too big to fail'? Should commercial banking be separated from investment banking? Have bonuses been responsible for the excesses leading to the crash? Should financial institutions be more tightly regulated? Will the financial sector shrink significantly in the foreseeable future? Will Wall Street and the City of London retain their world leadership or will they be upstaged by financial centres in Asia or the Middle East? Finance services play a central role in post-industrial societies and their future shape is of prime importance to all other questions, not least the exit from the current recession and the rebuilding of a more sustainable model of economic growth. It has repeatedly been said that this crisis offers a unique opportunity to reshape the financial system. Will the opportunity be seized, should it be seized, can it be seized? Is there much scope for reform in the face of the developments of financial activities since the 1980s? Is the current economic, political, social, and international context conducive to radical reform?

This book is an attempt to revisit the history of financial crises in the light of these very contemporary questions. In no way should this be seen as an instrumentalist approach to history. Historical research does not take place in a vacuum; its agenda has always been dictated, more or less directly, by the challenges faced by a changing world. Financial crises have periodically wrecked the financial system. To what extent have they also contributed to its shaping? Surprisingly no historical work has seriously attempted to deal with this question. The history of financial crises is in itself hardly a new topic. Innumerable accounts of individual crises are available—the most famous undoubtedly being John Kenneth Galbraith's *The Great Crash 1929*, published in 1954 and never out of print since then. Broader comparative analyses are of necessity less common. The classic work remains Charles Kindleberger's *Manias, Panics, and Crashes*, originally published in 1978 and also constantly re-edited—a masterful essay combining a long-term (1720–1975) historical perspective with a (non-mathematical) economic model. Kindleberger was interested mainly in speculative booms and the financial crises they provoked, the panics that followed, and the role of the lender of last resort.[3] Moreover, the crises of the late twentieth century have generated a new literature, of a more quantitative nature, based on comparisons over time and across countries, and mainly concerned with the macroeconomic aspects of financial crises.[4] Carmen Reinhart and Kenneth Rogoff's book published in 2009, *This Time is Different*, a quantitative analysis spanning eight centuries, belongs to this genre and is primarily concerned with showing that, however different financial crises appear to be, they display remarkable similarities, in both time and space.[5]

Less attention has been paid to another side of the history of financial crises: their effects on the financial architecture. We know, of course, about banks' bailouts, banking concentration, the lender of last resort, financial regulation. But our knowledge remains patchy, limited to a single country, the aftermath of a single crisis, or a single aspect of the financial system. Few historical studies have analysed, in a long-term historical and comparative perspective, the extent to which major crises have redesigned banking firms, increased or decreased the level of state intervention, reformed corporate governance, encouraged international cooperation, or provoked fundamental shifts in global financial and geo-political power—in other words how financial crises have not only undermined, but also reshaped the financial world. These are the main issues that this book intends to address.

Charles Kindleberger has described financial crises as being 'like pretty women: hard to define but recognizable when encountered'. Economists distinguish between currency crises, banking crises, and twin crises, combining banking and balance-of-payment problems. Hundreds of financial crises have broken out across the world since the mid-nineteenth century.[6] Their depth and, especially, their international character have varied considerably. The Financial Debacle of 2007–8 was a global crisis that started in advanced economies, in the first place the United States, and historical comparisons are most effective when involving countries presenting a relative homogeneity—in economic but also social and political development. Consequently, this study will concentrate on major financial crises—those whose reach can be considered to have been global or to have involved one, or several, of the main financial powers. Particular attention will be paid to banking crises, which are particularly relevant from our perspective; and the notion of 'crisis' will be understood in the broad sense of the word, including both short and acute shocks and longer periods of deep instability. Crises erupting in emerging economies have not been included in the analysis, because they present a different reality—at economic, social, and political levels. Financial crises have been far more disruptive in emerging economies, not only because of their lesser degree of economic and financial development, but also because of the balance of power between the core and the periphery. Some financial panics in advanced economies have been caused by financial crises in emerging ones—the Baring Crisis of 1890 and the International Debt Crisis of 1982—and in those cases due attention will be paid to both sides of the problem, and to the way the core industrial countries have been able to absorb the shock and transfer it to the periphery.

Eight financial crises will be taken into consideration for our analysis: the Baring Crisis of 1890; the American Panic of 1907; the Financial Crisis of July–August 1914; the banking crises of the Great Depression of the 1930s; the Financial Instability of the early 1970s and the ensuing bank failures; the International Debt Crisis of 1982; the Japanese Banking Crisis of 1997–8; and the Financial Debacle of 2007–8.

The number of cases might appear limited, given the hundreds of financial crises recorded in recent quantitative analyses. However, it should be remembered that, apart from the Great Depression, the vast majority of financial crises have taken place in emerging economies, and most were currency crises.[7] Other financial crises have broken out in advanced economies since 1890, but they have been confined, either to small or peripheral European countries (Italy, Spain, Portugal, and, especially, Norway in the early 1920s; Spain, Norway, Finland, and Sweden from the late 1970s to the early 1990s) with little spillover on, and limited interest aroused in, other countries; or to circumscribed episodes in a major economy (Continental Illinois in 1984 and the savings and loans crises in the 1980s in the United States, the Bank of Credit and Commerce International in Britain in 1991, the Crédit Lyonnais in France in 1993, and Long-Term Capital Management in the United States in 1998).

The eight selected crises have been the most serious, not necessarily in terms of loss of output, but in terms of systemic risk. Apart from the American Panic of 1907 and the Japanese Banking Crisis of 1997–8, it was during these crises that a real risk of collapse of the international financial system presented itself—even if the panic was not caused by financial recklessness, as in 1914, or the danger was not absolutely imminent, as in 1982. As far as the Financial Debacle of 2007–8 is concerned, it is with these crises that the most significant parallels can be established, especially, in connection with the main theme of this book, the opportunity to reform the banking system that they might have offered. The American and Japanese crises have, nevertheless, been included, because they affected respectively the world's largest (already by a significant margin in 1907) and second largest (and still the most dynamic in the 1980s) economies; and, especially for the American Panic of 1907, because their international impact was far from negligible.

Earlier crises could have been taken into consideration. The 'Bagehot principle' of lender of last resort, which was to play a decisive role in the development of central banking worldwide, evolved from the banking crises of the mid-nineteenth century in England, especially the Overend Gurney crisis of 1866. Overend, Gurney & Co. was Britain's largest bank when it closed its doors on Thursday, 10 May 1866, provoking previously unseen panic.[8] At the height of the crisis, the Bank of England lent without restriction to banks, discount houses, and merchants in the City. The fact was clearly acknowledged by the Governor, Lancelot Holland, at the meeting of the bank's proprietors later that year: 'We would not flinch from the duty which we conceived was imposed upon us of supporting the banking community'—prompting Walter Bagehot to conclude in *The Economist* and then in his influential *Lombard Street* that the bank had accepted its role of lender of last resort.[9] In France, the 'doctrine Henri Germain', from the name of the founder of the Crédit Lyonnais and its chairman until 1905, was shaped by the severe crisis that followed the crash of the Union Générale in January 1882.[10] Germain laid down the unwritten rule for commercial banks of maintaining liquid assets, in particular by avoiding industrial financing, an activity to be left to another type of bank, the *banque d'affaires* (investment banks). Our story starts a little later, with financial crises taking place in a globalized world, with their effects being felt beyond the frontiers of the country where they originated. The crash of Overend Gurney and the Union Générale remained respectively a British and a French affair. Yet their significance in the shaping of modern finance should not be overlooked.

The way financial crises have contributed to the shaping of modern finance has depended to a large extent on the type of shock they have provoked: its intensity, its duration, its causes, its broader economic consequences. It has also depended on the socio-political context in which the crisis has taken place, and the analysis of the event made by contemporaries. From this perspective, each financial crisis has been different from the other. On the other hand, financial crises have displayed common characteristics—in terms of causes, patterns of development, or economic consequences. Historians have always been confronted with this dilemma, without necessarily finding the two approaches antagonistic. With the exception of the panic of July–August 1914, caused by the coming of the First World War, all the crises discussed in this study, including the most recent one, fit in neatly with the anatomy of a typical crisis identified by Charles Kindleberger. They started with a 'displacement', an exogenous shock creating new profit opportunities, which was itself followed by a 'bubble', fuelled by a credit expansion. A period of 'financial distress', when investors, aware of the imminent crisis, started to sell but were still tempted to buy, preceded the 'crisis' itself, which was precipitated by a specific signal, such as a stock-market crash or the collapse of a major bank. 'Revulsion' and 'discredit' then led to a panic, which was quashed by the intervention of the lender of last resort.[11] The selected crises also fit in with the more quantitative analysis of Reinhart and Rogoff, emphasizing the systemic risks posed by excessive debt accumulation and the illusion that 'this time is different' prevalent in each boom.[12]

Quantitative analyses have their merits, but they also have their limits. They do provide wide-ranging correlations and categorizations enabling a better understanding of the causes of financial crises, their depth and length, their interaction with recessions, and the effects of policy responses. But they inevitably lump rather than split, emphasize the commonalities rather than the specificities, and, for some of them, run the risk of being anachronistic by comparing disparate periods and contexts. This book concentrates on a limited number of major crises and follows a qualitative approach—not as an alternative to quantitative analyses, but because it is more adapted to the purpose of the book. In the case of major crises, whose occurrence is not very frequent, the differences, in other words the singularity of each event, are of paramount importance—the more so if one is to understand how the opportunities for change have been identified and why they have, or have not, been seized. Such an analysis requires adopting a multiple point of view, taking into account not only the economic and business dimensions of the phenomenon, but also its political (at both national and international levels) and socio-cultural ones.

The book is divided into seven chapters. The first two briefly present the eight major financial crises that have affected the advanced economies between 1890 and 2010. Readers will not all be familiar with these events, whose history, surprisingly, is not always readily available, so it is important to set the scene. The following five chapters each address one central question that has been on the agenda since the outbreak of the 2007–8 crisis. The first is concerned with the banks themselves, in particular whether and since when they have been 'too big to fail', the concentration movement, and the level of performance. The second discusses governance, with special attention to ownership and control and bankers' responsibility in connection with banking crises. The third question deals with regulation, especially the link between the depth of a crisis and the demand for regulation; the regulation, or absence of regulation, of financial innovations; and the extent to which financial institutions and markets have been regulated and deregulated. The fourth has to do with international cooperation, its successes and failures, including the global regulation of the financial system. And the fifth pertains to the changes in the balance of power in international finance. Each of these five issues is discussed within the context of the 8 major financial crises of the last 120 years, looking, in particular, at how they have affected, and been affected by, each crisis. As will be seen, many factors have contributed to the shaping of modern finance. Financial crises have been only one of them—and not necessarily the forces for change that we would like them to be in the wake of the Financial Debacle of 2007–8.

1

Pre-War Crises

Four major financial crises broke out in the core industrial countries from the late nineteenth century to the Second World War: the Baring Crisis of 1890 in Britain, and the American Panic of 1907 in the United States, both with international repercussions; the Financial Crisis of July–August 1914, in all the leading financial centres; and the financial crises of the Great Depression, between 1929 and 1933, on a world scale—the last one thus consisting of several crises taking place at short intervals. There were, of course, others, but with little global impact. These four crises hit the advanced economies hardest during what has come to be known as the first globalization, an era that started around 1880 and ended with the Great Depression of the 1930s. The first part of this period, until 1914, was marked, in particular, by the surge in international capital flows (the stock of foreign investment increased nearly fivefold between 1870 and 1913, from under \$10 billion to nearly \$50 billion[1]); a monetary regime of fixed exchange rates, the gold standard; and Great Britain as the world's dominant economy. The First World War did not put an end to globalization, but it compromised it by profoundly disturbing the world economy. The gold standard was restored and capital exports resumed in the 1920s, but the legacy of the war (inflation, reparations and war debts, adaptation from a war economy to a peace economy, global imbalances, lack of world economic leadership) made any attempt at restoring the pre-1914 order extremely precarious.[2]

Significantly, the four major crises of the first globalization took place at four key moments in the period. The Baring Crisis erupted in the early stage in the process and shook the City of London at its apogee—which was to last another twenty-five years—as the financial centre of the world; the American Panic of 1907 hit New York as the

United States was fast moving from the position of an emerging to that of an advanced economy; the Financial Crisis of July–August 1914 came at a turning point in the world's history, and the Great Depression marked the end of the era. But the Great Depression was also a watershed in the history of financial crises—because of its severity; because of the amount of scholarly learning it has generated, not least in the field of macroeconomics; because of the lessons that have been drawn, if not in terms of prevention at any rate in terms of policy response; because of the establishment of international financial organizations that has taken place since the Second World War. The same mistakes might be continuously repeated, but financial crises took place in a different context before and after Bretton Woods.

THE BARING CRISIS OF 1890

The Baring Crisis is one of those few financial crises whose name is associated with a financial institution—in this case Baring Brothers & Co., one of the City of London's most prestigious and most powerful houses. Baring Brothers collapsed in November 1890. The catastrophic effects of the fall of a leading bank were avoided thanks to the preventive action of the Bank of England and the London banking community; but the panic shook the City and was followed by a deep recession. The Baring Crisis also had a global dimension—without, however, being a global crisis. It took place in a core industrial country, but was triggered by a financial crisis erupting in an emerging economy, Argentina, which had been the recipient of large capital inflows during the previous decade and where Barings was overcommitted. Moreover, the effects of the panic were felt in other Latin American countries and beyond.

In 1890, Baring Brothers was the oldest merchant bank in the City of London—the bank had been founded in 1763. Professionally, and for some of them also socially, the merchant bankers formed the 'aristocracy of the City'.[3] They remained in control of the two activities lying at the heart of London's position as the world's financial centre: financing world trade, through the acceptances of bills of exchange, and issuing foreign loans. Since the early nineteenth century, Baring Brothers had been the Rothschilds' great rivals. Definitely in the lead in the acceptance business (£15 million, out of a probable total of £90 million in 1890), it came second to the Rothschilds in the issuing business (especially the government loan market, though it dominated that of American railways, which were booming in the 1870s and 1880s), as well as in the City's overall standing.

It was in Argentina, however, that the bank was most active. Barings had been associated with the republic since 1824, with a loan for the province of Buenos Aires, but it was not until 1880 that its involvement became really significant. The election of General Julio Roca as President that year marked the beginning of a new era. Control had been secured over the pampas (by expelling and often exterminating the indigenous Indians), opening this vast and fertile land to cultivation; Buenos Aires was integrated into the federation and made its capital; and a new national currency, convertible in gold and silver, was enacted in 1881. Argentina entered a period of fast economic growth, fuelled mainly by immigration (the population rose from 1.8 million to 3.4 million between 1870 and 1890) and capital imports. The country appeared particularly attractive to foreign investors, with the prospects of building railways to link the pampas to the main ports and of greatly increasing the export of wheat and meat thanks to improved transport facilities. Low interest rates in Britain and other European countries unleashed a foreign investment boom from which Argentina was one of the main beneficiaries. Between 1880 and 1890, fifty foreign loans were raised by Argentina's national, regional, and municipal governments, for a total of £78 million (twice as much as Brazil, a far more populated country), to which must be added another £30 million on behalf of the public mortgage banks, as well as investments in private companies.[4] British investment in Argentina rose from just over £5 million in 1885 to £23.2 million in 1889.

Foreign investment was directed mainly towards state-run development projects, especially railways, ports, and urban modernization, which made a positive contribution to the country's development (the railway network expanded from 732 kilometres to over 9,000 kilometres between 1870 and 1890), but greatly increased the national debt. The servicing of the debt, immediate and mostly in the form of fixed interests payable in gold, was to prove difficult because of the slow maturing of the development projects financed through overseas investment.[5] The country's foreign obligations eventually reached unsustainable levels during the speculative boom of the late 1880s.

In 1889, property sales were ten times their level in 1886 and scores of new companies were registered on the local stock exchange, where total transactions reached sky-high levels.[6] A crash duly followed in 1890.

The national government could meet its foreign-debt obligations as long as foreign capital continued to flow into Argentina, though the bubble was going to burst anyway. Despite some dissenting voices, especially in the wake of the suspension of convertibility in January 1885, investors remained fairly confident until 1887.[7] By 1889, the London press was talking overtly of crisis. The failure of the first issue (out of a planned three) on behalf of the Buenos Aires Water Supply and Drainage Company, offered by Barings in November 1888, pointed to a changing mood: more than half the preference shares were left in the hands of the underwriting syndicate. Higher interest rates in Europe and the end of a long swing in capital exports also played their part. In any case, British capital exports to Argentina, which had reached a peak of £23.2 million in 1889, dropped to £16.7 million in 1890 and £5.8 million in 1891.[8] Revenues from exports, for their part, were hit by the fall in world prices. The growing budget deficit and the continuing issue of paper money led to further depreciation of the peso. The gold premium rose steadily from June 1889— from 135 to 240 in March 1890 and to a peak of 310 in April.[9]

By March 1890, the national Treasury, the Provincial Bank of Buenos Aires, and the Banco Nacional were on the verge of bankruptcy. In May, the latter announced that it was suspending its dividend. The government attempted to raise funds by selling profitable state-owned railways to British interests, only to provoke a political outcry. A failed coup on 26 July 1890 led, nevertheless, to the forced resignation of President Juárez Celman and his replacement by Vice President Carlos Pellegrini. The Argentine government still found it impossible to service its external debt entirely. In November, the Minister of Finance urged Barings to arrange a loan, but by then the famous bank was no longer in a position to help.[10]

Sovereign debt crises in the nineteenth and early twentieth centuries, including the Russian default in 1917, rarely threatened the leading banking institutions in the capital exporting countries. Losses were usually borne by investors, who tried to recoup them in various ways—through investors' associations, such as the Corporation of Foreign Bondholders in Britain or the Association Nationale des Porteurs Français de Valeurs Mobilières in France, support from the bank that floated the issue, or government intervention. The

Baring Crisis was different. As was written in *The Economist* in November 1890: 'Had Messrs Baring Brothers been able to shift the burden of their South American obligations upon the investing public they would now have been standing erect.'[11]

Baring Brothers was the main agent for the Argentine government, though it faced competition from other banks in Britain and continental Europe. Between 1880 and 1890 it raised, by itself or with others, £27 million (out of a total of £78 million) on behalf of the national government, the Provincial Government of Buenos Aires, and the Council of the City of Buenos Aires.[12] Another £5 million was issued for a number of British registered companies.[13] Given its enormous prestige and its privileged relationships with the Argentine government, Baring Brothers was a market leader and its name was seen as a guarantee of the quality of a new issue. However, despite the information at its disposal, Baring Brothers had greatly misjudged the risks associated with Argentina and found itself saddled with vast quantities of assets that it could sell only with very heavy losses.[14] A major mistake was its involvement, in association with the Buenos Aires firm Hale & Co., in the Buenos Aires Water Supply and Drainage Company, which left it with over £2.5 million of unsold ordinary shares and debentures.[15] The firm had also opened large credits to banks, railway companies, and merchant houses. By the autumn of 1890, Barings was no longer able to meet its commitments. Loans from trusted private banks in the City (Martin & Co., Glyn, Mills, Currie & Co.) eased its position in September and October, but by early November it was advised to go to the Bank of England.

Barings' rescue was successfully organized in five days, between 11 and 15 November 1890, and in complete secrecy under the leadership of William Lidderdale, the Governor of the Bank of England. He first ordered an investigation of Barings' accounts, which showed that the bank was solvent but needed an advance of between £8 million and £9 million to meet its commitments. He then secured, through the Rothschilds, an advance of £3 million from the Banque de France and £1.5 million from the Russian government in order to strengthen the Bank's position. He also tried to obtain direct help from the British government, a request at first declined, though on Friday, 14 November, ministers agreed to increase the government's balance at the Bank of England and to bear half of any loss that might result from Barings' bills taken in during the next twenty-four hours. Finally, Lidderdale set up a guarantee fund, in which all the City's leading banks took part, to cover the Bank of England against any loss that might result from the liquidation of Baring Brothers & Co.[16]—an innovative procedure that was to be repeated in subsequent financial crises.

News of the Baring Crisis broke in the City after the guarantee fund had been put in place. Panic was thus averted, but contemporaries were fully aware of the 'systemic' risks of the firm's collapse on the London discount market, not least Lord Rothschild, head of N. M. Rothschild, Barings' great rival, who admitted that 'had Barings been allowed to collapse most of the great houses would have fallen with them . . . about 6 millions' worth of Bills are drawn daily upon London and an enormous proportion of this business passed through their hands.' Nevertheless, the Baring Crisis was followed by a severe recession, which lasted until 1893. Capital exports from Britain fell from £123 million in 1889 to £32 million in 1893, before gradually increasing from 1894 but not reaching their pre-crisis level before 1900.[17] French capital exports also fell, from Fr.913 million to Fr.127 million between 1890 and 1891, though they picked up earlier than in Britain.[18] Banking crises broke out in several countries, not least in Australia, where fifty-four out sixty-four banks closed in the crash of April and May 1893.[19] European investors showed a clear disaffection with Latin American securities.[20] As to Argentina, it suffered a severe depression, with real GDP falling by 11 per cent between 1890 and 1891.

THE AMERICAN PANIC OF 1907

The American Panic of 1907 was the first financial crisis to shake one of the world's main financial centres, in this case Wall Street, since the Baring Crisis seventeen years earlier. It was a very serious financial crisis—so serious that it led to the creation of the Federal Reserve System a few years later—and was followed by a deep recession. The crisis also had a global dimension, because of the interaction between international financial centres, and because of the new role of the United States in world finance.

By the early twentieth century, the United States could no longer be considered as an emerging economy. It had already become the world's largest, in terms of GDP level, in the 1870s and overtook Britain in terms of GDP per capita in the early years of the twentieth century.[21] It had also become an industrial superpower, with about a third of world manufacturing output, the largest firms, and the highest level of productivity. The United States was the top destination for foreign investment before the First World War, yet by the turn of the twentieth century, especially during the years 1897 to 1908, it had also become a major capital exporter.[22] As an international financial centre, New York was no longer only an entry point into a capital-importing country but also, increasingly, an exit point from a capital-exporting nation, as well as the financial heart of the world's most dynamic economy.[23] Nevertheless, New York was still dependent on the City of London—for capital imports, for the financing of American foreign trade, and for obtaining liquid assets and, ultimately, gold. Moreover, the fragmentation of the American banking system—networks of branches were prohibited from being established across different states—was a source of instability.

The American Panic of 1907 thus took place in a different geo-economic context from the Baring Crisis of 1890. It was also a banking crisis in the proper sense of the word: there were runs on several banks, some of which had to close their doors. However, the two crises differed in two main aspects, which are particularly relevant in connection with the Financial Debacle of 2007–8. First, in 1907, the banks whose failure threatened to sweep away the financial system were new, unregulated institutions rather than pillars of the banking establishment, as had been the case in 1890. Second, the Panic of 1907 had to be overcome without the intervention of a central bank—which did not exist in the United States.

The crisis was sparked by the failed attempt by F. Augustus Heinze, in mid-October 1907, at cornering the stock of the United Copper Company.[24] Heinze was an adventurer who made his fortune through a number of lawsuits against copper mining companies. He subsequently moved to Wall Street, where he entered into association with the dubious figure of Charles W. Morse and became the president of the Mercantile National Bank and a director of several other banks linked together through what was known as 'chain-banking'—a cascade of controlling interests from one bank to another and interlocking directorships. United Copper Company's shares collapsed on Wednesday, 16 October, causing the fall of two brokerage houses, including Heinze's brother's firm, Otto Heinze & Co., and Augustus Heinze was forced to step down as president of the Mercantile National Bank. Concerns about risks of insolvency led to a run on the bank, requiring the assistance of the New York Clearing House,[25] while concerns about possible runs on other banks kept growing. On Sunday, 20 October, the Clearing House ordered Heinze and Morse to resign from all their banking directorships in New York and confirmed its readiness to lend to troubled banks. These measures appeared to have put an end to the risks of a banking panic in New York, and the Mercantile National Bank resumed normal business on Monday, 21 October.

On that very day, however, the news that Charles Barney, president of the Knickerbocker Trust, had been involved in the affairs of Charles Morse and Augustus Heinze started to emerge: he was forced to resign from his post, while the National Bank of Commerce announced that it would no longer act as the Knickerbocker Trust's agent. The National Bank of Commerce, often referred to as J. P. Morgan's bank, was the country's second largest bank: its vote of no confidence was a devastating blow for the Knickerbocker Trust. A run on the bank on Tuesday, 22 October, forced it to suspend payment a few hours later.

The trust companies' function initially consisted in collecting deposits from a better-off clientele than that of the 'savings and loans'— American savings banks—and investing them in stocks and shares. They turned into real banks in the late nineteenth century without, however, being subject to the regulations of the national banks and the state commercial banks as far as reserves were concerned. It was not until 1906 that they were required by New York State (they were state chartered institutions) to hold reserves against deposits—15 per cent, a third of which was to be in cash, as against 25 per cent for national banks, half of which was to be in cash. They also became active in investment banking, playing a major role in financing companies through investment and holdings in issuing syndicates. Trust companies enjoyed a spectacular growth in the decade preceding the crisis: in New York State, their assets grew 244 per cent (from $396.7 million to $1.364 billion) as against 97 per cent for the national banks ($915.2 million to $1.8 billion) and 82 per cent for the state banks ($297 to $541 million).[26] But they were perceived as more likely to become insolvent in a financial crisis: they were lightly regulated, their activities were considered more risky,[27] and, not being members of the New York Clearing House, they could not benefit from its protection.

From the Knickerbocker Trust, runs soon spread to other trusts, first the Trust Company of America, on 22 October, and then the Lincoln Trust Company the following day. These were all large financial institutions: the Trust Company of America was the second largest trust company in New York, with about $100 million in assets, and the Knickerbocker Trust was the third.[28] Their collapse thus posed a threat to the entire financial system. By 24 October, money at call was no longer available on the New York Stock Exchange, even for 60 per cent; a week later the largest New York brokerage house, Moore & Schley, was on the verge of collapse; in the meantime the City of New York was facing bankruptcy, having tried and failed to issue bonds the previous summer.

A collapse was avoided thanks to the joint intervention, in the following days, of the secretary to the Treasury, George Cortelyou, and the New York banking community led by John Pierpont Morgan, with John Stillman, head of National City Bank, and George Baker, head of First National Bank. The Treasury deposited $25 million in the main reserve banks of New York to enable them to cover withdrawals. And Morgan organized a pool of $25 million in order to prevent the collapse of the Trust Company of America and the Lincoln Trust, convincing, in particular, the presidents of New York's trust companies to raise the required funds. This was followed by a second pool of $10 million to prevent the Stock Exchange from closing down. Other measures included issuing loan certificates by the New York Clearing House to increase the supply of currency to the public; underwriting a $30 million loan for the City of New York; and, more controversially, organizing the takeover of the Tennessee Coal, Iron and Railroad Company by the US Steel Corporation in order to prevent the failure of the brokerage house Moore & Schley, thus replacing unwanted Tennessee Iron and Steel shares by US Steel bonds.[29]

The American Panic of 1907 was caused by a combination of factors. It came after a long boom—a decade of vigorous economic growth, strong capital formation, and monetary expansion, as well as financial innovation, not least through the rise of the trust companies[30]—and it erupted in a tense economic climate and just as credit had become much scarcer on the New York market, following the San Francisco earthquake, in April 1906,[31] and measures by the Bank of England (higher discount rates and discrimination against American finance bills) to control gold flows. Trust companies, seen as the more innovative but also the riskier component of the system, were the most exposed to runs once scandal and malpractice further shook confidence—and were most affected by the crisis. Loans at trust companies contracted by 37 per cent between August and December 1907, as against 11 per cent at state banks, while they increased by 8 per cent at national banks.[32]

The Panic of 1907 resulted in one of the biggest recessions that the country had ever known.[33] Commodity prices fell 21 per cent, industrial production about 40 per cent, and the Dow Jones Industrial Index more than 35 per cent; bankruptcies were up 47 per cent over the previous year and unemployment rose from 2.8 to 8 per cent. It was associated with financial crises in Amsterdam, Hamburg, Genoa, and Copenhagen, as well as Chile and, especially, Mexico, which was dependent on investment flows from the United States.[34] The Panic occurred in the autumn, at the height of demands for credit from cereal exporters, demands that could be met only by purchasing huge quantities of gold from London. The Bank of England had to raise its discount rate, at first to 6 per cent, then to 7 per cent at the beginning of November, its highest level since 1873, and maintained it until January 1908—a severe blow, with the prospect of an increase in the discount rate to 8 or 9 per cent paralysing the City until the situation calmed down in the United States.[35]

In the end, however, the Panic of 1907 was very much an American affair and to a large extent can be ascribed to the organization of the American banking system, in particular its atomized structure and the lack of a central bank. Moreover, the New York Clearing House did not take any responsibility during the crisis, delaying the issue of loans certificates, as the unregulated trust companies were not among its members.[36] In any case, it was no substitute for a central bank.[37] To a contemporary such as Oliver M. Sprague, Harvard economics professor and a student of the American banking crises, institutional failure was the main cause of the Panic of 1907: 'there is reason to believe that [the crisis of 1907] might have been confined to narrow limits even if it could not have been entirely avoided. Nothing in the general economic condition of the country . . . can be regarded as so hopelessly unsound as to have rendered the explosion of last autumn clearly unavoidable.'[38]

THE FINANCIAL CRISIS OF JULY–AUGUST 1914

Wars cause the deepest shock to a financial system. The First World War did so possibly more than any other—whether one considers the business of banking (financing the growing needs of the state), the financial market (suspension or restrictions on stock-market activities), monetary conditions (suspension of convertibility, inflation), international capital flows (government guaranteed loans supporting the war effort), or the financial capacity of the belligerent powers before, during, and after the war. And yet a war cannot be equated with a financial crisis in the strict sense of the word—that is, a collapse or near collapse of the financial system. The financial system continues to function, indeed must continue to function, albeit in different conditions. Acute crises tend to occur at the very beginning and/or immediately after the end of the conflagration.

The Financial Crisis of July–August 1914 is one of the most serious ever to have hit the financial world. Never before, and never again until September 2008, was the international financial system so near collapse and in need of state intervention to rescue it. The causes, however, were different: the growing rumours of war and then the outbreak of hostilities, not an uncontrolled financial boom. And so were the sequels: the panic of 1914 was followed by a total war, not a severe recession, but the war itself was, of course, responsible for the economic instability of the 1920s and, ultimately, the Great Depression of the 1930s.

War was not totally unexpected. Financial elites adhered to the prevailing nationalism of the day, not least in their support for colonial imperialism, but this by no means implied that they hankered after war between the great powers. On the contrary, they knew perfectly well that banking and financial activities flourish in times of peace, not of war. This contradiction probably explains the huge success of the book by the liberal journalist Norman Angell, *The Great Illusion*, published in 1910. For Angell, European countries had become so interdependent economically and financially that war risked ruining both the victor and the vanquished. A conqueror harming his adversary's trade or finance would suffer similar losses in return. While having some grounds for hope, bankers and financiers, at least the most clear-sighted among them, were well aware of the danger. 'War still remains a possibility,' declared Frederick Huth

Jackson, chairman of the Institute of Bankers in London, at a meeting devoted to discussing Angell's book in January 1912.[39]

On 28 June 1914, the day Archduke Franz Ferdinand of Austria was assassinated, few in the world's leading financial centres had anticipated that war could break out within five weeks. In London, the Rothschilds were busy preparing their Brazilian loan and during the following three to four weeks were apparently unaware of the worsening of the international situation. On 22 July, the day before Austria sent the ultimatum to Serbia, they remained confident that war could be avoided and were happy to report 'the well founded belief in influential quarters that, unless Russia backed up Serbia, the latter will eat humble pie and the inclination in Russia is to remain quiet, circumstances there not favouring a forward movement'.[40] Six days later, on 28 July, Austria-Hungary had declared war on Serbia and within a week Europe was at war.[41] The financial world was taken entirely by surprise: 'The war came like a bolt from the blue and no one was prepared,' admitted Gaspard Farrer, a partner in Baring Brothers, a few days after the outbreak of hostilities.[42]

The lack of preparation and the surprise effect explain in large part the reactions of the markets as soon as a European war became, not a vague possibility, but a strong probability. From Thursday, 27 July, panic gripped all financial centres, though severe tension had been apparent from the 24th. It followed a similar pattern everywhere, as investors rushed for liquidity: collapse of stock exchanges; withdrawals of funds from banks and, their corollary, banks' demands that loans be repaid; pressure on the foreign exchanges; drain on gold; interest-rate rises; on top of which came the risk of non-payment—all this cumulatively threatened to trigger a series of bankruptcies and completely paralyse the credit mechanism.[43]

As the world's financial centre, the City of London was the most exposed to these upheavals.[44] One major problem concerned the liquidity of the bill market. The bulk of international trade was financed through the medium of bills of exchange, generally for three months, drawn on, or accepted by, the City's merchant banks. Before reaching maturity, these bills were discounted by specialized houses, the discount houses, which then resold them to British clearing banks, as well as to the foreign banks present in the City, which kept them in their portfolio. These bills thus lay at the heart of the huge London discount market, in which the banks of the entire world took part, directly or indirectly. When war broke out, bills amounting to some £350 million were in circulation on the London discount market and would have to be paid when they fell due—in other words, within a period of three months, with about £3 million to 4 million being due every day. And yet, owing to the outbreak of war, a good third of these drafts (about £120 million), whose drawers were from then on in the enemy camp, or in Russia, with whom all normal trading relations had been cut off, were likely to remain unpaid, thus forcing the acceptors to honour the guarantee that they had provided to the holders of these bills. But the merchant banks were unable to do this, their own funds amounting to a mere £20 million. The merchant banks were threatened with collapse, taking with them the discount houses, while the clearing banks faced huge losses, with part of their assets now 'toxic'—not only illiquid but probably worthless.

Another liquidity problem concerned the London Stock Exchange. On the one hand, stockbrokers were owed vast sums of money by foreign clients on whose account they had purchased securities, but, with the outbreak of war, these debts had become irrecoverable. On the other hand, the members of the Stock Exchange collectively owed £60 million to banks and £20 million to other financial institutions, on top of the £25 million worth of unpaid and outstanding transactions among themselves. Moreover, bank loans amounting to a total of £250 million were secured by stocks and shares.[45] Given the drop in prices, the need to sell off these stocks to reimburse loans risked bankrupting several houses and triggering a chain reaction. The London Stock Exchange, the last stock exchange still open in Europe, ceased trading on 31 July 1914, reopening only on 4 January 1915.

The City's complete credit mechanism was thus in danger of collapsing. The commercial banks' huge assets, upon which the entire edifice was built, were at risk of being frozen.[46] The rather panic-stricken reaction of their managers, who called in their loans and refused gold payments to their depositors, did little to calm the panic that seized London's markets.[47] Disaster was avoided thanks to the combined intervention of the Bank of England, the commercial banks, and the government. Monday, 3 August, was a Bank Holiday: it was extended until Friday, 7 August. By 6 August, the main measures to deal with the crisis had been decided. They included a general moratorium on payments, the suspension of the 1844 Bank Act, and the issue of £1 and 10s. Treasury notes. Bank rate, which had been raised from 3 to 10 per cent at the height of the crisis, between 29 July and 1 August, was reduced to 6 per cent, and to 5 per cent the following day. As for the discount market, the Bank of England, with the Treasury's backing, agreed on 13 August to discount all drafts accepted before 4 August.[48] Convertibility was suspended in practice, though not officially, as some people, including Keynes, believed that abandoning gold at the first warning would be detrimental to London's reputation.

In Paris, the amount of bank loans on the Bourse reached Fr.625 million (£25 million), 400 million of which were in the form of carry-over transactions. On 29 July, the Compagnie des Agents de Change postponed, with the agreement of the minister of finance, the traditional monthly settlements. On 31 July, with banks facing sustained withdrawals of funds and mounting gold requests at the Banque de France, the government decreed that commercial maturity dates and protest periods would be deferred, and on 1 August it authorized banks to limit withdrawals from current and deposit accounts. This near suspension of payment was eased progressively from the end of the year. The convertibility of the franc was suspended on 5 August.

Berlin was also panic-stricken. Falling prices led the stock exchange to close its doors on 30 July, and a run on the banks reduced their deposits by some 20 per cent—though the Reichsbank did not introduce a moratorium on debt, setting up lending offices to obtain liquid assets for banks in difficulty, a stopgap measure whose effects turned out to be highly inflationary.[49] Convertibility was suspended on 31 July.

Neutral countries were not spared. The Swiss stock exchanges (Zurich, Geneva, Basle) closed, the convertibility of the Swiss franc was suspended on 30 July, a banking moratorium was established on 2 August, and de facto suspension imposed when the National Bank limited withdrawals to Fr.200 on deposit accounts and Fr.50 on savings accounts.

Wall Street did not avoid panic either. The New York Stock Exchange closed its doors on 31 July, a few hours after the London Stock Exchange had done so, following the huge sale of American securities, mainly by Europeans, and the growing difficulties confronting the banks and large numbers of brokers. The United States' liabilities also fuelled worries about the country's ability to pay its debts, leading to an outflow of gold and a fall in the dollar's value during the first months of the conflict.[50]

The crisis of July–August 1914 lasted only a few days. In all countries, state intervention enabled business to resume under conditions that few contemporaries imagined would persist longer than a couple of months. The panic, however, was soon forgotten as the war took over and changed the banking world and its broader economic and financial environment far more profoundly than any crisis could ever have done. At the end of the war, the assets of the big banks, in belligerent and neutral countries alike, comprised mainly Treasury bonds and similar stocks.[51] On the stock exchanges, government securities regained the part that they had played at the dawn of the first phase of globalization,[52] as war expenditure led to a huge increase in the level of public debt.[53] The war, rather than the financial crisis of August 1914, was followed by serious economic difficulties: steep downturn in 1920–1; financial crises in smaller or peripheral European countries (Italy, Spain, Portugal, and, especially, Norway); rampant inflation in others (Germany, Austria). The world economy had become very different from what it had been a few years earlier, even if contemporaries, in their eagerness to re-establish the pre-war order, were not always fully aware of this. The changes brought about by the war were sources of the imbalances and instability that lay at the root of the Great Depression that hit the world in the 1930s.

THE GREAT DEPRESSION OF THE 1930s

The Great Depression of the 1930s—sometimes referred to simply as 1929—remains the most serious economic crisis in modern history and the yardstick by which other downturns have been measured since then. Is it a repeat of 1929? The question has been raised time and again: in 1974, for instance, with the onset of 'stagflation' following the first oil shock; in 1982, when Mexico defaulted on its sovereign debt; or in 1987, when the New York Stock Exchange's fall in one day, on 19 October (over 22 per cent), was actually higher than in October 1929. There are many other examples. And, of course, 2008 has been repeatedly compared with 1929 and the ensuing Great Recession unanimously judged as the most severe contraction to happen since then. However, on account of its duration and its effects, the Great Depression was on a far grander scale than any other crisis. It consisted of four interrelated shock waves: the Wall Street crash of October 1929, a series of banking crises occurring over a period of five years, the collapse of the world's monetary order, and, of course, an economic slump of dramatic proportions. World industrial output dropped by 36 per cent between 1929 and 1932, world trade by 25 per cent in volume and 48 per cent in value; the price of manufactured goods fell by 26 per cent and that of raw materials by 56 per cent.[54] Between 1930 and 1933, the average unemployment rate was 28.4 per cent in the United States and 34.2 per cent in Germany, the two countries most affected by the Depression.[55]

Two main questions arise when comparing 2008 with 1929: one concerns the nature of the financial crisis, the other the relationship between the financial crisis and the economic crisis. Narrowly defined, 1929 was a stock-market crash on Wall Street, not a banking crisis. The New York Stock Exchange soared after 1925, partly as a result of the euphoria of growth that marked the Roaring Twenties, speculative fever, inexperience, and, at times, also fraud,[56] but largely because of the progress of the American economy and particularly the rationalization of production and the introduction of new management methods. The top-performing shares of the period, such as RCA (Radio Corporation of America) or General Motors, reflected the companies' profitability and growth prospects. However, a bubble was clearly forming from 1928, especially in the new technologies.[57] Public confidence started to be shaken in the summer of 1929 by increasingly clear signs of an impending recession, and share prices started to fall in early October. One thing then led to another. The brokers were overwhelmed by the volume of sales, there were more frequent margin calls, and the ticker tape fell further and further behind the transactions. Without constant information on the share price levels, traders lost track of their positions, and panic gripped the Stock Exchange on Thursday, 24 October, Monday the 28th, and Tuesday the 29th, after the attempts by the market's main players to stabilize share prices.[58] The New York banks, supported by the Federal Reserve, increased their loans and managed to prevent a lack of liquidity and a series of bank failures. Having lost 30 per cent since its peak in August, the New York Stock Exchange stabilized in the first few months of 1930, as did the production and employment indices.

Unlike the banking crisis of September 2008, which was clearly the cause of the Great Recession, the Great Depression was not caused primarily by the Wall Street crash of October 1929. Its main causes lay in the international monetary system of the time, the gold standard, which was a fixed exchange-rate system, and in the monetary policies that this system generated. As Barry Eichengreen has clearly shown, the first symptoms of the crisis were seen as early as 1928, and were mainly the result of the Federal Reserve's decision to raise interest rates from spring 1928 in order to curb the wave of speculation on the New York Stock Exchange. That decision led to the interruption of America's capital exports and forced the central banks of countries dependent on that capital to adjust their balance of payments, to adopt restrictive policies to defend their currency's parity, and to become more deeply entrenched in the crisis. This was typically the case with Germany, as well as with other non-European countries such as Australia and Argentina. In the United States itself, the economic downturn reflected in the fall in industrial output in August 1929 became a deep depression not because of the Wall Street crash, though this did not help, of course, but because of the restrictive policy adopted by the Federal Reserve from 1930 and, in particular, in 1931.[59]

The banking crises of the 1930s happened once the economic crisis was well under way, between 1931 and 1934. Unlike the Debacle of 2007–8, they were more caused by, rather than being a cause of, the economic crisis, even though they helped to exacerbate the situation. Moreover, these banking crises did not break out simultaneously in all countries—despite the global nature of the Great Depression. Some, like Britain, escaped them altogether. In others, such as France, the crisis was protracted, but never very acute. Not surprisingly, the most serious banking crises occurred in the countries where the economic depression was most severe, the United States and Germany.

The first banking crisis to hit a major economy took place in the United States, in the autumn of 1930: 256 banks failed in November (with $180 million deposits) and 352 in December ($352 million).[60] However, it appears to have been a regional rather than a national crisis, without incidence of panic. About 40 per cent of bank failures took place in the St Louis District, mainly as a result of the collapse of one bank, Caldwell & Co., of Nashville, Tennessee, the largest investment bank in the South. In terms of deposits of failed banks, 45 per cent were in two districts, St Louis and New York.[61] The share of New York, where only six banks failed, was due to the failure of the Bank of United States, a fairly large bank, with $160 million deposits,[62] which collapsed on 11 December. A poorly managed bank, as was the Caldwell bank, it had grown somewhat recklessly in the 1920s and had been insolvent for several months. A plan to rescue it through a merger with four other banks, organized by the Clearing House and the Federal Reserve of New York, came to no avail and, being insolvent, the bank was allowed to fail. Intervention by the Fed prevented panic from spreading to the New York money market, and the impact of the crisis remained limited, though confidence was never fully restored.[63]

The year of the banking crises during the Great Depression, especially in Europe, but also in the United States, was 1931, and in that respect it is more relevant than 1929 for comparisons with 2008, despite significant differences.[64] Austria was the first casualty. On 8 May, the Credit-Anstalt informed the Austrian government and the Austrian National Bank that it had ended 1930 with a loss of 140 million schillings, amounting to about 85 per cent of its equity and 7.5 per cent of its total balance sheet.[65] The bank was founded in 1855 by the Rothschilds and counted among Europe's leading financial institutions before the First World War. However, it suffered from the dismemberment of the Austro-Hungarian Empire, Austrian hyperinflation, and the poor state of the country's economy in the 1920s. Its problems were compounded by its heavy involvement in industrial finance and by its merger in 1929 with Austria's second largest bank, the Boden-Credit-Anstalt, a troubled bank that had turned to the government for help. On 11 May, the Credit-Anstalt's problems were revealed to the public, together with a reconstruction plan, whereby the state, the Austrian National Bank, and the Rothschilds provided new capital. Despite the plan's favourable reception, the announcement led to a run on the Credit-Anstalt, as well as on most other Viennese banks. The Credit-Anstalt lost about 16 per cent of its deposits in two days and some 30 per cent in two weeks. The bank was kept afloat by the Austrian National Bank and the government with the help of a foreign credit. Austria suspended convertibility on 9 October 1931, and the Credit-Anstalt was finally reconstructed in 1933.[66]

The run on Austria was followed by a run on Germany.[67] Panic erupted on Monday, 13 July 1931, when the Darmstädter und Na-tional Bank (Danat Bank), one of Germany's three largest banks,[68] did not open its doors. This provoked a run of depositors on all banks, from the other big banks to smaller regional banks, savings banks, and cooperative banks. Some had to suspend payments entirely, most partially, deciding to pay only 20 per cent of the sums that their clients wanted to withdraw. Government intervention managed to recover the situation. The Chancellor, Heinrich Brüning, immediately ordered all banks to close for two days, during which another major bank, the Dresdner Bank, declared itself bankrupt. The banks made only limited payments when they reopened and resumed business properly only three weeks later, on 5 August for the commercial banks and on 8 August for the savings banks. In the meantime, exchange controls were introduced on 15 July in order to stem capital outflows. Germany was thus the first country to leave de facto the gold standard: the parity of the Reichsmark was maintained, but it was protected by the restrictions imposed on the free movement of capital, gold, and currencies. With state backing, the Reichsbank set up a new institution, the Akzept- und Garantiebank, in order to obtain credit for commercial banks and savings banks: by providing a third signature, it enabled the Reichsbank to discount bills drawn between banks. And the banks were reorganized and recapitalized, in return for 35–90 per cent of their capital, depending on the institution concerned.

Germany's banking crisis in July 1931 thus shares a number of similarities with the events of September 2008, both in its manifestations, with the country's major banks standing on the edge of the abyss, and in aspects of the rescue operation. But the context, and thus the deep causes, were different—because of the weakness of the German banks, and because of the weakness of the German currency, the Reichsmark. The weakness of the banks was only partly due to poor investment decisions and undue risk taking. They had been badly affected by war, inflation, and hyperinflation: between 1913 and 1924, the nine big Berlin banks had lost 43 per cent of their equity capital and 50 per cent of their reserves.[69] During the period of relative stability, between 1924 and 1929, they had faced strong foreign competition on their own turf, and had themselves been highly dependent on foreign funds, always subject to withdrawals: foreign deposits represented as much as 43 per cent of liabilities for clients in 1928.[70] And they were hit by the stock-market crash and the Depression as they were reconstructing their balance sheet. The weakness of the Reichsmark stemmed from the conditions in which it was born, in the wake of the traumatic 1923 hyperinflation, and from lingering doubts about the sustainability of its parity given the problems of the German economy. Concerns about the Reichsmark were compounded by international tensions, not least those related to the payment of German reparations.

There had been previous alerts before the panic of July 1931, in the spring of 1929, following the breakdown of the reparations conference in Paris, and in September 1930, following the Reichstag elections, when the Nazi Party unexpectedly won 107 seats. In both cases, fears about the currency led to deposit withdrawals and capital flight, mainly from German rather than foreign depositors. But the Reichsbank was able to control the situation. In 1931, similar fears about the currency, triggered by the 'Reparations Declaration' of 5 June 1931,[71] led to heavy deposit withdrawals—the Danat Bank lost more than 40 per cent of its deposits that month, the Dresdner Bank nearly 11 per cent, the other banks around 8 per cent—and flight out of the Reichsmark, first by Germans and other Europeans, eventually by Americans.[72] But there were also increasing doubts about the banks' solvency. The news that Nordwolle, the large textile company, to which the Danat Bank was known to have extended ample credit, had made a loss of RM200 million in speculative transactions exacerbated the situation. How imprudent had the bankers been? They did use short-term foreign capital to finance long-term investments, though universal banking does not seem to have been the main cause of the crisis.[73] Banks' assets had been damaged by the crisis, and, of course, some errors of judgement had been made. And, in July 1931, they were no longer able to obtain refinancing from the Reichsbank, whose gold and currency reserves shrank constantly after it had failed, when faced with conditions imposed by France, in its attempts to bail them out by means of a foreign loan, making the gold cover for banknotes drop below its statutory minimum.

From Germany, the crisis moved to Britain.[74] But it was a very different type of financial crisis—a currency, not a banking crisis, which alleviated rather than aggravated the economic crisis. Pressure on the pound had been almost constant since its return to the gold standard in 1925; but it intensified from 1929, owing to a loss of confidence in a British currency generally considered overvalued, with the Bank of England having to face increasingly frequent withdrawals of gold. The situation worsened during the summer of 1931 under the triple effect of the German crisis, the gap between foreign short-term claims on London and the British gold and currency reserves, and the extent of the budget deficit. The crisis took on a political dimension when the Labour government resigned on 24 August, faced with the need to reduce its budget deficit in order to be able to obtain two loans, totalling £80 million, from the United States and France. A government of national unity, still chaired by the Labour Prime Minister, Ramsay MacDonald, was formed, but the announcement of a new budget on 10 September did not soothe anxieties. Withdrawals of funds continued, and on 21 September 1931 the British government suspended the pound's gold convertibility, which henceforth floated in relation to the main currencies. It was immediately followed by twenty-five countries, mainly from the British Empire, Eastern Europe, Scandinavia, as well as key trading partners such as Portugal and Argentina. Britain's abandonment of the gold standard marked the end of an era—the long nineteenth-century world economic order centred on Britain and the pound sterling. But its effects were highly beneficial to the British economy, as the Bank of England, relieved from its duty to defend the pound's parity, could embark on a policy of cheap money. Britain was the first country to emerge from the Depression, unlike the countries that remained on gold.

The effects of the pound's exit from gold were rapidly felt in the United States. A second banking crisis had already hit the country between April and August, with 563 bank failures totalling $497 million. However, it had remained fairly localized, with four federal districts accounting for about three-quarters of the casualties: Chicago, in the first place (one-third), as well as Minneapolis, Cleveland, and Kansas City.[75] The third crisis, in September and October, was more serious—817 banks failed, with deposits amounting to $747 million—and of a more nationwide character, despite the high share of three districts (Chicago, Philadelphia, and Cleveland) and the absence of crisis in New York. Pressure on the dollar and gold losses—more than $369 million between 21 September and 8 October—led the Federal Reserve to raise its discount rate from 1.5 to 2.5 per cent on that date, two and a half weeks following Britain's departure from gold, and to 3.5 per cent one week later. The suspension of the pound's convertibility appears to have aggravated the banking crisis in the United States—the number of bank failures increased significantly in October—mainly because, coming on top of the Austrian and German crises, it further undermined a badly shaken confidence in the financial system. However, the situation eased at the end the year, as confidence was this time boosted by the announcement by President Hoover, on 13 October, of the formation of the National Credit Corporation, whose objective was to rediscount banks' liquid but frozen assets.[76]

Unlike Germany, banking crises in the United States did not end in 1931. The number of bank failures remained comparatively high in

1932, without, however, the outbreak of a major panic. The open-market policy of the Federal Reserve and the loans by the Reconstruction Finance Corporation—a government-owned agency created in January 1932 to replace the National Credit Corporation, conceived as a banks' voluntary association—eased the situation. However, this action backfired in January 1933, when a decision by Congress required the Reconstruction Finance Corporation to publish a list of all the loans it had made the previous year. Such loans were seen as a sign of weakness and led to bank runs. The crisis was met with moratoria and bank holidays, starting, on a small scale, in Nevada in November 1932, followed by Iowa and Louisiana. But it was the decision by the Governor of Michigan to declare, on 14 February 1933, a state-wide bank holiday that sparked a panic that, in less than three weeks, was completely to paralyse the America banking system.[77] Moratoria and bank holidays accentuated the drain on banks in other states, not least in New York, where leading banks were dangerously dragged into the crisis. The National City Bank lost 33 per cent of its correspondents' deposits and 12.5 per cent of its domestic deposits in February 1933.[78] Roosevelt's uncertainty about a possible devaluation of the dollar during his long interregnum—he was elected on 8 November 1932—exacerbated the situation. By the time of his inauguration on 4 March 1933, forty-eight states had imposed banking restrictions, with banks being closed in thirty-three of them. On 6 March, Roosevelt declared a national bank holiday, at his first press conference on the 8th he stated clearly that the dollar would remain on the gold standard—it was eventually devalued on 19 April—and on 9 March Congress passed the Emergency Banking Act, which provided the legal basis for the reopening of the banks—a series of measures that restored confidence. One half of the country's banks, with 90 per cent of total banking resources, were judged capable of reopening for business on 15 March 1933, and their soundness was guaranteed by the government; another 45 per cent were to be reorganized before being licensed; and the remaining 5 per cent (about 1,000 banks) would have to close permanently.[79] In total, more than 10,000 banks, out of nearly 25,000 in existence in 1929, had closed their doors by 1933.

The banking crisis was less severe in France, the other financial power of the day. There was no real panic, despite the collapse of two big banks and a score of small regional and local banks. The Banque Nationale de Crédit (BNC), the country's fourth largest bank, suspended payments in 1931: it had lost about 20 per cent of its deposits between January and August when a run, starting in October, brought the loss to three-quarters by the end of the year.[80] In order to prevent a panic, depositors benefited from a state guarantee. The bank was built up again the following year, with help from the state, under the name of Banque Nationale pour le Commerce et l'Industrie (BNCI). The Banque de l'Union Parisienne, the second largest investment bank, shaken by the crises in Germany and central Europe, experienced serious difficulties that brought it to the brink of bankruptcy in 1932; but it was saved by the joint intervention of the Banque de France and the main Parisian banks.[81]

The financial crises of the Great Depression of the 1930s were thus very different from that of the Great Recession of the early twenty-first century—on account of their number, their duration, the type of banks affected, and the causes of bank failures. The crisis was global, its contagious effects spreading across the globe and contaminating most countries, yet each national crisis had a very specific configuration, determined as much by domestic as by international conditions. The reference to 1929 has been the prerequisite reference in all discussions of 2008, but it might well be that the post-war financial crises, to which we must now turn, provide a more suitable comparative framework.

2

———

Post-War Crises

Four major financial crises broke out in the core industrial countries between the end of Bretton Woods in 1971 and the early twenty-first century: the Financial Instability of the early 1970s and the ensuing bank failures, especially in Britain, Germany, and the United States, within the context of 'stagflation' and the end of fixed exchange rates; the International Debt Crisis of 1982, when the international financial system was threatened with collapse; the Japanese Banking Crisis of 1997–8, which undermined the financial system of the world's second largest economic power; and the Financial Debacle of 2007–8.[1] These crises were not the only ones to affect the advanced economies. More major financial institutions failed in the larger economies than during the first half of the twentieth century (the Continental Illinois in the United States in 1984, the Bank of Credit and Commerce International in Britain in 1991, the Crédit Lyonnais in France in 1993, Long Term Capital Management in the United States in 1998); an entire sector of American banking, the savings and loan industry, went through a disastrous crisis in the 1980s; and full-blown financial crises broke out in the smaller ones (Spain in 1977, Norway in 1987, and Sweden and Finland in 1991). However, their global impact remained limited—failures in the large countries were isolated cases, and crises occurring in small countries usually have few spillovers.

One striking feature of the period is the absence of any significant crisis during its first twenty-five to thirty years—from the end of the Second World War to the early 1970s, a period marked by regulation and controls over international capital flows. Financial crises broke out again with the opening-up of the world economy—the stock of foreign investment went up from $125 billion in 1960 (6 per cent of world GDP) to $29,000 billion in 2000 (92 per cent)[2]—and, from the late 1970s, increasing financial deregulation. While the first two crises, especially the International Debt Crisis of 1982, marked the beginning of the second globalization, it is too early to tell if the fourth and most recent one will signal its end.

THE FINANCIAL INSTABILITY OF
THE EARLY 1970s

The world was virtually free of financial crises for nearly forty years, from the depression of the 1930s to the recession of 1973–5. The latter put an end to what has come to be known as the 'Golden Age' of economic growth—a period of nearly thirty years, commonly known in France as 'les Trente Glorieuses', of unequalled economic growth. Between 1950 and 1973, Western Europe's GDP per capita grew at an average rate of 4.1 per cent per year, compared with 0.8 per cent between 1913 and 1950. Growth, though strong (2.5 per cent), was necessarily slower in the United States, given the country's much higher level of income at the beginning of the period; and spectacular (8.1 per cent) in Japan.[3] In one generation, Europe managed, if not to catch up, then at least to draw closer to the world's leader,[4] while Japan became the second world economic power by 1973. Growth was not only faster, it was also more stable: between 1948 and 1973, GNP never fell once, whether in the United States, Japan, or Western Europe. The business cycle took a new form, with absolute fall in GNP being replaced by decreases in growth rates.[5]

The economic stability of the 'Golden Age' was mirrored by the absence of financial crisis. There were a number of currency crises, requiring a readjustment within the Bretton Woods system of fixed exchange rates,[6] such as the devaluations of the pound sterling in 1949 and 1967, or the French franc in 1958 and 1969. But the banking system was stable, if highly regulated—nationalizations of the commercial banks in France, tight credit controls in the UK, Regulation Q (ceiling on interests paid on deposits) and others in the USA, to give but a few examples.[7] International capital movements were also restricted, reaching their lowest point in the twentieth century. Exchange controls remained in force in Europe until 1958, when free convertibility on current accounts was re-established. By then, the emergence of the Eurodollar market—an unregulated market for dollars held outside the United States—started circumventing the various national regulations and gave a new impetus to international capital flows.[8] The first transactions in Eurodollars took place in the late 1950s, and, from approximately $1.5 billion in 1958, the market expanded rapidly to reach $132 billion in 1973.[9] It was supplied mainly by American multinationals and European central banks, either directly or through the Bank for International Settlements. It provided credit on a worldwide scale in hitherto unprecedented proportions. This credit mainly provided inter-bank deposits; it also financed international trade and other short-term loans—all transactions involving extremely large sums.

The 'Golden Age' ended with the first oil shock of 1973—the decision taken in October by the OPEC countries to double the price of oil and then to double it again two months later. It hit the world economy at a time of strong inflationary pressure and monetary instability following the collapse of the Bretton Woods system in 1971 and the adoption of floating exchange rates in 1973, and more generally economic expansion running out of steam. GDP fell in absolute terms in the United States, Britain, and Japan in 1974 and in the OECD as a whole in 1975. But 1973 marked a turning point: other recessions followed, in 1979 and again in 1990, and economic growth never regained the same vigour, at any rate in Western Europe (1.8 per cent between 1973 and 1998) and Japan (2.3 per cent), and even in the United States (2 per cent).[10] But it also signalled the return of financial crises, which resulted as much from the economic downturn as from the new opportunities for investment and speculation offered by the first steps towards financial deregulation and the end of fixed exchange rates. Three banking crises broke out in 1973 and 1974, in Britain, the United States, and Germany. They were not the most acute in the history of financial collapses, but their happening in close proximity at a time of worldwide economic turmoil gave them particular significance. And, though mainly national in character, they also had a clear international dimension stemming from the opening-up of the world economy.

The first and most severe crisis, known as the secondary banking crisis, took place in Britain.[11] The 'secondary banks' appeared in the late 1950s to take advantage of the wholesale money markets that were growing fast in London, in particular the inter-bank market and the market for certificates of deposits. They were able to offer banking facilities that could not be provided by the highly regulated clearing banks, which had lending ceilings imposed on them, and which formed a tight interest rates cartel. By 1970, around ninety such banks were active in the City, with little supervision from the Bank of England. Some of them were founded by a new breed of entrepreneurs, remote from the City establishment; others were subsidiaries of the clearing banks or backed by powerful City institutions. Among the better-known names were Cedar Holdings, founded in 1958 and converted into a public company in January 1971;[12] London and County Securities, founded in 1961, and First National Finance Corporation, backed by Hambros Bank, were both floated in 1969. These 'fringe' banks, as they were also called, attracted short-term deposits by offering slightly higher rates, were highly leveraged and borrowed heavily in the inter-bank market, and lent for the medium term, mostly to the booming property market. They achieved spectacular growth in the 1960s and were generally perceived as far more dynamic and innovative than the old, and far larger, clearers. This trend was exacerbated by the new competitive climate established with the introduction of Capital and Credit Control in September 1971, which relaxed most controls on the clearing banks, and the government's expansionary policy in a context of 'stagflation'—the Barber boom. The rise of the money supply fuelled an increasingly speculative property market, with the clearing banks using their surplus of funds to lend to the secondary banks rather than to the manufacturing industry, from which there was little demand.

The crisis followed a typical pattern. By 1973, the economic situation had deteriorated gravely, and restrictive measures were introduced in November, creating a severe credit squeeze. The Bank of England minimum lending rate, which stood at 7.5 per cent in mid-June, went to 13 per cent within five months. Having made long-term loans based on short-term money borrowed at lower rates, the secondary banks found themselves in a critical position. Confidence was shaken by the resignation, on 27 November, of one of the directors of London and County Securities: its share price fell abruptly, and deposits were heavily withdrawn. Several other banks faced a similar reaction from depositors and shareholders alike and could no longer borrow or renew their loans. On 3 December, Cedar Holdings, whose profits had grown from £87,000 in 1967–8 to £1.9 million in 1972–3, was on the verge of collapse, with the risk of a domino effect on many other secondary banks and, possibly, the entire banking system. In a move reminiscent of the Barings rescue in 1890, the Governor of the

Bank of England, Gordon Richardson, organized, with the clearing banks, a 'Lifeboat' operation. Funds were provided to the fringe banks that were considered as solvent, twenty-one in total, reaching up to £400 million by March 1974. The situation, however, kept worsening, with rising inflation and falling property prices. The problems were compounded when the crisis took on an international dimension in the summer, with the failures of Franklin National Bank in the United States and I. D. Herstatt in Germany. The Franklin National and Herstatt debacles were not part of a general banking crisis, despite deteriorating economic conditions and mounting problems for banks. They were extreme cases of losses resulting from speculation in the foreign-exchange markets,[13] but carried risks of systemic effects.

Franklin National was a relatively small regional Long Island bank for most of its history, but by 1973 had grown into the twentieth largest American bank, with $3.7 billion deposits. It was granted permission to expand to New York in 1964 and opened a branch in London in 1969. Franklin National financed this rapid growth mainly through short-term funds, including the Eurodollar market, where it faced strong competition, made many high-risk loans, and achieved poor returns.[14] By 1970, Franklin was beginning to suffer steadily declining operating earnings—earnings per share fell from a peak of $4.67 in 1970 to $3.31 in 1971 and $2.21 in 1972. Costs had risen out of control, and larger than anticipated provisions had to be made for loan losses. In 1972, the Sicilian-born financier Michele Sindona bought a majority stake (22 per cent) in the bank, and, from 1973, the bank embarked on an aggressive international expansion: early in 1974, executives were claiming that 22 per cent of the bank assets and 35 per cent of its net operating profits derived from international operations. The situation became alarming in 1974, when it was revealed that Franklin had made heavy losses amounting to $63.6 million in the first five months of 1974—because of bad management, especially excessive reliance on short-term financing, and unauthorized trading in foreign currencies. Frightened depositors began making heavy withdrawals, and, in order to avoid the risk of a financial crisis caused by an abrupt failure, the Federal Reserve bailed Franklin out with loans totalling $1.75 billion. The bank, however, could not be saved, and the Comptroller of the Currency declared it insolvent on 8 October. In the meantime, a purchase was organized by the Federal Deposit Insurance Corporation. Bids were offered by First National

City Bank, Chemical Bank, Manufacturers Hanover, and European-American. The latter, a bank chartered in New York State and owned by a consortium of European banks, made the highest bid, and, on 9 October, Franklin reopened as European American Bank and Trust Company.[15]

The news of Franklin National's losses was followed by the announcement, on 26 June, of the collapse of the German private bank I. D. Herstatt. Founded in 1956 by Iwan Herstatt, it was the thirty-fifth largest in Germany in 1973, with total assets of just over DM2 billion. The bank specialized in foreign trade payments, an activity that became more risky after the end of Bretton Woods, but it was its speculation in the foreign exchanges that caused its fall. In March 1974, its open exchange positions amounted to DM2 billion, eighty time its authorized limit of DM25 million! In June, Herstatt's losses on its foreign-exchange operations were DM470 million, nearly its entire capital, and on the 26th the Federal Banking Supervisory Office withdrew its licence to conduct banking activities—the bank's assets (DM1 billion) were more than offset by its liabilities (DM2.2 billion).[16] The bank was closed by the German authorities at the end of the working day in Germany, but during banking hours in the United States, leaving a number of foreign-exchange deals half completed and heavy debts owed to several leading banks—a settlement risk that came to be known as the 'Herstatt risk'.

The collapse of the Herstatt Bank sent shock waves through the international banking system, especially in the foreign-exchange markets and the Euromarkets, both predominantly based in London. The impressive and regular growth of the Eurocurrency market came to an abrupt end, its gross value decreasing from a peak of $350 billion in mid-1974 to $345 billion at the end of the year. The decline of inter-bank transactions was even sharper, from $165 billion to $150 billion, with flights of deposits from many banks outside the ranks of the leaders.[17] A new wave of 'secondary banks', including larger houses such as First National Finance Corporation and United Dominion Trust, had to be rescued by the 'Lifeboat', which reached £1,200 million by the end of 1974. The Governor of the Bank of England, Gordon Richardson, was particularly adamant to avoid any failure in order to preserve the reputation of London as an international financial centre.

THE INTERNATIONAL DEBT CRISIS OF 1982

The International Debt Crisis was in many respects a continuation of the financial troubles of the mid-1970s. The recession of 1973–5 was soon followed by the even more severe recession of 1979–82; the oil shock of 1973 was followed by the second oil shock of 1979, with oil prices nearly trebling again; inflation was rampant, reaching double figures (for the OECD as a whole) in 1980; and the Euromarkets kept growing, with increasing international capital movements but also higher risks of financial instability. The Debt Crisis broke out on 20 August 1982, when Mexico declared a moratorium on paying the principal on its debt, putting many of the world's largest banks at risk of insolvency. The Debt Crisis thus affected both major international financial centres and emerging economies—like the Baring Crisis nearly a hundred years earlier, though on a bigger scale, as more developing countries, on the one hand, and more leading banks, on the other, were involved, giving the crisis an unprecedented international dimension, characteristic of a new era of globalization.

The new era of globalization had started with the emergence of the Eurodollar market in the late 1950s, which quickly gave rise to the Eurobond market. The idea of using funds deposited in this way not only for bank loans but also for issuing dollar-denominated bonds, in London rather than in New York, did not take long to form in City bankers' minds. The first Eurobond was issued in 1963 by Siegmund Warburg—a $15 million loan on behalf of Autostrade Italiane, a subsidiary of IRI, the Italian state holding company. Eurobond issues rose from $258 million in 1963 to $4.2 billion in 1973 and $20 billion in 1980.[18] However, its growth was less spectacular, especially in the 1970s, than that of the syndicated Eurocredits—a medium-term credit, lasting from two to ten years, between short-term, mainly inter-bank, deposits, which formed the Eurocurrency market proper, and long-term Eurobonds.

Eurocredits were international bank loans wholly financed by resources in Eurodollars and generally granted on the basis of floating interest rates, which made the borrower carry any risks associated with interest-rate fluctuations—a vital transfer of responsibility for the banks that financed these medium-term loans with very short-term deposits or even with demand deposits.[19] But the borrower found this a more flexible source of funding than a bond issue. They really took off with the issue in May 1966 of the first certificates of deposit in Eurodollars, introduced in London by their American creator, the First National City Bank.[20] Towards the late 1960s, in view of the growing demand for these loans and the size of the amounts required, the banks organized syndicated loans, bringing several of them together. Among the first syndicated Eurocredits was a loan for $15 million organized in June 1968 by the Bank of London and South America (BOLSA) for the Hungarian aluminium industry, and another for $100 million to Austria, orchestrated by Lehman Brothers and Bankers Trust International.[21] From barely $2 billion in 1968, Eurocredits quickly swelled to exceed $20 billion in 1973— or more than four times the amount of Eurobonds—and $78 billion in 1980.

This expansion was fuelled by a particular type of Eurodollars, the 'petrodollars', the dollars accumulated by OPEC countries following the explosion of oil price. Between 1974 and 1980, these countries accumulated $383 billion in liquid assets, half of which was invested as short-term bank deposits with the biggest American and European banks. These deposits had all the characteristics of Eurodollars— mobility and an absence of control by a national authority—and swelled the already existing pool of Eurodollars. The question of the risks that this influx of money posed to international financial stability was widely debated in the wake of the first oil shock, particularly in the United States: a solution for placing, or 'recycling', these 'petrodollars' had to be found. From the outset, the main banks involved—above all Citibank from New York—envisaged lending these funds to developing countries, whose public and trade deficits increased sharply following the oil price hike, with at least the tacit approval and at most the overt encouragement of Western monetary authorities, in particular the International Monetary Fund (IMF), the World Bank, and the Federal Reserve. Henceforth, up to the early 1980s, international capital movements were dominated by commercial bank credit to Third World countries. These were the largest international bank loans, increasing in amount from about $40 billion dollars in 1975 to $160 billion in 1980.[22] As for emerging countries' foreign debt, it went from $126 billion dollars in 1975 to $455 billion in 1982, with the share of private debt, mostly made up of bank loans, growing at the same time from 43 per cent to 56 per cent of the total.[23] Latin America absorbed the bulk—about two-thirds—of banks' loans to developing countries. Until the mid-1960s, capital flows to the region were mainly of an official character—60 per cent, as against 40 per cent for private funds. Ten years later, private capital flows made up 75 per cent of the total, reaching 87 per cent by the end of the 1970s. And, while bank loans accounted for only 8 per cent of total capital inflows in the years 1966–70, their proportion had reached 58 per cent by 1976–80. Bond issues then stood at a mere 9 per cent, up from 2.5 per cent a decade earlier.[24] Bank loans, usually in the form of syndicated floating-rate Eurocredits,[25] thus clearly had the edge over international issues.

This was a new way of transferring capital to sovereign states. Until then, and especially before 1914, banks had served as intermediaries between the borrowing state and the public, making the latter bear the risk of any possible default. This time it was the banks that were on the front line. They lived to regret it when Mexico decided to suspend payment on its foreign debt on 18 August 1982. The country was faced with the imperative to raise $500 million every week to service a debt that had climbed from $6 billion in 1970 to $80 billion in 1982. Yet the omens were good when, following the discovery of new huge oil deposits in the mid-1970s, Mexico embarked on a programme of rapid industrial modernization, mostly financed by foreign borrowing. Investments at first paid off, with oil exports earnings trebling from $3.7 billion to $10.4 billion between 1979 and 1980. However, despite peaking at $14.5 billion in 1981, they were below the expected $20 billion, prices having fallen as a consequence of the world's oil glut. With non-oil export stagnating, there was a growing feeling that the peso, which had remained stable since its 1976 devaluation, was overvalued. Massive capital flight forced the authorities to devalue the peso by some 30 per cent in February 1982. The wage compensation, which averaged 24 per cent, in turn fuelled inflation. At the same time, the current account deficit soared to $12.2 billion, or 6 per cent of GDP by 1981, increasing government borrowing and, with rising interest rates, the cost of servicing the debt, which was taking up the country's entire oil revenues.

American banks were particularly exposed to a sovereign default: they were owed more than 30 per cent of Mexico's outstanding loans ($25 billion out of some $80 billion). The nine largest banks alone were due $13.4 billion, representing nearly half their total capital of $27.1 billion.[26] The danger was compounded by the risks of default of other Latin American countries, especially Brazil (with loans amounting to $80 billion) and Argentina ($40 billion), where banks were equally exposed. Both countries wanted to renegotiate their debt soon after Mexico. Fears of a generalized debt crisis mounted in the late summer and autumn of 1982, with catastrophic scenarios painting a collapse of the international financial system being drawn in the press and elsewhere.[27] Panic, however, was avoided, and there was no bank failure or even bank rescue. Defaults were avoided through similar agreements with Mexico in August, Argentina in November, and Brazil in December 1982. The banks agreed to reschedule the debt and to provide new credits; a loan, together with a restructuring programme, was arranged with the IMF; and American monetary authorities offered guarantees and brokered the deals. By the end of the year, as Otmar Emminger, the head of the Deutsche Bundesbank in 1977–9, put it: 'No one believes any longer there will be a crash of the banking system.'[28]

The immediate cause of the Debt Crisis was the decision taken in October 1979 by Paul Volcker, the new Chairman of the Federal Reserve, to raise interest rates in order to fight inflation. In real terms, the US Prime Rate, which had been negative from 1974 to 1978, rose to 3.2 per cent in 1979 and to 8.1 per cent in 1981. Syndicated loans contracted on the basis of floating interest rates became far more expensive to service—and a huge burden in highly indebted countries. For emerging countries, this was aggravated by the deterioration of the terms of trade as commodity prices, which had been increasing in the 1970s, fell sharply in the 1980s. For the non-oil-exporting Latin American countries, interest payments increased from $5.4 billion in 1978 to $22.5 billion in 1982. Put another way, interest payments absorbed 15 per cent of exports in 1978 and 47 per cent in 1982—well above the 20 per cent ratio considered by bankers as a heavy burden.[29]

The question remains, however, whether bankers should not have known better. Did they manage risk poorly? Did they lack basic historical knowledge in view of both the level of exposure and Latin America's recurrent debt crises? Did they actually 'impose' loans on Third World countries? They were accused of these evils, after having been commended by national and international monetary authorities for so skilfully solving the problem of international imbalances caused by the oil-price hike. Mistakes were undoubtedly made. Syndicated loans were part of American banks' new strategy of international expansion, starting in the early 1960s with the emergence of the Euromarkets. The number of foreign branches of US banks, for example, rose from 124 in 1960 to 899 by 1986. By then a multinational presence had become the norm for an American bank of some significance: 151 of them had at least one branch abroad, up from 8 in 1960. The largest banks were obviously the most active internationally: for the top ten, overseas earnings represented 17.5 per cent of total earnings in 1970, 39.6 per cent in 1974, and 54.7 per cent in 1980.[30] They were also the most dangerously exposed to Third World debts—the top nine controlled 60 per cent of international lending, and the top twenty-four 80 per cent.[31]

This internationalization went hand in hand with a new banking culture, a new way of doing business. The financial journalist Anthony Sampson has well described how 'Putting together these syndicated loans . . . attracted a special coterie of cosmopolitan younger bankers . . . They enjoyed a social world of their own: finance ministers treated them as friends; they entertained each other lavishly; the final signing of the loan was celebrated by a huge banquet at the Ritz or the Berkeley.' Even more tellingly, one of them confided to him: 'When I first signed a loan agreement for twenty million dollars for a country I hardly knew anything about, I thought we must be crazy.'[32] Such attitudes were encouraged by the banks' top management. The analysis of country risks remained fairly rudimentary and clearly overwhelmed by the banks' determination to lend.[33] And Walter Wriston, Citicorp's president and the main proponent of Third World loans, had famously declared that 'countries don't go bankrupt'. Excessive risks were thus clearly taken in a booming climate fuelled by low interest rates.

Whatever the role of the banks, the Debt Crisis was primarily a crisis affecting developing countries. For Latin America, the 1980s was a 'lost decade'. Restructuring programmes took their toll, and at the end of the decade per capita incomes were barely higher than at the outset of the crisis. Attention turned to their plight, but also to their responsibility in the outbreak of the crisis. Bankers were criticized, very much in the same way as the 1st Lord Revelstoke and his partners had been at the time of the Baring Crisis—excessive risks, naivety, myopia about a crisis waiting to happen. But there was even more disapproval of the debtor countries' bad economic management, in particular their lack of fiscal and monetary discipline leading to unsustainable debt—in an adverse international economic context, with high oil prices, rising interest rates, and a prolonged recession.

THE JAPANESE BANKING CRISIS OF 1997–1998

The Japanese Banking Crisis of 1997–8 was more acute than any previous one affecting a rich country since the Second World War. Together with the depression that afflicted the country during the 'lost decade' of the 1990s, it put an end to the idea of 'Japan as number one' that had formed in the 1980s.[34] In many respects, the Japanese case conforms to the pattern of a typical financial crisis, especially as it happened at the end of a long stock-market and property boom, taking place during a period of high profits and high savings, and was fuelled by an expansion of the money supply. But the Japanese Banking Crisis was exceptionally severe—on account of its duration, though there was no real panic; of the number of failures of major financial institutions; and of the overall cost to the economy.[35] This peculiarity has much to do with Japan's specific banking and, more generally, business organizations and their relationships with government.[36] Japan's financial crisis was mostly confined to Japan—even more so than the Panic of 1907 was confined to the United States. But Japan was the world's second largest and, until the crisis, most dynamic economy. A crisis of this amplitude necessarily had implications on international financial relations and hence on the entire financial world.

The post-war Japanese banking system was geared primarily towards financing growth in heavy industry, with several legal categories of banks, each with, at least initially, fairly distinct roles. The major banks provided finance to the large companies, especially in the core industries of the catch-up effort—coal, iron and steel, ship-building, electricity. Long-term capital for investment in plant and equipment was provided by the 'trust banks', associated with each *keiretsu*,[37] as well as by 'long-term credit banks', which had no *keiretsu* affiliation. Long-term credit banks issued debentures to the public and provided credit to industry at low interest rates, thus contributing to Japan's international competitiveness. Short-term lending was granted by the large 'city banks', which were also affiliated to a specific *keiretsu* and took deposits. Small and medium-sized businesses were catered for by local regional banks and credit unions, while agricultural cooperatives and labour cooperatives also provided services to their members. However, this division of labour among major banks blurred in the 1970s, as long-term credit banks and city banks started competing in both the savings and the lending markets.

Two characteristics of the Japanese banking system are particularly relevant in connection with the Banking Crisis of the 1990s. The first is its management by the Ministry of Finance, in close cooperation with the banks if problems arose. One of the management principles was the so-called convoy system, under which the sector as a whole progressed at the speed of its weakest members. This was achieved by regulation that limited competition, in particular as far as branch opening and the setting of interest rates were concerned.[38] The 'convoy system' was primarily aimed at ensuring stability. A mechanism existed to deal with banks in distress: the Ministry of Finance arranged for a healthy bank to intervene by injecting new capital and dispatching staff. In exchange, the healthier bank obtained access to the other's branch network.[39] The second characteristic was the role of bank loans, which dominated the system to a greater extent than in the United States or Britain. In the 'main bank system', a bank had a long-term relationship with a firm, was its main source of funds (on average 20 per cent of total borrowing), and provided it with a number of other services, such as payroll management, foreign exchange, or settlement accounts.[40] On the basis of this deep insider's knowledge, the bank stood ready to support the firm in times of trouble. This implicit expectation of support acted as a sufficient guarantee for the firm's other lenders. Within this system, cutting off funds to a struggling client could damage a bank's standing, since such an act would be perceived as a breach of trust not only towards the client but also towards all the client's other creditors. Main banks faced up to their responsibility and effectively took over borrowers in financial distress.

The Japanese asset-price bubble started in 1986, when, in response to the revaluation of the yen following the Plaza Accord in September 1985, the government decided to pursue a policy of domestic-led growth. The Bank of Japan greatly expanded the money supply, and the value of assets began to rise as long-term interest rates fell below the return on stocks. The Nikkei Index nearly quadrupled in less than six years, from just over 10,000 in 1984 to just over 20,000 in June 1987 and nearly 40,000 in December 1989; while urban land prices doubled between 1980 and 1990. As a reaction to lower profit rates and, since the mid-1970s, diminishing use of bank finance by large industrial companies, banks sought to raise profits by lending to the booming property sector—opting for extensive rather than intensive growth.[41] The upshot was that much of the collateral for these new loans was land at increasingly inflated prices; and that, in the urge to lend to promising clients, banks relaxed their inspection requirements, making risky lending more likely. Much of the banks' more risky lending was done through 'non-bank' affiliates, so called because they were non-deposit-taking institutions and were thus more lightly regulated. However, while guaranteeing their affiliates, banks controlled their lending activities only imperfectly and could end up with far more exposure to risky borrowers than their managers were conscious of.

In order to limit speculation, the Bank of Japan raised its interest rate, which it had kept at 2.5 per cent after 1985, to 6 per cent between late 1989 and mid-1990; market rates had already been driven up by high private-sector investment in plant and equipment. This rise in interest rates was followed by a sudden depreciation of assets, first stocks and then property, as the speculative climate dissipated and expectations turned bearish. The Nikkei was back at just over 20,000 in September 1990, falling by nearly half in nine months; it would fluctuate around that level throughout the decade, falling under 10,000 in September 2001. The land price index faltered a year later, in 1991, and began a steady fall of about 5 per cent a year: supply had outstripped demand as construction of new office and residential buildings continued apace, while rising prices put downward pressure on demand. Recession gradually spread to the rest of the economy. Consumer spending stopped growing in 1990; corporate profits went down, bringing a drop in investment as companies faced excessive fixed costs; and small businesses, which had been the main actors in the bubble, were primarily concerned with paying back debts. Real GDP growth averaged 1.7 per cent during the 1990s, with several years of zero or negative growth.

Financial institutions reacted to these changed conditions by retaining rotten assets. Rather than cut their losses, they continued to lend to troubled or failing companies and held on to falling stocks. Later, when they came into possession of land used as collateral, they likewise tended not to sell it. Such a strategy could work only if asset prices recovered quickly. It also meant that banks could not cut off struggling companies, as they would risk systemic failure, as well as damaging their own reputation—a corollary of relationship banking wherever it is practised, especially in Austria or Germany. Non-performing loans mounted, possibly to as much as ¥100 trillion in the mid-1990s, but banks were unwilling to take decisive action and sought to conceal the problem—by reporting risky assets to the limited extent required by law, and by moving non-performing loans off their balance sheets, selling them to affiliated companies, often ad hoc creations located in their buildings. Since consolidating accounting was not required by law and affiliated companies were assumed to be financially sound, by virtue of being owned by a major bank, loans to them were not considered as risky.

No financial institution actually failed until 1994, when the Tokyo Metropolitan Government declared bankrupt two small credit unions under its regulatory responsibility; they were rescued by the intervention of the Bank of Japan.[42] Three other credit unions failed the following year. In 1996, seven mortgage companies collapsed almost simultaneously. They had been founded by banks in the 1970s and had turned their attention to property development during the boom. After a fierce debate in the Diet, public funds were used to rescue them. This was interpreted as a bailout of the founder banks, and the public response was such that future recourse to public funds to rescue financial institutions would be politically unacceptable.

The actual Banking Crisis broke out in 1997, even though the financial system had been near-paralysed by the non-performing loans problem for over five years. The Asian crisis of that year increased the pressure on distressed banks. The first sign of trouble was the announcement of a restructuring plan by Nippon Credit Bank, one of the world's top fifty banks, which received an injection of capital from the Bank of Japan in July. The following November a brokerage house, Sanyo Securities, went bankrupt, followed three weeks later by the near simultaneous though unrelated failures of two major companies: Hokkaido Takushoku Bank, a city bank and the largest in Hokkaido; and Yamaichi Securities, one of Japan's four largest brokerage houses. Confidence was shaken to such an extent that, when Tokuyo City Bank, a minor bank in a northern region, failed that same week, a general run on banks—mostly regional and targeted by rumour—was narrowly averted. The Ministry of Finance and the Bank of Japan issued a joint statement confirming that deposits were protected and that sufficient liquidity would be extended if necessary. According to Hiroshi Nakaso, of the Bank of Japan: '[26 November] was probably the day that Japan's financial system was closest to a systemic collapse.'[43] The failure of Hokkaido

Takushoku Bank, however shocking, given that the failure of a reputable city bank was unthinkable, was, not surprisingly, due to reckless lending in the property boom. Yamaichi Securities voluntarily ceased business on 24 November 1997 following huge off-balance-sheet losses and a scandal involving alleged profit sharing with *sôkayia*—racketeers specializing in the disruption of shareholders' meetings. Yamaichi had debts of ¥3.5 trillion, making its bankruptcy the largest since 1945. The government managed to 'wind down' the firm in an orderly way, keeping it in business long enough to settle existing contracts and avoiding sudden shock to the international financial markets. Funds were injected by the Bank of Japan without collateral, with the question of ultimate payment remaining unresolved.[44]

The crisis deepened further in 1998, with the largest bank failure in Japanese history: that of the Long-Term Credit Bank of Japan, better known as LTCB. With assets of ¥23 trillion, LCTB was Japan's tenth largest bank.[45] Originally one of the country's three long-term credit banks, it had lost much its specificity and become the equivalent of a highly respected city bank; with heavy industry needing little bank financing, it had to find new sources of profits. A plan for turning it into an investment bank more actively involved in the foreign markets was rejected in 1985. Instead, LTCB favoured the domestic market, in particular small and medium-sized enterprises and the booming property sector. The new strategy led directly to massive overlending and the accumulation of bad debts, which took place during the bubble and ultimately brought down the bank. The bank was temporarily nationalized on 23 October 1998.

In the years following the burst of the bubble, all Japanese financial institutions faced the same adverse environment, even though only a minority went bankrupt. The high-profile failures of LTCB, Hokkaido Takushoku Bank, and others had one significant consequence: they revealed the true extent of the damage to the financial system. There was no doubt that other banks, too, held massive amounts of non-performing loans and were using similar techniques to conceal them. The bankruptcies of 1997 and 1998 severely damaged the credibility of the Japanese banks. Analysts published estimates of the total amount of bad debts that were far above the official figures.[46] Banks and regulators were slow to tackle the problem. Politicians, especially the ruling Liberal Democratic Party, were extremely reluctant to let companies go bankrupt in great numbers and fought any solutions that involved cutting credit to troubled firms. Meanwhile, lack of credit continued to affect the wider economy. The banks' lending capacities were further eroded by the Basle Accords, which were adopted in 1987 and fixed at 8 per cent the ratio of equity capital to liabilities. The Japanese authorities had authorized their banks to consider their unrealized stock-market earnings to be equity capital. By the time the new standards came into force in 1992, much of the banks' capital had melted away and their ratio had fallen below 8 per cent, forcing them to reduce new lending as well as lending to existing clients.[47] At international level, the crisis meant a temporary disappearance of Japanese banks from the world's top ten, their retreat from foreign markets, as well as the withdrawal of numerous international players from Tokyo, thus altering the configuration of the international financial world.

New legislation made it possible to deal with bad loans. In particular, the criteria for non-performing loans were brought closer to worldwide standards and consolidated accounting was made the rule, making it less easy for banks to shift bad debts off their balance sheet. Securitization schemes involving special purpose companies gave banks new ways to write off unrecoverable securities. The ratio of non-performing loans to total loans began to decrease in 2002 and had fallen below 2 per cent in 2005. Apart from small regional banks, no deposit-taking institution went bankrupt after 2002. Japan eventually took the opportunity to modernize its financial sector, and banks, especially the big ones, were stabilized and became solid institutions once more.

THE FINANCIAL DEBACLE OF 2007–2008

The Financial Debacle of 2007–8 marked the culmination of over thirty years of unbridled financial development, unleashed by the end of fixed exchange rates, the opening-up of the world economy, the advent of a post-industrial society, widespread financial deregulation, the rise of market fundamentalism, and a historically unprecedented wave of financial innovations.[48] Not only did the size of financial institutions and the volume of financial operations grow exponentially,[49] but the process of financial intermediation was transformed by the rise of the financial markets and the decline of traditional banking. The credit crunch did not happen in a world devoid of financial crises, even though the financial innovations of the late twentieth century claimed to have greatly reduced if not eliminated the risks inherent in all financial transactions. Several studies observed that the number of financial crises had been regularly increasing since the end of Bretton Woods.[50] The collapse of Long Term Capital Management, a high-profile hedge fund whose rescue had been orchestrated by the Federal Reserve, in 1998, and the bursting of the dot-com bubble in 2000 rang alarm bells. But the most serious crises affected emerging economies—Mexico in 1994 and 1995, East Asia in 1997 and 1998, Russia in 1998, Argentina in 2001 and 2002. The advanced economies seemed immune to financial cataclysms. Admittedly, all the ingredients for a crisis were assembled: property boom, cheap money, high leverage, global imbalance, but few saw it coming and anticipated the violence of the shock.

The first indication of the reality and the severity of the crisis came on 9 August 2007, when BNP Paribas, France's leading investment bank, suspended three of its investment funds, giving as a reason the impossibility properly to value their assets. BNP Paribas's announcement 'officially' signalled the beginning of the credit crunch: banks became increasingly reluctant, if at all prepared, to lend to each other—a situation not only dangerous for the financial system but potentially damaging for the real economy and, if it were to last, carrying high risks of a worldwide recession. The gravity of the moment did not escape the monetary authorities, with the Federal Reserve and the European Central Bank immediately injecting substantial liquidity into the system by making loans available to banks.

How did the inter-bank lending market come to freeze and liquidity evaporate from the system? The immediate cause lay in the US subprime mortgage market. The housing market had boomed in the United States since the mid-1990s, fuelled by low interest rates as well as favourable demographic trends and an ideological climate promoting an 'ownership society'. House prices more than doubled between 1995 and 2006, when, following two years of rising interest rates, the bubble eventually burst, with ensuing mortgage defaults. The collapse of the housing market was aggravated by two interrelated factors: on the one hand, the very low credit and high level of indebtedness of the recipients of these mortgages; and, on the other hand, the securitization of this debt, in the form of mortgage-backed securities (MBS), whose value soared during the first years of the twenty-first century. With increasing defaults from subprime borrowers, MBS not only lost their value, they became impossible to price, exposing banks and other financial institutions, in all financial centres, to huge potential losses.[51]

Despite the shock and concern about the seriousness of the crisis, it was widely assumed in the following months, within both the financial world and the monetary authorities, that a major financial crisis, leading to a deep recession, could be avoided. If anything, the stock market continued to climb, reaching its highest point in October 2007—the Dow Jones peaked at 14,093 and the FTSE at 6,730 on 12 October. The situation, however, was not improving. One of the first casualties of the credit crunch was a British bank, Northern Rock, one of the country's largest mortgage lenders, which relied mainly on the money market to fund its operations. A run on the bank took place on 14 September 2007, the first on a British bank for more than a century, with customers withdrawing some £2 billion—it was nationalized a few months later, in February 2008. Another casualty, whose difficulties sent alarm signals to the markets, was Bear Stearns, Wall Street's fifth largest investment bank. Its market value had fallen from $18 billion in April 2007 to $3.5 billion on 14 March 2008 and a mere $240 million three days later, the day it was bought by J. P. Morgan Chase, with the backing of the Federal Reserve.

Bank losses were a serious cause of concern. In May 2008, asset write downs and credit losses, including reserves set aside for bad loans, were estimated to have reached $379 billion since January 2007 at the world's 100 biggest banks and securities firms.[52] The leading banks withstood the heaviest losses: Citigroup headed the list with $42.9 billion, followed by UBS ($38.2 billion) and Merrill Lynch ($37 billion). Global stock markets fell sharply—by 10–15 per cent—in January 2008 and then again in June and early July.[53] Warnings about the risks of a serious recession became increasingly louder. In its *Global Stability Report of April* 2008, the IMF considered that the effects of the credit crunch were likely to be 'broader, deeper and more protracted' than in previous downturns because of the degree of securitization and leverage in the financial system. Central banks continued to pump liquidity into the system, conducting several auctions to provide funds to banks, including through internationally coordinated actions;[54] accepting a wider range of collaterals; allowing swaps of less liquid assets for more secure government bonds;[55] and lowering interest rates.[56] Faced with mounting write downs,[57] banks attempted to strengthen their position by raising capital, mainly tapping sovereign wealth funds in Asia and the Middle East.[58] By August 2008, Citigroup had raised nearly $50 billion, Merrill Lynch and UBS nearly $30 billion, the Royal Bank of Scotland and the Bank of America more than $20 billion.[59]

These sums proved vastly insufficient as things took a turn for the worse in the late summer of 2008. On 7 September, the two mortgage companies Freddie Mac and Fannie Mae were taken over by the US government. They owned or guaranteed $5 trillion of debt, nearly half the home loan market, and the failure of either of them was judged to present too high a risk for the financial markets in the United States and worldwide. A different view was taken about Lehman Brothers, America's fourth largest investment bank, which filed for bankruptcy protection on 15 September. The same day, Merrill Lynch, one of Wall Street's 'big three' investment banks, announced that it had agreed to be taken over by the Bank of America.

The fall of Lehman Brothers marked a turning point, the passage from a severe downturn to an acute crisis—or from crisis to panic. The entire banking system was contaminated by hundreds of billions of 'toxic assets', not only mortgage-backed securities, but all types of structured products—asset-backed securities, collateralized debt obligations, credit default swaps—now possibly worthless. No bank, whatever its size and reputation, appeared to be sound or safe, and other big banks might be allowed to fail. This was not to be the case, and Lehman Brothers remained the sole major casualty. Governments stepped in to rescue banks directly and to prevent the financial system from collapsing—in moves reminiscent of August 1914 in most financial centres and July 1931 in Germany, with increasing talks of banks' 'nationalizations'. On 16 September, the Federal Reserve came to the rescue of AIG (American International Group), the world's largest insurance company, offering it an $85 billion loan and taking an 80 per cent stake in the company.[60] During the following months, more than thirty banks in Europe and America, including HBOS and RBS in Britain, Goldman Sachs, Morgan Stanley, and Citigroup in the USA, Commerzbank in Germany, and UBS in Switzerland, to quote but the most famous, were bailed out in various ways by their governments, mostly through direct loans or equity injection. State intervention proved quite efficient, and, by early 2009, the acute financial crisis appeared to have ended.

However, the effects of the Financial Debacle on the real economy were felt rapidly, with GDP shrinking by 2.0 per cent in the OECD area in the third quarter of 2008, and by 2.1 per cent in the first quarter of 2009; and unemployment rising from 5.6 per cent in April 2008 to 7.8 per cent in April 2009.[61] These trends were, initially, comparable with those observed in 1929–30. On the other hand, the expansionist policies pursued by the political and monetary authorities, in contrast to the deflationist policies of those in charge in the early 1930s, seem to have had a positive effect and prevented the Great Recession from becoming a Great Depression.[62]

The causes of the Financial Debacle of 2007–8 are both general—and frightfully similar to those of all previous crises—and specific. Low interest rates during the boom years and the oversupply of capital on the financial markets led to excessive risk-taking in the search for higher yields. Much of this can be put down to the accommodating policy of the central banks and the widening global imbalances since the start of the twenty-first century—between countries with a balance-of-payments surplus and those with a deficit; between excessive saving in the former, primarily China, and a worrying level of debt in the latter, primarily the USA; and through the accumulation of enormous currency reserves in the emerging economies, mainly invested in American treasury bonds.[63] This macroeconomic climate unquestionably favoured the triggering of a financial crisis, especially when coupled with unregulated markets, inadequate supervision, and the total failure of the credit-rating agencies. Financial innovations have also been blamed for the Debacle of 2007–8, in particular the increasingly opaque nature of derivatives and other structured products, based on extremely complex mathematical formulae, which few bankers can really understand and for which, therefore, few can assess the risks involved. Warren Buffett famously referred to derivatives as 'weapons of mass destruction'.[64] However, it is not financial innovation per se but how it is used and regulated that generates risk. Derivatives are certainly complex, but recent generations of bankers are highly trained enough to handle this complexity. It is risk supervision, both by the regulators and within firms themselves, that all too often seems to have been lacking—as witnessed by the banks' incredibly high leverage ratios hidden in off-balance-sheet operations. This, in the end, is where the causes of the debacle are to be found.

But the Financial Debacle of 2007–8 was also different from previous experiences. As a strictly financial crisis, it can be considered as the most severe in history: never before did so many leading banks, in so many advanced countries, find themselves, at about the same time, in a situation requiring state intervention in order to avoid collapse. The nearest parallel in terms of systemic risks is August 1914, but the reasons for the panic—the outbreak of a world war—make that an altogether different crisis. The International Debt Crisis of 1982 was similar, because of the number of major banks facing serious threats, but the danger was never as imminent. A single bank was involved in the Baring Crisis of 1890, but the systemic risks were at least as high. The financial crises of the Great Depression were of another type: they did not affect all countries at the same time or with the same degree of intensity, and at no point was the global financial system on the verge of collapse. Taken together, however, over a period of five years and with thousands of bank failures, they were more traumatic and caused greater damage to the real economy than the credit crunch and the crisis of 2007–8. Is 1929 the most significant reference if we want to understand the effects that the Financial Debacle of 2007–8 had on the financial system—on banks, governance, regulation, international cooperation, and balance of power? This is the question to which we must now turn.

3

Banks

What happens to banks during a banking crisis? The question is not entirely incongruous. Massive bank runs and a succession of bank failures are only one aspect of banking crises, and not necessarily the main one as far as large banks are concerned. The collapse of Lehman Brothers is the exception that proves the rule, a rare case in the history of an advanced economy since the late nineteenth century of a large bank being allowed by the financial authorities to fail in a sudden and disorderly way. The fact is little appreciated, but it has undoubtedly left its mark on the debates that have followed the Financial Debacle of 2007–8. The main issue, repeatedly raised, has been whether the banks had become too big to fail, which implies that big banks no longer fail in times of financial crises, though they can run into serious difficulties. One corollary of this situation is that banks could or should be cut down to size in order to avoid pitfalls: on the one hand, the 'moral hazard' created by the certainty of being bailed out in case of failure, and, on the other hand, the systemic effects of the collapse of a big bank. Cutting banks down to size has usually been envisaged by separating commercial banking from investment banking, but the possibility of creating smaller units by forcing demergers has also been put forward. This chapter discusses these issues from a historical perspective, by considering how banks have fared in the wake of the eight major financial crises that have shaken the advanced economies since 1890. Three main questions are addressed. First, to what extent have big banks actually been allowed to fail? Second, have financial crises been followed by waves of consolidation? And, third, how have large banks performed in the aftermath of a crisis—especially in terms of growth and profits?

TOO BIG TO FAIL

The suggestion that the big banks had become too big to fail was apparently first mooted in 1984, at the time of the collapse of Continental Illinois, the seventh largest US bank, with $40 billion in assets.[1] As a matter of fact, large banks have been too big to fail for a much longer time. Very few large banks have failed in one of the leading economies since the late nineteenth century; and when they did, they were immediately rescued, in one way or another, by their government. Bailouts, however, have usually come at a price for the rescued institutions.

Before the Financial Debacle of 2007–8, bank bailouts proved necessary in three major financial crises. The first was the Baring Crisis, in 1890. Baring Brothers was already too big to fail—more so than Lehman Brothers in 2008. The fact is often overlooked: because it was a family-owned merchant bank, it is usually assumed that Barings had fallen well behind the fast-growing joint stock banks— in terms of size though not of overall influence. Rankings are difficult for this period, but with a total balance sheet of some £25 million in 1890, Baring Brothers then ranked among Britain's top five and Europe's top seven banks, including deposit banks. In Britain, only three London-based joint stock banks—National Provincial (the world's largest), London and County, and London and Westminster—were larger.[2] N. M. Rothschild, Sons & Co., also a family-owned merchant bank, was about the same size, but with a much larger capital.[3] Elsewhere in Europe, Barings was surpassed only by de Rothschild Frères in Paris and Crédit Lyonnais. It was then larger than Deutsche Bank in Germany, Société Générale and Banque de Paris et des Pays-Bas in France, the Société Générale de Belgique, Crédit Suisse in Zurich, National City Bank in New York—to name the most obvious possible contenders.

William Lidderdale, the Governor of the Bank of England between 1889 and 1892, might not have had these figures to hand when he decided to mount a rescue operation. But he acted with extreme decisiveness as soon as he was informed, by Lord Revelstoke, Barings' senior partner, of the bank's critical position on Monday, 11 November 1890, successfully setting up a guarantee fund to cover the Bank of England against any loss that might result from the liquidation of Baring Brothers & Co.[4] For the liquidation of the old partnership was a condition of the rescue. On 25 November 1890, a circular announced that the business had been transferred to a new company, Baring Brothers & Co., Ltd, with a capital of £1,000,000 taken up by members of the family (though not the old partners, whose liability was unlimited), together with allies and friends, including Hottinguer & Co. in Paris and Hope & Co. in Amsterdam.[5] Liquidating the assets of the old firm took several years, alongside Argentina's financial recovery—the Bank of England and other participants to the guarantee fund were eventually relieved of any responsibility in 1895. As to the new Baring bank, it was, interestingly, quickly back on its feet. By the turn of the twentieth century, it was once more a force to be reckoned with in the world of international finance, especially in Argentine matters, and in Russia, where it regained the Russian government's confidence—a success attributable in no small part to the family's huge social assets (five peerages and an entrenched position within the British establishment) and the firm's extended networks of relationships.

The second financial crisis requiring the bailout of big banks was the German banking crisis of 1931. The 'Big Six' Berlin banks[6] were, even more clearly than Barings, too big to fail. The two banks that actually went under—the Darmstädter und National Bank (Danat Bank) and the Dresdner Bank—were Germany's second and third largest, not far behind the national leader, the Deutsche Bank und Disconto-Gesellschaft;[7] and they ranked amongst Europe's top ten. The Danat Bank's failure on Monday, 13 July, was followed by a two-day bank holiday, during which the Dresdner Bank also declared itself bankrupt. Both banks reopened on 15 July, with government guarantees, as part of a rescue programme destined to salvage the entire banking system. Assistance, however, came at a price. The government made some RM1.25 billion available to cover the losses and restructure the capital of the main banks, of which nearly 20 per cent, about RM223.5 million, was never repaid. The bulk, RM845 million, consisted of advances, and the remainder, RM187 million, was in equity participation. In return, the government undertook major restructuring of the banking system, which was completed by the spring of 1932 and boiled down to the near nationalization of the big banks. The Dresdner Bank and the Danat Bank were forced to merge into a new institution, named after the former. Its initial capital of RM220 million was reduced to RM150 million, 91 per cent of which was held by the state and the Reichsbank. At the same time, the authorities ended up owning more than 50 per cent of the Commerzbank's equity capital and approximately 35 per cent of that of the

Deutsche Bank und Disconto-Gesellschaft, whose capital was first reduced to RM144 million and then to RM130 million a year later, in 1933.[8] Of the Berlin big banks, only the Berliner Handels-Gesellschaft passed through the crisis without incident. State intervention in the financial sector would not diminish with the advent of the Third Reich, despite the reprivatization of the big banks.

The third crisis was the Japanese Banking Crisis of 1997–8. It was the crisis where large banks had to pay the highest price for their rescue, especially in terms of size and corporate identity. They were four in total: two 'long-term credit banks' (Nippon Credit Bank and LTCB), one large 'city bank' (Hokkaido Takushoku Bank), and one of the top four brokerage houses, Yamaichi Securities. Of these, one, Yamaichi Securities, actually never reopened for business, a rare instance of disappearance of a large failed bank. The two 'special banks' were at first both temporarily nationalized, in 1998, and sold to private consortia. LTCB was sold in 2000 to a consortium of foreign investors led by Ripplewood, a small American private-equity firm, and was reorganized as an ordinary city bank, under the name of Shinsei Bank.[9] Nippon Credit Bank, the smaller of the two, was sold in 2000 to a Japanese consortium led by Softbank, an Internet investor, and ORIX, a leasing company, and reorganized the following year under the name of Aozora Bank. Both long-term credit banks have thus remained in business, but performances have been lacklustre. In 2008, each bank was about half its 1998 size in terms of assets. As for Hokkaido Takushoku Bank, one of Japan's most reputable city banks, it was absorbed by North Pacific Bank, a small regional bank based in Sapporo.

A financial crisis can happen without bank runs, failures, and bailouts. This was clearly the case in the Financial Crisis of July–August 1914. The liquidity crisis was exceptionally severe, and, for a few days, there were fears of a complete paralysis of the financial system. State intervention was required in order to restore confidence. Exceptional measures, such as a moratorium on payments, limitation on deposit withdrawals, or suspension of convertibility, were taken. Financial support was temporarily provided. But none of the big banks in any of the belligerent countries faced bankruptcy. This was also the case during the International Debt Crisis of 1982. There was a real possibility that several of the world's largest banks would become insolvent, in this case because of the excessive risks they had taken in their lending policies rather than the disruption created by a world war. Here again, state intervention, as well as international coordination, were necessary in order to avoid debtors' default, through debt rescheduling and restructuring programmes. However, there was no need for the emergency rescuing of a failing bank.

The real victims of financial crises have been small banks. This was especially the case during the Great Depression. Whatever the severity of the banking crisis—or rather crises, as there were four between 1930 and 1933—in the United States, there was hardly any large bank among the 10,000 or so casualties. During the first crisis, between November 1930 and January 1931, the deposits of the 761 failed banks amounted to $708 million, that is less than $1,000,000 ($930,000) per bank.[10] The exception was the Bank of United States, in New York ($160 million deposits), which closed its door on 11 December 1930. However, it did not rank among the country's largest banks, and the consequences of its collapse remained limited. The banks that suspended payments in the crises of 1931 were on average equally small, with no bank of any significance among them.[11] In 1933, the declaration of a banking holiday in Michigan on 14 February, which played a major role in the ensuing panic, was connected with the problems of two fairly large banks in Detroit,[12] but, with the banking system near complete paralysis in the first week of March, the crisis took on a new dimension; and in any case, the big New York banks remained highly liquid throughout the national bank holidays.[13]

In Germany, the number of private banks declined by more than a third (from 1,100 to 709) between 1929 and 1932. While the big banks benefited from government support at the height of the crisis in July 1931, the private banks suffered from the reluctance of the Reichsbank to refinance them.[14] In France, where the banking crisis was protracted but less acute, 670 banks failed between October 1929 and September 1937.[15] Most of them were small, often family-owned local and regional banks. They played a dynamic role in the French economy during the 1920s, especially through their support of local industry. However, unlike the big deposit banks, which remained highly liquid throughout the period, they overcommitted themselves during the years of prosperity, becoming extremely vulnerable in times of crisis. Their difficulties could be aggravated by the attitude of the local branch of the Banque de France, as some of them dramatically tightened the conditions at which they were prepared to rediscount bills.

A number of crises were confined mainly to small or medium-sized banks, especially in the United States.[16] The banks and trust companies that failed during the American Panic of 1907 were either small (Morse and Heinz group of banks) or medium-sized (Knickerbocker Trust), though the two trust companies that were supported throughout the crisis under Morgan's leadership, the Trust Company of America and the Lincoln Trust, were fairly large as well as solvent—a typical case of a panic extending from small and weak firms to large and healthy ones. However, the big New York banks were unaffected and able to provide the required liquidity. More recently, the savings and loans crisis of the 1980s, which was also in the United States, and the secondary banking crisis in Britain during the Financial Instability of the early 1970s, primarily involved small and medium-sized banks.

The bank bailouts of 2008–9 must be seen in this historical context. It was certainly not the first time that big banks were judged too big to fail. And the types of bailouts were not particularly new, taking the form of direct loans or equity injection—rather than outright nationalization.[17] As in the past, some failing banks were rescued through a merger with a larger and, apparently at least, healthier competitor.[18] And yet 2008 was different, in three main respects. First, a large bank, Lehman Brothers, was allowed to fail. Second, the banks benefiting from government support for their very survival were able to escape very lightly—in terms of restructuring, loss of autonomy or of corporate identity, purge of senior executives, or reduction of remuneration levels, which we will discuss in the next chapter. A higher price might still be exacted from the banks, but, at the time of writing, in early 2010, it was still much lower than in previous comparable instances, even though the costs of the rescue were higher than ever before. The third difference was the sheer scale of the operation, both because of the unprecedented number of very large banks simultaneously needing to be bailed out—Germany in 1931 and Japan in 1997–8 came close, but within a national not a global context—and because of the size of the largest banks. Global financial assets represented 318 per cent of world GDP in 2005, up from 109 per cent in 1980.[19] And, while a single bank had total assets worth more than 50 per cent of its home country GDP in 1990, more than half the world's top twenty-five banks were in this position in 2010.[20] The world's largest banks were no longer too big to fail, but they might well have become, as has been suggested, too big to save. In other words, the cost of a bailout had become extraordinarily expensive and possibly beyond the means of the financial authorities of a single country, including financial powers such as Switzerland, or even Britain. This puts the question of banking consolidation following a financial crisis in a different perspective.

CONSOLIDATION

Have banking crises led to a consolidation of the banking system? The answer is apparently a straightforward yes. As banks disappear during a crisis, some closing their doors, others being taken over by a competitor, surviving institutions would be expected to grow bigger, if not necessarily stronger, while the level of concentration, in other words, the share of the business held by the top players, should proportionally increase. Such a pattern can undoubtedly be perceived in most crises, but constitutes only one aspect of the historical process of banking consolidation. In fact, banking crises have played an indirect role in the major restructurings of the banking system. A degree of rationalization has taken place in all crises marked by the disappearance of a high number of small banks—the banking crises of the Great Depression, the Financial Instability in Britain in the early 1970s, and, to a lesser extent, the Japanese Banking Crisis of the 1990s.[21] Conversely, and not surprisingly, there have been few changes in the absence, or near absence, of bank failures—during the Baring Crisis of 1890, the American Panic of 1907, the Financial Crisis of July–August 1914, and the International Debt Crisis of 1982. Interestingly, however, in most countries these crises were followed, after a short time lag, by a wave of consolidation.

Hardly any bank failed during the Baring Crisis—Barings itself having been reconstructed as a limited liability company.[22] However, the 1890s were the most intense period of amalgamation in English banking history, with 1891 the year with the highest number of mergers—eighteen—ever recorded.[23] The Baring Crisis was certainly one of the major causes of the acceleration of the movement, as smaller institutions endeavoured to grow stronger in a post-crisis climate of high uncertainty. The prestigious London private bankers, who had held out strongly until then, were the first to go.[24] The outcome of this merger wave was the emergence of a group of

London-based giant banks, with a network of branches extending throughout the country and controlling nearly two-thirds of the country's deposits.[25] The main predators were Lloyds Bank and Midland Bank, two provincial banks originally based in Birmingham, which moved to London respectively in 1884 and 1891 by acquiring a smaller bank member of the London Clearing House. Lloyds Bank took over thirty-three banks between 1890 and 1914, the Midland twenty-three.[26] By the early twentieth century, they had become the country's two largest banks.

However, apart from the initial shock following the Baring Crisis, there is little evidence that the merger wave of the late nineteenth and early twentieth centuries was linked to the course of economic activity.[27] In fact, the rise of the great commercial banks was a characteristic of the banking sectors of all industrialized countries. Consolidation was based on the formation of common-interest groups rather than outright mergers in Germany. The big banks hardly opened any branches outside Berlin. Instead, they established a 'community of interests' (*Interessengemeinschaft*), based on cross-shareholding and pooled profits, with a number of provincial banks.[28] Internal growth, by contrast, was the dominant feature in the consolidation of French banking: the leading banks established a national network of branches without taking over local banks. Despite these different patterns of consolidation, Europe's, and indeed the world's, top five banks on the eve of the First World War were of nearly equal size, with total assets of about $500 million. Three were British (Lloyds, Midland, and Westminster), one was French (Crédit Lyonnais), and one was German (Deutsche Bank).[29] American banks were smaller than their European counterparts, mainly because they were prohibited by law from opening branches in another state. Consolidation thus remained limited, and the number of banks actually increased substantially in the early twentieth century—from 13,000 in 1900 to over 22,000 in 1908 and 26,000 by 1913.[30] However, there was a concentration of big banks in New York (seventeen of the country's top twenty-four, as against two for Chicago), where bankers' balances were mostly held (43 per cent in 1915, as against 11 per cent for Chicago).[31] Moreover, the leading banks experienced fast growth during this period. National City Bank, in particular, the country's largest bank, succeeded in gaining the accounts of numerous large American companies and taking up issue activities.[32] From being 10 per cent of the size of Crédit Lyonnais in 1890, it had become half as big by 1913.

Having been triggered by politico-military rather than primarily economic factors, the Financial Crisis of July–August 1914 did not lead to any restructuring of the banking system. The war and its aftermath, however, did. One of the greatest merger movements in banking history took place in Britain in 1918, even before the end of hostilities: five mergers brought together, two by two, the ten largest banks in the country and gave rise to five giant clearing banks, immediately called the 'Big Five': the Midland Bank, Lloyds Bank, Barclays Bank, the Westminster Bank, and the National Provincial Bank. They all ranked among the word's ten largest banks until the Second World War. In Germany, in the inflationary climate of the early 1920s, the great banks were encouraged to take over the provincial banks with which they were already linked through 'communities of interest'.[33] Mergers involving medium-sized and large banks gave rise to new big banks—the Commerz-und-Privat Bank (Compri-Bank) in 1920 and the Darmstädter und National Bank (Danat Bank) in 1922. Consolidation also took place in the United States. The leading banks strengthened their position as a result of the new financial power of the United States in the post-war world, sustained economic growth in the 1920s, and extension of their business activities through the takeover of small and occasionally large banks—the 1929 merger between Chase National and Equitable Trust is a case in point. By 1929, three New York banks—Chase, National City, and Guarantee Trust—had total assets of around $2 billion, a size comparable to that of the three largest British clearing banks.

The effects of the banking crises of the Great Depression were different, not least because of the high number of failed banks—in an exceptionally severe economic downturn. The drastic reduction in the number of small banks did lead to some rationalization of national banking systems. Central bankers actually saw the crisis as an opportunity to achieve that goal. In the United States, the most influential figures in the Federal System appear to have been rather contemptuous of small banks and rather complacent about their disappearance.[34] In Germany, Hjalmar Schacht, President of the Reichsbank from 1933 to 1939 and Economics Minister from 1934 to 1937, actively promoted a rationalization of the German banking system, which implied the liquidation of hundreds of small and weak private banks. This policy was perpetrated within the sinister context of Nazi anti-Semitism. Admittedly, until 1936 Schacht prevented as much as possible any discrimination against Jewish bankers at the economic level, though this defence did not extend to their civic and political rights.[35] Nevertheless, most of the private banks disappearing during this period were Jewish. This did not mean that they were necessarily the weakest, though some had been severely shaken by the banking crisis, including the famous Frankfurt house Lazard Speyer Ellissen. But, in the prevailing racist climate, several Jewish bankers preferred to transfer or sell their business to non-Jewish concerns.[36] Likewise in France, Henri Ardant, the leading banker under Vichy, attempted to rationalize the banking system by getting rid of what he called its 'most sordid' elements—no less than 63 per cent of French banks. However, small banks still enjoyed protection in Vichy France, and the number of local banks fell by only 22 per cent (from 262 to 205) between 1940 and 1944.[37] As in Germany, rationalization and anti-Semitism went hand in hand, with selective measures against 'specialized banks', which included a high proportion of Jewish houses, and the liquidation and 'aryanization' of most Jewish banks.[38]

Nevertheless, banking concentration did not really increase as a result of the banking crises of the Great Depression. On the contrary. In all countries, the forward march of the great banks was halted by the Depression, with deposits moving towards savings banks and other types of public and semi-public banks. In Germany, the share of the commercial banks in the total assets of the entire banking system declined from 33 to 15 per cent between 1929 and 1938, while that of the savings banks increased from 31 to 45 per cent during the same period.[39] In France, the deposits of the private sector's commercial banks decreased from Fr.89.5 billion to Fr.67.4 billion between 1930 and 1937, while those of the public and semi-public banks increased from Fr.67 billion to Fr.113 billion.[40] In the United States, commercial banks' deposits fell by 17 per cent between 1929 and 1933, those of the savings and loans associations, which were even more badly hit by the crisis, by 28 per cent, while deposits in the postal savings system increased sixfold.[41] Even in Britain, where a banking crisis hardly featured in the 1930s, the assets of the savings banks and building societies rose from 17 per cent of those of the clearing banks in 1920 to 37 per cent in 1937.[42] This trend persisted until after the Second World War, and the great banks did not regain their advantage before the 1960s.

The Financial Instability in Britain in the early 1970s was a classic case of weakened banks either disappearing or being absorbed by stronger and much larger competitors. Of the twenty-five banks with which the Lifeboat support was concerned, eight collapsed and fourteen eventually passed under the control of larger groups, mainly Barclays Bank, Lloyds Bank, and National Westminster Bank.[43] Moreover, with the adverse business climate created by the crisis, several other small banking and financial firms passed under the wing of larger ones.[44]

However, the financial crises of the 1970s and 1980s played only a marginal role in the consolidation of British and American banking, as major mergers took place before and after them. In Britain, where an oligopolistic structure had existed since the mergers of 1918, the two smallest of the 'Big Five', the National Provincial Bank and the Westminster Bank, merged in 1968 to form the National Westminster Bank; while the largest, Barclays Bank, took over Martins Bank, one of the few remaining independent provincial banks, based in Liverpool, after a tripartite merger with Lloyds Bank had been blocked by the Monopolies and Mergers Commission. These manoeuvres started once it became clear that, after nearly fifty years, the Bank of England and the Treasury would no longer oppose mergers between major clearing banks. The move was partly motivated by the growing strength of American banks, now the world's largest.[45] A merger wave among the leading New York banks had taken place earlier, in the mid- to late 1950s, mainly as a response to the 'funding squeeze' they were experiencing. Demand for bank loans was growing much faster than deposits: the rise of interest rates led corporate clients to reduce their bank balances, on which little or no interest was paid, and to invest their surplus into marketable securities or Treasury Bills. One solution for the banks was to grow bigger and to expand their deposit base through mergers. Significantly, most of them were between wholesale banks needing to increase their resources to meet the demands of their corporate customers, and retail banks needing to find proper use for their deposits. Six major banks merged in 1955: Chase National Bank with the Bank of Manhattan, Bankers Trust with Public National Bank, and National City Bank with First National Bank; in 1959, J. P. Morgan merged with Guarantee Trust, and in 1961 Central Hanover Bank with Manufacturers Trust.[46]

The clearer case of major consolidation resulting from a banking crisis was the 'mega-mergers' between the largest Japanese banks at the turn of the twenty-first century—on a scale comparable to the 1918 mergers between British banks, though the latter were operating from a position of strength. The first took place in 1996, when the Bank of Tokyo and Mitsubishi Bank merged into the Bank of Tokyo Mitsubishi (BTM), but most followed after the Japanese Banking Crisis of 1997–8. In 2000, the merger between Dai-Ichi Kangyo Bank, Fuji Bank, and the Industrial Bank of Japan created Mizuho Financial Group. And in 2001, Sumitomo Bank and Sakura Bank (formerly known as Mitsui) combined to form the Sumitomo Mitsui Banking Corporation (SMBC); while Sanwa Bank and Tokai Bank formed UFJ Bank. These four banks became, not surprisingly, known as the 'mega-banks'. The playing field was reduced further in 2006 with the merger between BMT and UFJ, to become the Bank of Tokyo Mitsubishi UFJ (BTMU). All these major banks became consolidated into holding companies, which became legal in 1998.[47] The initial impetus for concentration was the change in the regulatory environment following the 1997–8 Crisis: banks faced new, more stringent accounting and capital standards. But they were also encouraged to consolidate by the government and could take advantage of new stabilization policies, in particular capital injection, directed at banks considered to have become 'too big to fail'.[48]

Interestingly, mega-mergers had taken place in the United States a few years earlier, not because of a financial crisis, but because of the opportunities offered by the removal of regulatory constraints, in particular the possibility to set up a network of branches throughout the country (Riegle–Neal Interstate Efficiency Act, 1994) and to combine commercial and investment banking (abolition of the Glass–Steagall Act, 1999). The most significant mergers involved the country's largest banks: Chase Manhattan Bank and Chemical Bank (which had itself bought Manufacturers Hanover) in 1996; Citicorp and Travelers, under the name of Citigroup, in 1999; J. P. Morgan and Chase Manhattan, under the name of J. P. Morgan Chase, in 2000, and the takeover by the latter in 2004 of Bank One, the sixth American bank based in Chicago, and it too the result of numerous mergers.

Will the Financial Debacle of 2007–8 lead to further consolidation? History sends contradictory messages. On the one hand, as in most crises, there is room for rationalization in countries where there are still a great number of inevitably weakened small banks, not least in the United States. Recent research suggests that concentrated banking systems are less prone to crisis than decentralized ones.[49] Talks of European-wide consolidation, which have subsided with the crisis, will resurface sooner or later. On the other hand, there appears to be limited scope for mergers between large banks. A few large banks have indeed passed under the wing of even larger competitors: HBOS was taken over by Lloyds TSB in the UK, Wachovia by Wells Fargo in the USA, Bear Stearns and Washington Mutual by J. P. Morgan Chase, Fortis by BNP Paribas in Belgium. Such mergers, however, have been the exception rather than the rule. With banks deemed not only too big to fail, but too big to save, there have been calls for the largest banks to be downsized, including from within the banking world.[50] The declaration by US President Barack Obama, in January 2010, that banks should be banned from proprietary trading, and from 'owning, investing in or sponsoring' hedge funds and private equity groups—the so-called Volcker rule—pointed towards the possibility of demergers, rather than further mergers, at any rate in the United States. Regulation, which will be discussed in a subsequent chapter, will obviously play a major role. However, a weakening of the big banks along the lines of what happened during the Great Depression seems less likely than the trend towards consolidation following, after a time lag, a financial crisis.

PERFORMANCE

With big banks rarely failing and some being able to strengthen their position, how badly have banks actually performed in times of financial crises? A proper answer to this question would require a vast research programme on banks' performance, as, surprisingly, the issue has not been systematically explored before. To the extent that banks are linked to the 'real' economy, their level of performance, whether measured in terms of profitability or of growth, will of necessity be determined mainly by the prevailing climate. However, it should not be forgotten that, throughout their history, the big banks have suffered losses, as opposed to falling profits, only in exceptional circumstances. Banks' performances are also likely to have been affected by the nature of the crisis, in particular whether their troubles have primarily been a cause or a consequence of the wider economic crisis. In that respect, three moments in the twentieth century deserve particular attention in order to put the events of the early twenty-first in historical perspective: the 1930s, the mid-1970s, and the early to mid-1980s. The economic crisis was the dominant aspect during the Great Depression of the 1930s and the Financial Instability of the early 1970s, the financial crisis in the International Debt Crisis of 1982 and indeed the Financial Debacle of 2007–8. A few pointers to the big banks' performances, rather than a systematic analysis of profits and profitability, will underlie the comparison of the four periods.

Banks' performance during the 1930s varied very much between countries, and between banks themselves. There was a sharp contrast between Britain and to a lesser extent France, on the one hand, and the United States and Germany, on the other hand. The differences had much to do with the severity of the crisis in each country. The clearing banks remained highly profitable in Britain throughout the 1930s, with a return on equity of 7–8 per cent, with a minimum of 7.14 per cent in 1932.[51] The return was, on average, 8.8 per cent for the Midland, 7.8 per cent for Barclays, and 6.9 per cent for Lloyds. Barclays's shares appreciated by 38 per cent between 1930 and 1935 and Midland's by 21 per cent, while Lloyds's remained unchanged.[52] France did experience the orderly failure of the country's fifth largest bank, the Banque Nationale de Crédit, in 1932, as well as the collapse of a myriad of small banks. The great deposit banks, however, performed on the whole satisfactorily during the Great Depression, especially the largest, the Crédit Lyonnais, with a stable return on equity averaging 6.8 per cent between 1930 and 1938.[53] The Depression was deeper and the financial crisis more acute in Germany, and banks' profits remained depressed throughout the decade. Despite recovering somewhat after 1936, Deutsche Bank did not declare any profit from 1931 to 1934, allocating its entire operating income—as well as half of its share capital and most of its reserves in 1931—to write off losses, while its share price lost two-thirds of its value between 1929 and 1933.[54] Similarly, American banks' profits recovered very slowly in the second half of the 1930s. National City Bank suffered heavy losses between 1931 and 1934—amounting to over 30 per cent of shareholders' equity in the latter year. Profits recovered only slowly from 1935, and the bank actually achieved a negative return on equity (3 per cent) over the years 1930–8.[55] By 1932, the value of its share had fallen to a mere 4 per cent of its highest price in 1929. Chase National was about as badly hit, as it too suffered losses

on all its operations and a heavy exposure to loans to Germany and
Latin America. Other New York banks, however, such as Bankers
Trust, Central Hanover, or Guarantee Trust, fared better, having
expanded more cautiously in the pre-crash years.[56] And more generally, the profits of the banking sector held better than those of the
United States' entire domestic industry during the Great Depression,
falling by 40 per cent between 1929 and 1932, as against 85 per cent
for corporate America.[57]

The recession of 1974, while marking a turning point in the post-
war years, bore no comparison with the Great Depression, nor did the
banking crises that broke out in the middle of the decade. This is
reflected in the performance of the big banks, in particular in terms of
earnings and growth of their international business. According to *The
Banker*, the pre-tax earnings of the ten leading American banks grew
at a compound rate of 100 per cent during the 1970s, German banks
at 200 per cent, and British banks at 600 per cent.[58] Significantly,
especially from the perspective of the International Debt Crisis of
1982, the international and domestic earnings of American banks
followed opposite paths. While the former grew at a compound rate
ranging from 24 per cent for Chase Manhattan to 65 per cent for
Continental Illinois, First Chicago, and Security Pacific between 1971
and 1976, the latter stagnated or grew moderately, ranging from −14.5
per cent for Chase Manhattan to 2.2 per cent for the Bank of America
and 11.2 per cent for Continental Illinois.[59] The opportunities for
growth were limited on the internal market; the Euromarkets, on the
other hand, were open, unregulated, and highly profitable. Of course,
the markets were not free of turbulences, with, in particular, the
Financial Instability in Britain in 1973 and the collapse of I. D.
Herstatt in Germany and Franklin National Bank in the United States
in 1974. But the decade, especially its second part, was highly profitable for the banking sector, and the fact that no major bank experienced any loss was all the more remarkable given the travails of the
real economy. Banks were able to take advantage of lax supervision,
cheap lending, with interest rates remaining negative until 1979, and
profitable lending opportunities, through the enormous surplus accumulated by the oil-exporting countries since the first oil shock of
1973.

The 1980s, by contrast, were less favourable to commercial banks.
Their profitability was not affected by the International Debt Crisis of
1982[60]—at any rate not until 1987, when Citibank decided to make a

$3 billion reserve provision against its Latin American loans, resulting in the biggest loss recorded until then in banking history. Nevertheless, their margins were being squeezed, as a result of two main factors. The first was the progressive decline of the lending functions of commercial banks and the shift towards capital markets. The second was the more stringent capital ratios imposed on them in the wake of the International Debt Crisis. The measures were first taken by the American authorities, and, while aimed at protecting customers in a period of renewed financial turmoil, they contributed to the creation of an asymmetric regulatory framework—comparatively strict towards commercial banks and indulgent towards other market participants, especially investment banks, the rising stars of the new era.[61] The diverging trend between commercial banks and investment banks is well reflected in their profitability. In the United States, between 1979 and 1983, the net return on equity of the ten largest bank holding companies ranged from 13 per cent to 17 per cent, as against 20–30 per cent for the large investment banks.[62]

The losses sustained by several of the world's leading banks between 2007 and 2010 have hardly any historical precedent. The International Monetary Fund (IMF) has estimated total write downs for American banks at more than $1 trillion and at more than $900 billion for European banks, including more than $300 billion for UK banks alone.[63] Banks saw their annual profits shrink and their shares plunge accordingly.[64] Between January 2007 and March 2009, the Bank of America fell from $46 to $6.80 (with write downs and losses reaching $21 billion); Citigroup from $50 to $1.50 ($55 billion); RBS from 681p to 22p ($15 billion); Lloyds Bank from 581p to 58p ($5 billion); UBS from CHF75 to CHF10 ($44 billion). A few institutions, however, managed to limit the damages, such as J. P. Morgan Chase, which fell from $47 to $22, or HSBC, down from 690p to 375p.[65] After March 2009, the rise in the stock markets benefited all financial shares, though the major banks underperformed on the Dow Jones in the United States, with the exception of Goldman Sachs and J. P. Morgan; and on the FTSE 100 Index in the United Kingdom, with the exception of HSBC. In that respect, comparisons with the Great Depression are the most relevant. However, they also highlight the exceptional character of the Financial Debacle of 2007–8: losses and share-price collapses were on a higher and more global scale than during the Great Depression, even though, as in all previous crises, some financial institutions have performed far better than others. The debates surrounding the governance and regulation of the banking sector must be considered in the light of the magnitude of the disaster.

4

Governance

The manner in which the affairs of the world's leading banks have been conducted has obviously attracted a great deal of attention in the wake of the Financial Debacle of 2007–8. How have decisions been made? What have been the various levels of responsibility? Have the remuneration and incentives, especially bonuses, had a pernicious effect on strategic choices? The technical literature on corporate governance deals with these questions in terms of relationships between 'principal' and 'agent'—in other words how, in a firm where ownership and control are separated, dispersed shareholders, the principals, can control the behaviour of salaried managers, their agents.[1] Corporate governance is thus a matter of organizational structures and legal arrangements. But it is also a matter of personal and collective responsibility, of people's involvement in business and finance: bankers and financiers make short-term decisions and long-term strategic choices that have repercussions not only on their firms but also, in certain circumstances, on the global financial markets. The two levels must thus be taken into account: the structural and the personal. Two questions seem particularly relevant in the context of financial crises and will be discussed in this chapter. The first concerns the extent to which bankers and financiers have been held responsible for the outbreak of financial crises. The second is the impact of financial crises on the governance of financial firms, in particular the evolution of ownership and control. Both questions are linked to the place and role of financial elites in economy and society.

RESPONSIBILITY

The question of the responsibility of financial elites for the outbreak of financial crises cannot be avoided. It has, of course, very much attracted the public's attention. This is important, because public opinion is at the interface between the economic and the politico-cultural sides of financial crises. Financial institutions are business enterprises, with managers, directors, shareholders, and customers, but to some degree, and especially as far as banks are concerned, they are different, not least in terms of responsibility, from other businesses. On the one hand, by definition, banks work with the financial resources of others: deposits are not the same type of liability as equity or even debt, and their safety is paramount. On the other hand, by providing credit to firms in the entire industrial and commercial spectrum, banks play a vital role in the functioning of the economy. Conversely, banks can cause great harm to the economy—by failing to provide adequate credit, by fuelling or themselves engaging in reckless speculation, and because of the systemic consequences of their possible failure. Hence the view that banks are public-service companies rather than mere profit-making undertakings, with special rights, but also special duties—a view that is far from being unanimous but tends to gather strength in times of financial distress. The responsibility of individual bankers cannot be entirely distinguished from that of banking institutions, but the former are more likely to be personally asked to answer for their action in connection with a financial crisis.

Whatever the criticism directed towards Argentinean financial and monetary management, Edward Baring, 1st Lord Revelstoke, took the brunt of the Baring Crisis of 1890, both morally and materially. There was no doubt about the firm's, and in particular its senior partner's, responsibility in the crisis—the consequence of his 'insatiate vanity and extravagance', as his brother Tom Baring put it.[2] Baring Brothers' liability was unlimited, like that of all City merchant banks at the time, which meant that the partners were liable for their entire fortune. As senior partner, Lord Revelstoke was entitled to the largest share of the profits, but he also had to bear a similar proportion of the losses. His house in Mayfair, with its collection of French furniture and pictures, and his country estate in Devon had to be sold. Interestingly, however, and despite the long recession that followed the crisis, there was some sympathy, though not unanimously shared, for the firm and the family.[3] In any case, the family's solidarity and its social assets and networks of relationships in finance, politics, and society remained intact and enabled the firm to bounce back and regain much of its power and influence in less than ten years.

On 14 November 1907, Charles Barney, the former President of the Knickerbocker Trust Company, committed suicide in his home in the Murray Hill neighbourhood in Manhattan. Barney was very much part of New York's financial establishment, though not quite in the same league as Barings in London. He had been forced to resign a few weeks earlier, on 21 October, because of his business association with Charles Morse and Augustus Heinze and their failed attempt at cornering the copper market.[4] However, despite Barney's tragic end and the speculative manœuvres that triggered the bank runs, the American Panic of 1907 did not lead to a general outcry against bankers. Bankers, especially the most prominent among them, J. P. Morgan, seemed rather to have saved the day. Yet suspicions remained about the excessive concentration of power in the hands of Wall Street's financial elite and were fuelled by Morgan's initiatives during the crisis. In particular, the takeover of the Tennessee Coal, Iron, and Railroad Company by the US Steel Corporation that he organized in order to prevent the collapse of the New York Stock Exchange brokers Moore & Schley was seen as having greatly benefited his own interests. By then, a sizeable part of the population appeared to believe in the existence of a 'money trust' controlling the country's business.[5] In April 1912, the Pujo Committee—named after its chairman Arsène Pujo—was appointed to investigate the heavy involvement of bankers on the boards of manufacturing companies and the concentration of issues in the hands of a few investment banks. However, the inquiry's findings were inconclusive, and the committee's recommendations (tighter control of the stock exchange, higher standard of information in relation to issues) had no effect.[6]

The war was, of course, the cause of the panic that engulfed the financial markets in August 1914, though, here and there, bankers were seen as bearing their share of responsibility, if not for the outbreak of the crisis, at least for its aggravation. In Britain, in particular, the clearing bankers were strongly criticized by the governor of the Bank of England, and publicly by Keynes, for calling in loans, withdrawing gold and notes from the Bank of England, and refusing to pay out gold coins to their customers: 'Our system was endangered, not by the public running on the Banks, but by the Banks running on the Bank of England.'[7] He subsequently softened his position on account of the risks of illiquidity faced by the banks, though the claim retained its validity.[8]

But it was not until 1929 that bankers were really put in the dock. They were blamed for making mistakes or being incompetent, but they were also accused of greed, and some of dishonesty and embezzlement, all of which provoked public opprobrium and consigned the profession to years in purgatory. Some bankers were dismissed, others were tried; public inquiries looked into the issues and public opinion turned against bankers. As with other aspects of financial crises, there were significant variations between countries, depending not only on the depth of the crisis, but on the socio-political climate and each country's idiosyncratic financial culture.

Not surprisingly, nowhere were bankers more severely criticized than in the United States. A Senate investigation into banking and stock-exchange practices greatly contributed to the pillorying of Wall Street's leading bankers and financiers, with its findings echoed in the popular press and resonating with the public. The hearings went on for two years, from April 1932 to May 1934, and took a particularly energetic turn with the appointment, in January 1933, of Ferdinand Pecora as counsel of the Senate Committee on Banking and Currency. Witnesses included Charles Mitchell, chairman and former president of National City Bank and its investment bank affiliate, National City Company; Albert Wiggin, his counterpart at Chase National Bank and Chase Securities Corporation; Jack Morgan, senior partner of J. P. Morgan & Co., and Thomas Lamont, the firm's foremost partner; Albert Kahn, a senior partner in Kuhn Loeb & Co., Wall Street's second largest investment bank; Clarence Dillon, senior partner of Dillon Read & Co., another top investment bank, which rose to prominence in the 1920s; Richard Whitney, chairman of the New York Stock Exchange; and others.[9]

These Wall Street grandees were not held responsible for bringing their banks to the brink of collapse: the major banks had indeed survived four banking crises and, however weakened, still stood firm in the depth of the Depression. They were accused mainly of malpractices judged harmful to investors and condemned by a public opinion increasingly hostile to the financial world. Abuses, breach of trust and self-enrichment, in various guises, were recorded. National City Company, for example, advised investors to buy South American stock (especially two loans for Minas Geraes, a state in the Brazilian Republic, and three Peruvian government loans) that it had issued, and knew to be low grade, with no information about risks or market conditions. Kuhn Loeb issued investors in a holding company (the

Pennroad Corporation) not with actual shares but with certificates carrying no voting rights. Dillon Read structured the capital of two of its investment trusts (United States and Foreign Securities Corporation and United States and International Securities Corporation) in such a way as to exert complete control with less than 10 per cent of their capital. J. P. Morgan allocated the stock of one of its holding companies (the Alleghany Corporation) to a 'preferred list' of influential friends. National City Bank, through its affiliates, took part in stock pools, especially in copper; and National City Company was used to trade in the stock of its parent company in order to prop it up. Albert Wiggin sold short the shares of his own bank, Chase National, in the midst of the stock-market crash, netting $4 million. Charles Mitchell, whose earnings exceeded $1 million in 1929 (his basic salary was $25,000), did not pay any income tax in that year, nor did Jack Morgan and his partners in 1931 and 1932.[10]

Such manœuvres were clear failings in governance practices, though they did not actually breach the letter of the law, nor, in some cases at any rate, did they contravene the code of conduct of the day. Disclosure requirements became more stringent following the New Deal legislations, and capital losses incurred through selling stock to one's wife were no longer tax deductible. But they were scandalous enough to shock public opinion deeply, especially in the depth of the Depression, and discredit the entire banking profession. The stock-market crash rather than the banking crises was the main cause of concern, and bankers were held responsible for having fuelled the speculative fever. Charles Mitchell was acquitted of the indictment of tax evasion, but had to resign as chairman of National City Bank in 1933. Albert Wiggin had resigned as chairman of Chase National at the end of 1932, with the board voting him a life salary of $100,000, a decision soon considered as unfortunate; he subsequently renounced his compensation. Beyond these casualties, Wall Street as a whole paid a heavy price for the crash, the banking crises, and the Depression—in terms of loss of prestige and loss of political influence. From being an object of respect and admiration, the banking profession had become an object of opprobrium. And bankers were no longer in a position to dictate the political agenda and had to accept the New Deal reforms, with greater or lesser enthusiasm.

German bankers were also held responsible for the financial crisis, in a more direct though less spectacular way than their American counterparts. Their responsibility was directly involved, because virtually all the country's big banks were on the verge of collapse in July 1931 and had to be bailed out by the government. This led to a general outcry against bankers. There was strong popular resentment, as massive subsidies were granted to the banks at a time when expenses were cut and sacrifices asked from all citizens.[11] Business-men, for their part, complained about the way banks had called back loans before the crisis and were still doing so after. Politicians embraced the public mood, but the crisis made them deeply distrustful of bankers; in the first place, Brüning, the German Chancellor, accused them of having misinformed him about the extent of the crisis. The banks' rescue was accompanied by a purge of their top management: one-third of the directors of the Deutsche Bank, half of the Commerz-bank, and all but two of the new Dresdner Bank were sacked.[12]

An inquiry, the *Bank Enquête*, took place in September 1933, after the Nazis had seized power. There were denunciations by state officials of the banks' dominant position in the economy and its ill effects on trade and industry. However, bankers emerged relatively unscathed from the inquiry. Both their evidence and that of major industrialists and small businessmen alike convinced the authorities that banks had sound relationships with other enterprises. Hjalmar Schacht, who had been reappointed as Reichsbank president, had apparently set the stage for the point of view of the practical man of business to prevail over that of the Nazi ideologue.[13] Nevertheless, the government considerably strengthened its hold over banking institu-tions, and the big banks became increasingly marginalized in a regime with which they never gained favour. And Jewish bankers, who formed a significant proportion of their leadership, and featured prominently in the anti-bankers propaganda, were gradually ex-cluded from economic life.[14]

Anti-banker outbursts also took place in Britain and France, though they were less clearly directed at their responsibility for bank failures. In Britain, there were talks on the Left of a 'bankers' ramp', accused of having brought down the Labour government on 24 August 1931—the government resigned in the face of demands for spending cuts, in particular a big reduction in unemployment bene-fits, and was replaced by a government of national unity, still chaired by Labour Prime Minister Ramsay MacDonald.[15] In France, a num-ber of politico-financial scandals, such as the failure of the Oustric bank in 1930 and, especially, the Stavisky affair in 1934,[16] tarnished the reputation of the banking world. In October 1934, Édouard

Daladier, one of the leaders of the 'Popular Front', a left-wing electoral alliance between the radical, socialist, and communist parties, denounced the 'Two Hundred Families' and their control over French economy and politics. The origins of the slogan went back to the original statutes of the Bank of France in 1800, which limited shareholders' power to the largest two hundred—though the real power was in the hands of the *régents*, the bank's directors, who were recruited mainly from the ranks of the *haute banque*, an exclusive group of leading Parisian private banks.[17] In 1936, the Popular Front government modified the statutes of the Bank of France, replacing the *régents* by representatives from all sectors and interest groups, including workers' and peasants' organizations.

Banks and bankers were tamed for a generation and were only emerging from a long torpor when a financial crisis struck again in the mid-1970s. Perhaps understandably, the profession as a whole was not incriminated. The extent of the crisis was limited, the number of banks involved remained circumscribed, and speculation on foreign exchanges had only recently started. Even in Britain, where the secondary banking crisis had the most serious repercussions, the public remained unaware of the immense scale of the episode, not least because of the efforts of the Bank of England to prevent any collapse.[18] Nevertheless, failure of governance and management was addressed directly on a case-by-case basis. In Germany, the Federal Banking Supervisory Office (BAKred) withdrew Herstatt's banking licence. In the United States, the Comptroller of the Currency reorganized the management of the Franklin National Bank, installing, in particular, a new director of foreign-exchanges operations and a new president of the bank.[19] In Britain, the ownership structure of the secondary banking industry was radically transformed as a result of the Bank of England's 'Lifeboat' support operation.[20]

Bankers were not much more criticized in 1982, despite the broader scope of the International Debt Crisis. They were, of course, held responsible for a series of serious errors. One was their poor assessment of sovereign risks and fairly rudimentary analysis of country risks—with 'good management of the economy' as its main criterion and special attention paid to the availability of foreign exchange for debt service.[21] Another was of aggressively pushing loans on Third World countries, far beyond the latter's actual needs. And a third was their herd behaviour and, in the case of British banks, an inability to use their historical knowledge of emerging markets.[22] However, there was no general outcry against bankers: there were no resignations among the heads of the leading banks or even testimonies in public inquiries, whatever the fulminations against bankers' irresponsibility in Congress. The Debt Crisis was a real crisis for the borrowing, not the lending, countries.

Things were far more dramatic in Japan some fifteen years later, partly on account of the country's specific business culture, mainly on account of the number of bank failures and the depth of the slump. There were high-profile suicides: Takayuki Kamoshida, Bank of Japan's chief director, in May 1998, Takashi Uehara, a vice president of LTCB, and Kazunori Fukuda, the bank's Osaka branch manager, in May 1999. Some bankers were arrested: Hiroshi Yamauchi and Sadamasa Kawatani, former presidents of the Hokkaido Takshoku Bank, in May 1999, were charged for breach of trust.[23] Others were indicted: Katsunobu Onigi, president of LCTB, Yoshiharu Suzuki, vice president in charge of domestic lending, and another vice president, in June 1999, on charges related to hiding the bank's insolvency in 1998.[24] The task of establishing the responsibility, in terms of criminal and civil liability, of the executives of failed financial institutions fell to the Deposit Insurance Corporation of Japan (DICJ) along with its sister organization, the Resolution and Collection Corporation (RCC): they brought 125 cases for civil compensation, amounting to ¥127.1 billion, between 1997 and 2009.[25]

Japanese bankers thus paid a high price for the crisis, possibly higher than even American and German bankers in the 1930s. They were primarily brought to account for the failure of individual banking institutions, as were German bankers after the crisis of 1931, though with more allegations of malpractices. But they were also held responsible for the country's severe depression, mainly because of the excesses of the 1980s, though to a lesser extent than American bankers during the New Deal. Significantly, the bad-debt mess persisted well into the economic crisis, with resignations of high-ranking executives taking place only when problems became public, and politicians continuing to inject funds into their constituents' firms in order to keep them in business.[26]

In line with the nature and severity of the Financial Debacle of 2007–8, bankers have been widely considered as the prime culprits of the catastrophe by public opinion, with greed and excessive risk-taking as the main charges—whatever the role of global imbalances or a loose monetary policy. However, it is also striking that, at the time of writing (early 2010), indictment had not gone far beyond the level of public opinion, whether in the press or through public declarations. In none of the countries affected by the crisis has there been any trial—as, admittedly, there was no breach of law—of leading bankers. A number of investigations have taken place, and, in particular, a 'Financial Crisis Inquiry Commission' was created in the United States on 20 May 2009 in order 'to examine the causes, domestic and global, of the current financial and economic crisis', with powers comparable to that of the Pecora Commission. Four of the country's leading bankers appeared as witnesses in its first public hearing on 13 January 2010.[27] They escaped very lightly: '"Sorry" still seems to be the hardest word on Wall Street' was the *Washington Post* comment.[28] A few leading bankers have been forced to resign. Some, such as Charles Prince of Citigroup or Marcel Ospel of UBS, did so as a result of the heavy losses suffered by their bank; others, most notably Richard Fuld of Lehman Brothers, following their bank's collapse. The reputation of the profession has been badly tarnished, yet the standing of a few individual bankers has been enhanced by their performance through the crisis—for example, James Dimon, of J. P. Morgan Chase, or Lloyd Blankfein, of Goldman Sachs, the *Financial Times's* 'Person of the Year' for 2009.[29]

The situation is thus paradoxical. On the one hand, the links between the financial debacle and the global economic downturn are stronger than in any previous crisis, whether in terms of intensity (think of the Baring Crisis or the International Debt Crisis) or causality (think of the Great Depression or the Japanese Banking Crisis); likewise, the responsibility of bankers for both shocks has been better understood than ever before. On the other hand, it is not at all clear, at any rate in early 2010, that this will lead to significant changes in the banks' governance—as witnessed by the most vividly debated issue, that of bankers' bonuses. It might be that the crisis has not bitten deep enough. It might also be that the structures of banks' ownership and control are not fundamentally altered by financial crises—apart from measures of (usually temporary) nationalizations taken to stem major financial crises.

OWNERSHIP AND CONTROL

Banks were the first companies, alongside railways, where ownership was separated from control. Yet big business in the financial sector has never entirely freed itself from the dominance of private interests. The 'banking revolution' of the nineteenth century saw the advent of the joint stock bank, in Britain in the 1830s, in continental Europe in the 1850s. By the late nineteenth century, a group of large commercial banks had emerged in most European countries and were extending their network of branches nationwide.[30] Banks were smaller in the United States, since opening branches in another state was prohibited by law.[31] The 'new banks' had several thousand shareholders and were managed by a board of directors who usually delegated the running of the bank's daily business to full-time salaried managers.[32] Banks had thus become typical managerial enterprises.[33]

There were, however, some limits to the rise of managerial capitalism within the financial world. In the first place, private bankers not only survived but remained highly influential. Their position was particularly strong in the then undisputed financial centre of the world, the City of London. The number of private deposit banks had been steadily diminishing in England since the 1870s, but they had held their own in London. They were old-established family concerns whose very wealthy partners were well integrated into the English aristocracy; and, in terms of collective size, they were still comparable to their joint stock rivals.[34] The Baring Crisis dealt them a fatal blow and thus altered the ownership structure of English banking[35]—but only partially. Another group of private banks, the merchant banks, were enjoying a golden age that was to last until the First World War. From a socio-professional point of view, merchant bankers formed the aristocracy of the City: Rothschild, Baring, Morgan Grenfell, Schröder, Kleinwort, Hambro—the names by themselves evoke this status. From an economic point of view, they kept their hold on the two financial activities that were at the heart of London's role as the world's financial centre: the acceptance business, with a 70 per cent market share in 1913, and the issuing business, with 40 per cent. In the United States, the most powerful banks—the investment banks—were mostly private banks. They were instrumental in financing railway construction in the 1870s and 1880s, the large manufacturing companies in the 1890s, and the merger wave in American business at the turn of the twentieth century, with J. P. Morgan and

Kuhn Loeb in the lead. In New York, their status was comparable to that of the merchant banks in London, with whom they had close business, social, and sometimes even family ties. Elsewhere, the leading private bankers were no longer in a dominant position, despite their wealth, prestige, and influence—as witnessed by the position of the Paris *haute banque*, where only the Rothschilds remained a force to be reckoned with.

Moreover, the separation between ownership and control was far from complete within the joint stock banks. Managerial hierarchies remained thin and family interests fairly strong. In the United States, the presidents of the largest banks often had a controlling stake in the company: James Stillman, for example, held 22 per cent of the capital of National Citibank by the turn of the twentieth century.[36] Likewise George Baker, the president of the First National Bank of New York, was its largest shareholder. The divorce between ownership and control was more advanced in Europe. Nevertheless, in England, former private bankers and partners in merchant firms and merchant-banking firms made up the bulk of the directors of the major London clearing banks. Professional bankers—in other words, salaried managers—often remained in their shadow.[37] Dominant figures among salaried managers, such as Edward Holden, chairman and managing director of the Midland Bank, were the exception rather than the rule.[38] In the big German banks, by contrast, the salaried managers were in control. They sat on the bank's executive board, which meant that they were actually managing the bank, the supervisory board having been reduced to a mere controlling body representing shareholders, many of them private bankers.[39] In France, too, the big banks were run by powerful *directeurs généraux*, with little interference from the board.[40]

This situation was reflected in the respective levels of remuneration and fortune of private bankers and salaried managers of joint stock banks. Two questions require particular attention: one has to do with how much bankers actually earned and how rich they were, the other with whether they earned more and were richer than other business people. Starting with this latter point, bankers and financiers were the wealthiest business group in Europe in the early twentieth century, whether in 'financial' Britain (where they represented some 25 per cent of the businessmen worth $2.5 million or more who died between 1900 and 1939, as against 9 per cent for ironmasters) or in 'industrial' Germany (where the proportions were respectively 27 and

12 per cent of those worth $1.5 million or more).[41] Incomes are harder to compare for this period, but there are clear indications that salaries in the financial sector were, not surprisingly, among the highest in the business world. In Britain, the salaries of the top managers were above average,[42] probably of the same order as those of the managers of the big railway companies, which were considered to be particularly high.[43] In Germany, they were at the same level as those of the executive directors of the heavy industry companies—the foremost sector in German business.[44]

The highest incomes and the largest fortunes in the financial sector were made by investing one's own money—in other words, as a partner of a private bank rather than as a manager of a joint stock bank. The wealthiest were the partners in the most prominent firms. In the Unites States, John Pierpont Morgan was the richest banker, though the $80 million estate he left on his death in 1913 fell short of the greatest fortunes made in industry by the likes of Carnegie or Rockefeller.[45] In Europe, the Rothschilds, as a family, came first by a significant margin, while individually the French Rothschilds ($50 million each for Alphonse and Gustave) came ahead of their English cousins. In the City of London, most of the multimillionaires (more than $5 million) were partners in a leading merchant bank: Baring Brothers, Schroders, Hambro, Samuel Montagu, Robert Fleming.[46] In Germany, private bankers in both Frankfurt and Berlin were far wealthier than the managing directors of the big Berlin credit banks. Interestingly, however, the latter were the richest among the salaried managers, with several fortunes in excess of $2 million. This reflected the governance structure of German business. Profit-sharing plans and bonuses are difficult to compare for this period. However, unlike their counterparts in Britain and France, senior managers in German banks sat on, and often chaired, the supervisory boards of a myriad of companies (usually at least twenty for the managing directors of the big Berlin banks), for which they received a not insignificant fee. However, this was not enough to bridge the gap with owner managers.[47]

Managerial capitalism became more firmly established in the banking world in the decades following the First World War, not so much as a reaction to a specific financial crisis, but rather in line with the general trend in business development. In Britain, with the emergence of the 'Big Five', professional bankers increased their power not only within their bank, but within the City at large. The phenomenon

is perhaps best epitomized by the election in 1917 of Frederick Goodenough as chairman of Barclays Bank, this former 'corporate home
for private bankers'[48]—Goodenough had been appointed secretary in
1896 and general manager in 1903. In the United States' largest bank,
National City, the separation between ownership and control was
finally achieved with the appointment as president in 1921 of Charles
Mitchell, who, unlike Stillman, had no stake in the bank. 'Agency
problems' were addressed, and a bonus plan, known as the management fund, was adopted in 1923, linking the remuneration of senior
executives to the bank's performance. In practice, after a deduction of
8 per cent, senior executives shared between themselves 20 per cent of
the bank's profits. Mitchell's fixed salary was fairly modest, $25,000—
less, for example, than Frederick Goodenough's $42,000 plus bonuses
on his appointment in 1917. His total pay package was far higher,
especially in the boom years of the late 1920s, reaching $3.5 million
between 1927 and 1929, to which must be added his individual
participations in the bank's flotations, as revealed in the Pecora
hearings.[49]

Bonuses were not the foremost issues in the inquests into the
financial crisis and the Depression, but they did raise concerns,
much more in the United States than in Europe.[50] Mitchell and
other National City top executives saw themselves as 'the equivalent
of partners in a private banking or investment firm'. However, questions were raised about 'the propriety of permitting executives to
share to such an extent the net earnings of financial institutions
without having to bear any part of the losses'. Questions were also
raised about the risk of a 'lack of care in the handling and sale of
securities to the public'. Interestingly, Mitchell admitted that the
incentive plan carried such risk and may have had 'some influence'
on the fact that almost a fifth of the securities that had been issued by
the National City Company, the investment banking arm of National
City Bank, in the previous ten years were in default. Other bankers
concurred. Winthrop Aldrich, who succeeded Albert Wiggin as
chairman of Chase National, declared that the 'the spirit of speculation should be eradicated from the spirit of commercial banks' and
that 'the only compensation [bank officers] should receive should be
their salary or such other compensation as is permitted by the board
of directors where full disclosure is made'.[51] The issue of executives'
bonuses died out as banks operated under a tight regulatory regime in
the following decades.

In any case, private banks remained at the apex of international finance throughout the 1920s—and they still worked with their own capital. In London, merchant bankers continued to form the City's aristocracy, in terms of wealth, status, and power. The group of leading houses was the same as before the war—Rothschilds, Barings, Morgan Grenfell, Schroders, Kleinworts, Hambros. Despite their comparatively modest size and in face of fiercer competition from the clearing banks, these houses remained dominant in both the accepting and the issuing businesses, even though they suffered from the decline of foreign issues on the London market. Ultimately, it was at the crossroads of finance and international politics that merchant bankers benefited from a decisive advantage—an advantage that they owed to their social status; to their network of relationships and to their presence on the court of directors of the Bank of England and their closeness to the governor, Montagu Norman; and to their expertise in the monetary questions that dominated the problems inherited from the war. On Wall Street, large-scale international financial operations continued to be the preserve of the investment banks, and they greatly benefited from the fact that New York had overtaken London as the main centre for the issue of foreign loans. Private banks—J. P. Morgan, Kuhn Loeb, Kidder Peabody, Lee Higginson, Dillon Read, and a few others—still dominated the field. The 1920s were undoubtedly J. P. Morgan's apogee, and in many respects the bank's decade—through the sheer volume of its operations, the strength of its international connections, not least with Morgan Grenfell in London, and its unique position at the hub of the world of business and politics, particularly in the field of financial diplomacy.

The financial crises of the Great Depression did not fundamentally alter the ownership structures prevailing within the banking sector of the advanced economies. Local private banks were decimated. The big banks strengthened their position and became more bureaucratized institutions. However, in Britain and the United States in particular, a powerful group of merchant banks and investment banks was able to survive the Depression, the war, the decline in international capital flows and, for American firms, an anti-trust trial at the end of the war, abandoned in 1953. They were no longer regal, but still enjoyed prestige and influence and perpetuated the tradition of the partnership form of organization in a banking world increasingly dominated by corporate giants. The change took place in the 1960s, with the conversion of most merchant banks and investment banks into public companies. J. P. Morgan & Co., a commercial bank following the Glass–Steagall Act, had done so as early as 1940—commercial banking required higher capital levels. Morgan Stanley, the investment bank offspring of the House of Morgan, founded in 1935, followed thirty years later, in 1970, with partial incorporation, and in 1975 with full limited liability. Most leading investment banks had converted earlier—Merrill Lynch, for example, in 1959, Dillon Read in 1964.[52] The trend had started earlier in Britain: Baring Brothers was registered as a limited company after its near collapse in 1890, Hambros and Morgan Grenfell in 1934, Schroders in 1959. However, they had remained in family hands. What changed in the 1960s, in Britain and the United States, was the opening of both ownership and control to outside interests, which, ultimately, meant the end of the private bank character of these venerable institutions.

Nevertheless, aspects of the partnership form of organization did not completely disappear, even after conversion into public companies. The appellation 'partner' was often preferred to that of 'director': at Morgan Stanley, for example, where the number of partners increased from more than twenty in the early 1960s to nearly forty by the mid-1970s.[53] At Schroders, the number of directors increased from twenty to thirty-three between 1962 and 1973.[54] Some firms, such as Dillon Read, were owned and controlled by their management.[55] Other firms, most notably Goldman Sachs, remained a private partnership until the very end of the twentieth century, by which time it had 174 partners. Even after going public in 1999, the firm retained a type of partnership structure—though closer to the modern corporation than to the private bank of old.[56] In new fields of financial activities, such as hedge funds and private equity, firms were set up by independent financiers, often with a partnership form of organization. These remnants of the partnership model were increasingly present in the governance of the world's leading banks, especially those operating in the two global financial centres, London and New York. They all became universal banks and had to accommodate investment bankers in their ranks—though a different culture and, especially, significant differences in remuneration levels continued to separate commercial banking from investment banking within the same institutions. Former partners in the merchant or investment banks they had taken over were usually offered senior positions in the acquiring institution, often foreign banks setting up in London or New York. More generally, investment bankers became highly mobile, with star traders or even entire teams being lured from rival banks, enjoying a more autonomous status than that of a typical salaried manager.[57] As in other sectors, markets and networks played an enhanced role while global enterprises remained in force.[58]

FINANCIAL ELITES

The position of financial elites has thus, not surprisingly, changed in the course of the twentieth and early twenty-first centuries. On the one hand, this has been a classical story of increasing separation between ownership and control. The financial elites of the late twentieth and early twenty-first centuries are no longer made up of private bankers, who lost ground to joint stock banks in the last quarter of the nineteenth century and were marginalized if not entirely eliminated after the Great Depression, but of salaried managers in large public companies—banks, insurance companies, investment companies, and their specialized subsidiaries. But, on the other hand, these new financial elites have retained some of the characteristics, and also some of the prerogatives, of the old private investment bankers.

The professional status deriving from the persistence of the partnership form of organization is one of them. Another is a high degree of cosmopolitanism—a characteristic of financial elites in a global economy. Bankers and financiers have always been attracted to the most dynamic international financial centres. German and Swiss bankers decisively shaped the Parisian *haute banque* in the first half of the nineteenth century. A more cosmopolitan immigration swelled the ranks of international finance in London throughout the nineteenth century. In New York, an entire area of investment banking was built up by German Jewish immigrants during the second half of the nineteenth century. In the 1930s, the anti-Semitism of the Nazi regime made numerous Jewish bankers from Germany and central Europe leave, bound mainly for New York and London. These foreign bankers and financiers usually established their own firm, immigrated for good, and became assimilated in the local elites from the second generation onwards, even if the international networks continued to operate.[59] The cosmopolitanism of the financial elites changed in the last quarter of the twentieth century, with the reopening of the world economy. It became based on much more transient migrations, those of the senior executives of the big multinational banks, who moved from one financial centre to another according to the responsibilities that they were called upon to assume. Expansion abroad, carried out by purchasing major banks, especially in the United States and Britain, greatly contributed to this development.

The most important prerogative shared by the old and new financial elites has been their level of remuneration, traditionally higher than in other sectors, but which has reached unprecedented levels in the new era of global finance.[60] The scale of the highest rewards might not have exceeded that achieved by the financial magnates of the first globalization, and such opportunities have remained the preserve of a fairly small elite. However, while it is difficult to ascertain whether the proportion of bankers benefiting from a very high income was higher in 2000 than in 1900,[61] this seems to have been the case, because of the vast expansion of the financial sector and the far greater complexity of financial transactions; and because salaried managers and traders, and no longer only self-employed entrepreneurs, were able to make their fortune—thanks not only to salaries but, especially, to incentives such as bonuses and stock options. In particular, membership of the governing bodies of major financial institutions—boards of directors and boards of management—has markedly increased. In the early twentieth century, the top management of a big London clearing bank usually included a general manager and one or two deputies. A modern bank's top management has become much larger and more complex. From the 1960s onwards, the big banks reorganized themselves, often with the help of management consultants, first and foremost McKinsey. Citibank adopted a divisional structure from 1967 and the National Westminster bank from 1970. In 2005, the governing bodies of UBS were made up of a board of directors with ten members, a group executive board of eight members, and a group managing board of more than fifty members. Similar structures were found in all big banks. The senior management of Citigroup, the then largest bank in the world, was made up of a management committee of fifty-seven people, including the group's chairman and vice chairman.

Moreover, high incomes have not been the sole privilege of members of these governing bodies, but also of star traders and others in sales (of equity or structured products), or in mergers and acquisitions, thanks to special fees and bonuses. This has been reflected in the investment bankers' culture on Wall Street—and also in the City of London—a culture of high risks and high rewards, in a climate of high uncertainty regarding job security; a culture of 'smartness', of being at one with the market and capable of mastering risk. Bonuses have been at the heart of this culture, rewarding deals, whatever their impact on the economy and society.[62]

The changes were thus more complex than a mere replacement of owner managers by salaried managers—the move had been more or less completed before the Second World War. If anything, there had been a retreat from the ideal-type of managerial capitalism by the turn of the twenty-first century. On a far greater scale than in any other period, the leaders of the major financial institutions, who were not significant shareholders of their company, were in a position where they enjoyed some of the privileges of the partners of a private bank, in particular in terms of level of remuneration, without having to bear the concomitant responsibilities, in particular loyalty to the firm and risking their own capital. A number of commentators have observed that changes to the pre-crisis order, if they are to happen, will have to be cultural.[63] History suggests that cultural values—attitudes towards profits, rewards and entitlements, public and private responsibility, ethical standards—have changed very little and only as a result of a violent shock. Has the shock of the crisis and recession of 2007–10 been violent enough? In early 2010, this appeared doubtful, though the outcry against bonuses, the absurdly high remunerations of top executives, and the ensuing short-termism signal more than a simple awareness of the problem. Regulation can help change cultural values, and vice versa.

5

Regulation

Financial crises and regulation are closely linked. Good regulation, it is commonly assumed, should prevent the outbreak of financial crises. This seems to be confirmed by historical evidence: the number of banking crises breaking out in advanced economies has increased markedly since the end of Bretton Woods, reaching a level of frequency, if not of depth, comparable to that of the Great Depression.[1] But what is good regulation? The debates taking place in the wake of the 2007–8 Financial Debacle have shown just how difficult it is to find the right answer.[2] Financial crises have tended to spark off a strong demand for a change in the regulatory environment. And yet crises have kept recurring. It is true that measures taken in the wake of one crisis can prove woefully inadequate to contain the following one—a classical case of fighting the previous war. The opportunity properly to design a regulatory framework can easily be missed— whether in the gloom following a crisis or in the euphoria of a boom, or because of the difficulty of coping with a major innovation. Economic, political, ideological, or technical divergence, if not outright conflict—between bankers, customers, politicians, and regulators themselves—can easily blur the picture and compromise the outcome. Striking the right balance between insufficient or excessive control, self- or state regulation, national or international compliance has historically proved a huge challenge.

The demand if not the need for regulation is at its highest during and especially immediately after a severe financial crisis. This is when the opportunity for real change, as opposed to an accommodation of the existing order, presents itself. This chapter first looks at the perception and understanding of the major financial crises, on which the degree of intensity of the need for change ultimately depends. It then turns to the question of the regulation, or absence of regulation, of financial innovations, especially those associated with a major crisis. Finally, it considers how the opportunities for improving the existing regulatory framework have actually been seized. Regulation and deregulation must be seen as the two sides of the same coin. Regulation can be understood as measures taken by the financial authorities in order to stabilize the financial system and requiring a degree of compliance on the part of financial actors. But the objectives of the authorities can also be to improve the efficiency of the capital markets, or to promote financial innovation, by removing restrictions—in other words, through deregulation. The balance among these purposes has changed over time, but there have been permanent tensions and contradictions between them. Financial regulation has primarily been a national prerogative. This chapter will be concerned with this level of intervention, to the extent that it can be isolated from external pressures. Attempts at setting up an international regulatory framework will be discussed in Chapter 6.

PERCEPTION

The 'never-again' feeling is a good indicator of the perception of a financial crisis—of its severity, its causes, the risks of a relapse, and how to prevent it. Perhaps surprisingly, the 'never-again' feeling, while present in all crises, has only occasionally been very strong in the eight financial crises that have hit the major economies since the late nineteenth century. The financial crises of the Great Depression marked a watershed, because of both the strength of the feeling and the fact that financial crises would never be perceived in the same way again.

The Baring Crisis of 1890 shook the City but did not traumatize it, or not for long. The news that Barings had fallen was, of course, astounding, but it was revealed once the crisis had actually been solved and the panic was short-lived. More significantly, the Baring Crisis did not lead to much soul searching in the City or Westminster about the national or international financial system. The severity of the crisis in Britain was primarily due to Barings' immense reputation and role in the markets. Its problems were attributed to individual mistakes rather than structural deficiencies. The other giant, Rothschilds, was above suspicion, doubts about the creditworthiness of other leading houses were soon dissipated, and the joint stock banks were rapidly gaining power within the banking community. The other correlated cause of the crisis was, of course, Argentina: the Argentine foreign debt was renegotiated with a group of London bankers known as the Rothschild Committee.[3] Foreign issues did decline in the years following the crisis, but, unlike what would happen nearly a century later, there was no debate about the risks associated with sovereign loans and more generally emerging markets. The City of London had a long experience of capital exports, the first Latin American debt crisis had taken place in the 1820s, and in 1875 a Select Committee on Loans to Foreign States had inquired on the conditions in which such loans were issued, centring on the role of the stock exchange—without, however, making binding recommendations.[4] A country's risk was evaluated on the basis of its budget, more precisely through the ratio of the cost of servicing its debt to its income from taxes. And the reputation of the issuing house offered guarantees to investors.[5] The main concern raised by the Baring Crisis was about Britain's gold reserves: were they really insufficient or was it acceptable to count on London's ability to attract gold if need be? There was also the matter of safeguarding these reserves: should the gold reserves accumulated by the clearing banks be deposited at the Bank of England? Or should each bank keep its own gold bars and coins and publish their total amount on its balance sheet? At the heart of the matter lay the contradiction between the Bank of England's responsibility as a central bank and its commercial activities as a private bank. No solution was found before 1914.[6]

Unlike the Baring Crisis, the American Panic of 1907 was not radically different from the recurrent banking crises that had marked American banking history in the nineteenth century,[7] even though it mainly involved a new type of financial institution, the trust company. The crisis was widely perceived as exceptionally severe—'the industrial paralysis and prostration was the very worst ever experienced in the country's history', according to the *Commercial and Financial Chronicle*[8]—and was primarily attributed to deficiencies in the American banking system, in particular the absence of a central bank. The fact that banking crises in the United States were more frequent and more severe than in Western Europe or in its northern neighbour Canada did not escape contemporaries. On 30 May 1908, Congress passed the Aldrich–Vreeland Act, which, in addition to enacting a scheme allowing banks to issue emergency notes, created the National Monetary Commission, whose mission was to 'inquire into and report to Congress . . . what changes are necessary or desirable in the monetary system of the United States or in the laws relating to banking and currency'. The Commission, chaired by Nelson Aldrich, a Republican Senator close to Wall Street banking circles, embarked on a formidable international inquiry, commissioning reports, written by leading national experts, and conducting interviews on the banking and currency systems of all major economies.[9] Another concern, of a more political nature, underlay the perception of the 1907 crisis: the concentration of power in the hands of Wall Street's financial elite. J. P. Morgan might have single-handedly saved the financial system, but the country's fate could not be left in the hands of one man. The Pujo Committee was appointed in 1912 to investigate the 'concentration of money and credit' and the fears aroused by the possible existence of a 'money trust' helped overcome the resistance to the creation of the Federal Reserve System in 1913—the major regulatory outcome of the Panic of 1907.

The Financial Crisis of July–August 1914 was, of course, different. The crisis was caused by the approach and then the outbreak of hostilities, and subsequent financial disturbances were overwhelmed by the magnitude of the demands of a total war. And yet the war acted as a revelator, first of the fragility of the financial system, both nationally and internationally. As one of Baring Brothers' partners wrote in a letter: 'It is mortifying in the extreme to find how instantaneously the credit edifice which we have built for generations could tumble to pieces in a night.'[10] The war also revealed the new role of the state in financial affairs—saviour, customer, but also supervisor. To a remark made by Edward Holden, chairman of the London City and Midland Bank, one of the world's largest banks, that the state should take the responsibility if it had forced the banks to lend a lot of money wrongfully, David Lloyd George, the Chancellor of the Exchequer, answered: 'It takes the responsibility and the control.'[11] The relationship between the state and financial world would never be the same again. However, this was not yet clearly perceived in the aftermath of the war, nor that the world economic situation was very different from what it had been four or five years earlier. On the contrary, both financial and political leaders were determined to return to the pre-war order, longingly remembered as the *Belle Époque*. Nowhere was this clearer than in monetary matters, with the restoration of the gold standard in the early 1920s, which proved to be the most important contributory factor to the severity of the Great Depression.[12]

Unlike other crises, the Great Depression has been analysed time and again by economists and historians. As Ben Bernanke put it: 'To understand the Great Depression is the Holy Grail of macroeconomics.'[13] This particular status of the Great Depression as one of the defining moments in the world's history somewhat blurs the distinction between the perception of contemporaries and that of ensuing generations. The financial regulations inherited from the Great Depression go beyond the immediate measures taken as a response to the banking crises, whatever their significance, and include the war and even the post-war years. The same goes with the analyses and interpretations of the crisis. Not only has the Great Depression become the reference against which subsequent crises have been judged; it has also altered the way subsequent crises have been dealt with—not least thanks to a far better understanding of economic and financial crises, from Keynes onwards.

Discussing how the banking crises of the 1930s were perceived by contemporaries would go far beyond the scope of this chapter or even this book. A few remarks can be made in connection with our general purpose. The first is the sense of the sheer enormity of the Depression— the worldwide dimension of the crisis, the human misery of mass unemployment, the apparent collapse of capitalism, and also the rise of political extremism and growing international instability. The banking crises were only part of a much broader phenomenon, however intricate their links with the state of the economy. A second point to bear in mind is that, whatever the global character of the slump, it was felt very unevenly across countries, and analyses differed greatly as to the causes, nature, and impact of the financial crises. Britain was more concerned with the fate of the pound than its fairly stable banking system. In France, politico-financial scandals tended to overshadow a lingering though never really acute banking crisis. Opinions were divided in Germany, between those who attributed the crisis to the banks themselves—excessive foreign liabilities, insufficient equity, and ultimately the pernicious effects of universal banking—and those who saw the problem in the international politico-economic context—German foreign policy on reparations.[14] In the United States, the banking system remained, as in 1907, the main culprit, despite the creation, in the interval, of the Federal Reserve, which was supposed to have stabilized it. More than elsewhere, the blame was put on the speculative excesses of the 1920s and the financial crisis, and more generally the Depression, linked to the Wall Street crash of October 1929.[15] Reactions to the crisis, in particular the necessity to do something, were thus motivated by a combination of economic and political considerations and, despite national differences, had their roots in a common zeitgeist—a sense that solutions should be found in state intervention rather than market mechanisms.

Like the financial crises of the 1930s, though in a far less dramatic way, those of the early 1970s were part of a broader economic crisis. Despite a number of bank failures (Bankhaus Herstatt in Germany, Franklin National Bank in the USA, fringe banks in the UK), which required the intervention of the monetary authorities, it was the general economic climate—oil shock, 'stagflation', rising unemployment—and the crisis affecting other industries, not least iron and steel, that mostly exercised the minds of decision-makers. More generally, there was a pervasive feeling that an era was coming to an end—a change best expressed, in the field of economics, by the mounting neo-classical challenge to Keynesianism—to which the end of the regime of fixed exchange rates strongly contributed. As far as banking was concerned, the awareness of potential risks lying ahead was particularly strong. The crises marked the end of a long period of stability—these were the first banking failures of any significance since the Great Depression! While banking difficulties were seen as part of the adverse economic climate, in particular inflation and higher interest rates, this new instability was primarily attributed to the internationalization of financial activities and the higher risks they entailed—risks deriving from the growth of the foreign-exchange market and the Eurocurrency interbank market. The frailty of the international banking system became apparent, raising the question of an international lender of last resort.[16]

The Mexican default in August 1982 came hard on the heels of the banking crises of the early 1970s, and, though different in many respects, the near panic was also linked to the development of the Euromarkets and, more generally, to an increasingly unstable international financial system. What became known as the International Debt Crisis was, on the one hand, a violent though short-lived shock—there might have been less noticeable bank failures than in 1974, but the feeling that the international financial system could collapse was more vivid. On the other hand, it was a protracted affair, as what was also called the Latin American—and also the Third

World—Debt Crisis lasted throughout the 1980s and beyond. The International Debt Crisis triggered off much debate and analysis—politico-strategic, academic, and journalistic. Three interrelated problems came to the fore: the lending policy of the commercial banks; the level of indebtedness of Third World countries; and the global character of the crisis. Banks were judged severely—for lending at all costs and taking excessive risks. Attention, in particular, was drawn to their exposure to a single borrower, considered too high; and to their capital ratios, considered too low.[17] In Europe and, especially, in the United States, there were demands for stricter capital requirements and banking supervision, which increased after further bank failures—Continental Illinois in the United States and Banco Ambrosiano in Italy. On the other hand, as with the Baring Crisis nearly a hundred years earlier, the problems at the periphery caused far more concern than those in the core industrial countries. Banks might have overlent, but, for most analysts, the unsustainable debt level reached in countries such as Mexico, Brazil, or Argentina was due to the poor conduct of their economy, in particular their lack of fiscal and monetary discipline. For some, however, the consequences of such mismanagement were compounded by adverse global economic conditions, in particular oil-price increases and higher interest rates.[18] In any case, the 'structural adjustment' programmes of the International Monetary Fund (IMF) and the World Bank were seen as the right solution here—despite being subjected, in several quarters, to strong criticism. More than ever before, the International Debt Crisis of 1982 was perceived as a global financial crisis, calling, not only for an international response, but also for international cooperation in order to prevent the outbreak of another crisis.

The Japanese Banking Crisis of 1997–8 broke out several years into the slump, as the public was becoming progressively aware of the degradation of the economic climate—through rising unemployment, reductions in employee benefits, overtime hours, wage reductions, and inability to sustain mortgage payments. The big banks had indeed fuelled the stock-market and property booms during the 1980s. However, the causes of the crisis were not seen as lying exclusively with the deterioration of the Japanese economy. The Japanese banks appeared to be suffering from structural problems—in particular with regards to bad loans—and in need of radical reforms going beyond the type of regulatory measures usually taken in the wake of financial crises, such as tightening supervision and imposing higher capital requirements. In fact, the country's entire financial regulatory framework, especially the informal and personal relationships between the Ministry of Finance and the banks, was judged by Japanese and foreign observers alike as ill suited to the demands of a severe crisis, hence the slow response of the authorities to the banks' problems.[19] Similar views were held about the Japanese economy as a whole. Public opinion has tended to eschew business-cycle explanations of the economic crisis, implying targeted macro-economic measures, in favour of structural explanations, implying a fundamental reform of the system.[20]

The perception of financial crises has been transformed during the last quarter of the twentieth century. The analysis and discussion of events were no longer confined to a small group of financiers, politicians, senior civil servants, and special advisers. The internationalization of financial activities, the greater role played by international institutions such as the IMF, the World Bank, and the Bank for International Settlements, the expansion of the economic profession, not only in universities but also in banks and other organizations—all these factors made financial crises become the subject of an ever-increasing number of published studies in books and journals, and, later, on the Internet. The International Debt Crisis set up a trend that accelerated with the Japanese Banking Crisis and, a few years later, the financial crisis in East Asia and Russia. These crises were analysed not only in the country or the region where they took place, but worldwide, especially in international financial organizations. The use of economic models has standardized their analysis in an attempt by the economic profession to draw prescriptive lessons from past experiences.

The reactions to the Financial Debacle of 2007–8 were as global as the crisis itself. In comparison to previous experiences, its perception was at first that of a predominantly financial meltdown, more so than in the 1930s, the early 1970s, or the 1990s in Japan, when the banking crises were part of a broader economic downturn; the International Debt Crisis of the early 1980s was also primarily financial as far as advanced economies were concerned, but was closely linked with the deep economic problems of Latin American and other developing countries, as was the Baring Crisis in 1890. The global character of the 2007–8 crisis was also underlined, with particular attention being drawn to the destabilizing effects of the world's growing economic imbalances since the turn of the twenty-first century; and the need for an internationally coordinated response to the crisis, including in terms of a global regulation of the financial system—a recurring theme since the 1970s. As the effects of the financial crises started to be felt on the real economy, attention turned to the nature of the recession, the risks of sliding into depression, the merits of fiscal stimuli, and exit strategies.

The 'great recession' of the early twenty-first century is still unfolding and its perception is still being shaped by new events. Less than two years after the fall of Lehman Brothers, three main observations can be made. First, no other crisis in history has ever been debated in such an extended way—by being for long and recurring periods on top of the political agenda; by sustained media coverage, despite the aridity of the topic; and by a flurry of publications, from highly academic analyses to popular books. It will be up to a new generation of historians to reflect on this phenomenon. Second, the 'never-again' feeling has been very strong and almost unanimous, especially at the height of the financial collapse, with the spectre of 1929 reappearing more vividly than at any time since the end of the war. However, and this is the third point, with time passing, the determination to push for radical change has been tempered by the inevitable return to business as usual. Financial innovations and their proper regulation have been at the heart of this growing tension, and their links with financial crises require further examination.

FINANCIAL INNOVATION

During a visit to the London School of Economics in June 2009, Queen Elizabeth II asked why nobody had seen the credit crunch coming. She was answered in writing, a month later: 'Many people did foresee the crisis. However, the exact form that it would take and the timing of its onset and ferocity were foreseen by nobody.'[21] The same general answer could be given about all financial crises—though the specific arguments developed in the letter are entirely illuminating within the context of the recent crisis.

The financial press had been warning about the inevitability of a crash in Argentina since 1887, but the collapse of Baring Brothers was not thought possible until it actually happened in November 1890. The conditions of the New York capital market had deteriorated badly during the summer of 1907, but nobody had predicted the effects that a failed corner on copper could have on trust companies, the weak link in the American banking system. The First World War was a far more devastating catastrophe than any financial crisis, but its outbreak was strikingly similar to that of many of them: the possibility of a war between the European powers was envisaged and preparations, including financial, were made for this eventuality, and yet the assassination in Sarajevo in June 1914 and the July crisis came as a storm out of a blue sky. Stock-market bubbles are known to burst eventually, and there were warnings in 1929 in New York and in 1990 in Tokyo, yet the depth of the following depressions was not foreseen. By the late 1970s, many could see that the level of foreign lending to developing countries was no longer sustainable, but the Mexican default in 1982 and its possible generalization to other borrowers came as a surprise. And, as a group of economists told the Queen in 2009: 'There were many warnings about imbalances in the financial markets and in the global economy.'

One of the reasons for the unpredictability of financial crises might well be the destabilizing effects of financial innovations on financial markets—a 'displacement', to use Charles Kindleberger's expression, in other words an exogenous shock offering new profit opportunities.[22] The difficulty, and sometimes the unwillingness, to regulate new financial products have compounded the risks they have carried, the more so as innovation has been a way of legally circumventing existing regulation. Three major innovations have been more closely associated to financial crises: investment trusts to the Baring Crisis in 1890 and, more directly, to the crash of 1929; the Euromarkets to the Financial Instability of the early 1970s and the International Debt Crisis of 1982; and derivatives and securitization to the Financial Debacle of 2007–8.

Investment trusts originated in Britain in the late 1860s. In England, the Foreign and Colonial Government Trust, founded in 1868, was the first to apply the principles of an investment trust—namely, to spread risks over a number of investments (in this case foreign and colonial government bonds) and to use a part of the surplus as a redemption fund to reimburse the initial capital. In practice, investment trusts invested the capital of their shareholders and paid them a dividend based on the average yield of their diversified investment as well as the gains from a few other operations. Their investment usually exceeded the amount of their share capital, as, in addition to issuing debentures, they borrowed from banks, using their capital as security. Investment trusts also participated in underwriting syndicates and granted long- and medium-term loans to other companies. However, they did not seek to exert any form of control over the companies in which they invested.[23]

Investment trusts enjoyed a remarkable boom in Scotland, epitomized by the foundation in 1873 of the Scottish American Investment Trust, whose secretary Robert Fleming is considered the 'father of investment trusts'. Following his Scottish successes, he moved to the City of London in 1888. His arrival coincided with a wave of foundation of investment trusts, which had been only marginally successful in England until then. In the boom years preceding the Baring Crisis, between 1886 and 1890, the number of registered companies rose from 12 to 101 and their nominal capital from £5 million to £50 million, mostly invested in foreign securities.[24] Investment trusts were viewed with a great deal of suspicion by the City establishment. *The Bankers' Magazine* considered them as one of the fashions of the City, acting as a front for company promoters making their fortunes through the manipulation of founders' shares, the watering of stock, and the underwriting of doubtful companies.[25] From the outset, *The Economist* was sceptical, noting that, despite their popularity with the public, few of them had been able to start in business and had experienced great difficulty in acquiring proper investment. It claimed that this was due to the fact that many trusts shared the same directors and bought, on the whole, the same securities, thus forcing prices up against themselves. Shortly before the Baring Crisis, *The Economist* warned that the investment of investment trusts' capital in established undertakings could not suffice to pay a dividend of 7 per cent on ordinary shares boasted by many companies, and that they had therefore gone into promoting and underwriting doubtful concerns.[26]

Investment trusts were heavily involved in the capital exports boom of the late 1880s, especially in Argentina, but also in Australia and the United States, and they suffered badly in the aftermath of the Baring Crisis. Their ordinary and preference capital had depreciated by 29 per cent by 1893, while 50 of the 101 companies registered in 1890 went into liquidation. The regulation of investment trusts was no different from that of other companies. They were subject to the admittedly permissive company law, consolidated in 1862. The 1900 Company Act intended to deal with the problem of frauds on shareholders committed by unscrupulous company promoters and introduced a few reforms related to the process of company formation.[27] In the end, investment trusts won acceptance. A new wave of companies came to the fore after 1905—this time with the blessing of the City aristocracy.

Investment trusts were hardly known in the United States before the First World War, but experienced tremendous growth in the 1920s. There were only 40 investment trusts in 1921; their number had reached 770 in 1929, including 591 founded after 1927. Between 1926 and 1929, their assets went from $1 billion to $7 billion. Investment trusts were founded mainly by investment bankers, brokers, and other banks and finance companies, from the most respectable to the most dubious. Powerful groups bringing together several investment trusts were also set up. The largest among them, the Founders' Group, established in 1921, brought together ten companies, whose total assets reached $626 million in 1929. The next largest was the Goldman Sachs group, which, with three companies, including the largest in the country—the Goldman Sachs Trading Corporation—came close to $500 million.[28] On the whole, however, the investment trusts had a bad reputation, with incompetence, greed, and dishonesty being the three main criticisms made of them. Their modus operandi was basically the same as that of their British counterparts, which served as role models, and thus fundamentally sound. But the practical application of these principles often left something to be desired, especially as far as the structure of their capital and the nature of their investment were concerned.

Parallels were made with the excesses of British investment trusts in the years preceding the Baring Crisis of 1890, with one insider warning that, 'unless we avoid these and other errors and false principles, we shall inevitably go through a similar period of disaster and disgrace. If such a period should come, the well-run trusts will suffer with the bad as they did in England forty years ago.'[29] John Kenneth Galbraith has described investment trusts as 'the most notable piece of speculative architecture of the late twenties'—thanks to the 'magic of leverage'—and 'the most important corporate weakness' in America in the 1920s, linking in this view the crash to the Depression.[30] Their organizational principles, which had become very different from those of their British counterparts, also explain their disastrous performance in the stock-market crash of 1929 and its aftermath. American investment trusts were larger, held a smaller number of stocks, had a capital structure dominated by preferred stock, maintained an investment strategy dominated by domestic equity, and favoured capital growth over income, speculation over investment, and market-timing over diversification of risks.[31] They lost over 70 per cent of their value between 1929 and 1932, from $7 billion to $2 billion.[32] Attempts at regulating them had been made in the 1920s—in 1924 by the New York Stock Exchange, in 1927 by the National Association of Securities Commissioners, in 1928 by the Attorney General of New York State and by the Investment Bankers Association of America. All were concerned with the protection of investors' interests, but no legislation was passed before the Investment Company Act of 1940.[33]

The Euromarkets did not arouse the same criticism as investment trusts, even though they were closely associated to the outbreak of financial crises. In 1974, the growth of the inter-bank market—making up a good 50 per cent of the Eurocurrency market—was seen as having greatly facilitated transactions relying on a dangerous mismatch between short-term borrowing and long-term lending. In 1982, the wave of soaring bank lending to Third World countries appeared to have been sustained by the innovative types of syndicated Eurocredits.[34] Rather than malpractice, it was the irruption of an unregulated and international market within a still highly regulated and nationally centred financial world that was a cause for concern. The novelty of the Euromarkets was the combination of their international, offshore, and unregulated character. Indeed, they elected domicile in London, because this is where these conditions could be met.

Dollars left the United States because of Regulation Q, which imposed a ceiling on the interest that banks could pay on deposits. And they came to London, because the City, with its financial expertise and traditions, was particularly well equipped to welcome them; but also because the monetary authorities of continental European countries, suspicious of capital considered speculative, took various measures intended to discourage foreign deposits, leaving no chance to Zurich, Paris, or Frankfurt. In 1960, the Swiss National Bank reached a 'gentlemen's agreement' with the banks in order to curb the inflow of 'hot money': banks agreed not to pay interest on foreign deposits and to charge a commission of 1 per cent on deposits withdrawn from Switzerland within six months; France and Germany also prohibited the payments of interest to foreigners, while in 1963 the French banks were advised by the Banque de France to reduce their Eurodollar business.[35] This contrasted with the more relaxed attitude of the British monetary authorities—an attitude clearly dictated by the willingness to promote the City's position as an international financial centre. This goal overrode any fears aroused by these new financial products, especially the volatility risks associated with such transactions, the possible inflationary effects of these capital inflows, and the greater difficulties that these might pose to the conduct of monetary policy. Their choice meant differentiating between domestic financial activities, denominated in sterling, which were tightly regulated, and international activities in foreign currencies on behalf of non-residents, which enjoyed far greater freedoms.

The Euromarkets thus remained unregulated in the centres where the bulk of the transactions took place—namely, London and, for Eurobonds, also Luxembourg. Their very nature called for an international supervision and the Bank for International Settlements (BIS) was well placed to play a coordinating role, though for monetary rather than banking matters.[36] Central bankers' main concern was about the effects of the Eurocurrency market on domestic monetary policy. On this front, the BIS was able to provide vital statistical information on the size and turnover of the market; to organize inquiries on its pros and cons; to set up discussions between central banks' governors and within the Group of Ten; a number of joint interventions with central banks was carried out in order to reduce the differentials between interest paid on Eurocurrency domestic currency deposits; and, in 1971, a Standing Committee on the Eurocurrency Market was created. However, any attempt at controlling the market failed, mainly as a result of the opposition from the United States and Britain. On the other hand, not much could be achieved in the field of prudential regulation, despite questions being raised about the overexposure of certain market participants and the increasing maturity mismatch between banks' lending and borrowing.

No financial innovation has been more closely associated to a financial crisis, in this instance the 2007–8 Financial Debacle, than 'derivatives', understood in the generic sense of the word and including a number of financial products and processes, such as hedge funds, structured products, or securitization. Compared to investment trusts or even to the far more encompassing Euromarkets, the financial innovations of the late twentieth century mark a radical change, despite their gradual but regular application to the financial markets. They accelerated the process of disintermediation and securitization, with bank finance giving way to direct financing through the markets and, for banks, the shift from interest income to fee and commission income. These new financial products were also highly complex, often based on mathematical formulae not always fully comprehensible to senior bank executives, thus adding to the risks inherent in all financial innovations.

Derivatives can be defined as contracts whose value 'derives' from an underlying asset. There are two main types: futures—standardized forward contracts—and options.[37] Forward contracts, as such, are not new: those relating to the price of raw materials have commonly been traded on the large commodity markets since the last quarter of the nineteenth century, and those relating to shares are as old as the stock exchanges themselves. The recent innovation is on a different level. On the one hand, futures are continuously listed on a secondary market, which limits the risks for the brokers; on the other hand, along with currencies, they focus increasingly on synthetic financial assets, such as notional interest rates or the various stock-market indices, called financial futures. The second main type of derivative—options—which have also been around for a long time on various stock exchanges, have made outstanding progress—first on individual shares in the United States, then on almost all other financial assets, including futures. Modern derivates came into being in Chicago, the world leader in forward markets. In 1972, the Chicago Mercantile Exchange launched the first futures market, the International Monetary Market, where currency contracts were traded; and the following year its great rival, the Chicago Board of Trade, founded the Chicago Board Options Exchange, where options were traded on shares. These initiatives coincided with major theoretical breakthroughs in the field of finance, in particular by Fisher Black, Robert Merton, and Myron Scholes on the pricing of options.[38]

Derivatives have also been combined with a new investment medium: alternative management funds, better known as hedge funds, which appeared in the 1980s. While they do not easily fit a single definition, they have displayed a certain number of characteristics: a domicile in an offshore centre; a predilection for short positions, through derivatives or forward operations; frequent use of leverage; and ongoing control of risks taken. They have often been organized in the form of unregulated investment pools or closed funds with rather limited exit possibilities. And their managers have earned high bonuses—generally reaching 20 per cent of profits above a certain threshold plus 1.5–2 per cent management fees—and, as a rule, invested their own funds alongside those of their clients. Their growth has been phenomenal since the 1990s, from a few hundreds to nearly 3,000 by 2006, with nearly $1,000 billion of funds managed—a development somewhat reminiscent of that of the investment trusts in Britain in the 1880s and the United States in the 1920s, with which in their early stages they shared an uncertain reputation, for being too risky and too highly leveraged. Hedge funds have experienced spectacular successes, perhaps best personified by George Soros; and resounding failures, the best-known case being the collapse in 1998 of Long-Term Capital Management (LTCM).[39] Since the early 2000s, they have nevertheless been taken up by more conservative portfolio managers, their average debt ratio has dropped considerably—from ten times equity capital in 1998 (and twenty-eight times in LTCM's case) to two to four times in 2005—as has their annual return, around 8–10 per cent, compared with two- or three-figure returns in the 1990s.

The transformation of banking and financial practices is best embodied in what has become known as securitization. Defined as the conversion of debt, especially loans, into marketable securities, securitization is hardly a new phenomenon. The novelty was the type of assets converted into securities and the type of financial products emerging from this conversion—typically, they were derivatives. Mortgages were the first debts to be securitized. Rather than kept on banks' balance sheets, they were bundled together, issued as Mortgage-Backed Securities (MBS) and sold to investors—banks, insurance companies, hedge funds, and other financial institutions across the world. Other assets were in turn securitized, in particular consumer debt, such as insurance policies, car loans, credit-card loans, student loans, and so on, the so-called Asset-Backed Securities (ABS). A third group of securitized assets was known as Collateralized Debt Obligations (CDO) and was backed mostly by loans and corporate bonds. Credit derivatives were also developed in these years, in the first place Credit Default Swaps (CDS), which offered protection against the risk of default on a debt through a contract between two parties, the seller, as it were, insuring the buyer in return for the payment of a regular fee.[40] Securitized debt grew spectacularly in the early twenty-first century. In the United States, ABS issuance quadrupled between 2000 and 2006, from $337 billion to $1,250 billion; while non-agency MBS issuance (those not guaranteed by a government agency such as Fannie Mae or Freddie Mac) rose from about $100 billion to $773 billion during the same period.[41] The notional value of CDS rose from about $600 billion in 2001 to more than $60 trillion at the end of 2007.[42]

One of the main advantages of securitization was that it allowed far greater leverage, as these transactions mainly took place off the banks' balance sheet, through the medium of ad hoc instruments, such as bank conduits and structured investment vehicles (SIV). Though usually linked to a bank, they mostly funded themselves by issuing short-term commercial paper and invested these funds in long-term assets, typically securitized debt. Through off-balance-sheet operations and other devices, including credit default swaps, banks were able to fund a far greater volume of assets with the same amount of equity, while officially remaining within the regulatory requirements regarding capital ratios. Leverage was even higher in the so-called shadow banking system, made up of unregulated entities including SIVs, hedge funds, private equity, and others. By 2007, this shadow banking system, together with the lightly regulated investment banks, had grown as large as the traditional banking system in the United States, reaching about $10 trillion.[43]

Securitization made credit more easily available worldwide, to all sectors of the economy and all segments of society. Ironically, it was also supposed to have reduced if not eliminated risk by spreading it more widely and assessing it through highly sophisticated models. This illusion partly explains why the financial innovations of the late twentieth century remained very lightly if at all regulated. A large chunk of the derivatives contracts, those traded 'over the counter' rather than in an organized market, remained entirely unregulated. Hedge funds have also remained unregulated, being able to escape the legal constraints on public offerings by being registered offshore or by making private offerings; and those on investment companies by, in particular, having 'qualified' investors—with assets of $5 million or more.[44] However, an important reason for the failure to regulate financial innovation has been the intense climate of deregulation that has marked the financial world since the 1980s.

REGULATION AND DEREGULATION

The level of regulation following a financial crisis has, to a large extent, been determined by the intensity of the 'never-again' feeling, and the damage caused by unregulated innovation. From this perspective, the Great Depression apparently stands apart: it was the worst economic downturn in modern history and never before, or since, has such a battery of regulatory measures been adopted in order to tame financial activity. While there is some truth in this vision of events, the history of financial crises presents a more subtle picture. In the first place, financial crises have not automatically led to more regulation; on the contrary, this has been the exception rather than the rule. Secondly, state intervention and regulation, which marked the nearly half-century extending from the 1930s to the late 1970s, were the upshot of historical circumstances reaching beyond the Great Depression. Third, significant differences can be observed between the United States and Europe. And, fourth, deregulation has also followed financial crises.

The Baring Crisis of 1890 is the clearest case of no regulatory measures being taken in the aftermath of a financial shock. The Bank of England's preventive action was a model of intervention, which has been followed many times, not least during the secondary banking crisis in 1973, the International Debt Crisis in 1982, and the Long-Term Capital Management collapse in 1998, but things ended there—because of the absence of panic, no real fear about the recurrence of such an event, and the strength of Britain's laissez-faire tradition. Conversely, the American Panic of 1907 led to one of the most important pieces of legislation in US banking, the creation of the Federal Reserve System. The panic was real, the likelihood of its happening again strong, and the crisis widely attributed to the inadequacies of the American banking system. However, if there was a broad agreement behind the necessity of a central bank, there was much disagreement about the type of institution to be established—centralized or decentralized, under financial or political control? Antagonism against Wall Street remained vivid among Midwest country bankers, and the solution could only be a compromise.

The Federal System aimed, above all, at solving the problem of the inelasticity of the money supply and the absence of a lender of last resort. It did so by setting up a decentralized structure, dividing the country into twelve districts, each provided with a Federal Reserve Bank located in the district's main city. Membership of the Federal Reserve was compulsory for the national banks though not for the state banks and trust companies. The Federal Reserve banks had the power of rediscounting bills, serving as a clearing house for member banks and monitoring banks. The entire system was overseen by the Federal Reserve Board, a body with eight members based in

Washington and responsible for defining overall policy in agreement with the twelve Federal Reserve banks. How successful were the reforms that followed the Panic of 1907? The creation of a central bank was undoubtedly a leap forward. However, all the opportunities for change were not and, for historical and political reasons, could not be seized. The creation of the Federal Reserve did not really alter the structure of American banking. On the one hand, it did not solve all the problems it intended to, in particular the pyramidal system of correspondent banking, by which money centre banks held the reserves of provincial banks and which was seen as a destabilizing factor in times of crisis; and the separation between national banks and state banks, as many among the latter did not become members of the Federal Reserve. On the other hand, for many contemporaries and later observers, the main problem of the American banking system was the prohibition of branch banking—a question that was politically too sensitive to be addressed.[45] The pre-1914 legislation did not prevent the outbreak of nineteenth-century-type banking panics in the early 1930s.

The 'never-again' factor was especially strong during the First World War. This was indeed 'the war to end all wars'. The feeling, however, did not really extend to banking crises, whatever the acuity of those affecting some smaller European countries in the early 1920s. Legislative measures related to the banking sector, while being concerned with financial and monetary stability, were not primarily designed to prevent a return of the panic of August 1914. In the event, neither diplomacy nor finance was able to prevent the outbreak of another crisis and another war—the Treaty of Versailles and the restoration of the gold standard loom large in this context.

The Great Depression, on the other hand, was 'the crisis to end all crises'. In many countries, regulatory measures were taken to that effect, and in none more than in the United States. A series of radical reforms to the American financial market were introduced within the framework of the New Deal.[46] Two laws were passed in 1933, one on the capital market (the Securities Act) and the other on banks (the Banking Act, better known under the name of its two promoters as the Glass–Steagall Act). The first contained various provisions aimed at improving the quality of information about the securities offered and traded on the stock exchange. The second decreed the complete separation of commercial banking activities (taking deposits and making loans) from investment banking activities (issuing, distributing, and trading securities), including if these activities were shared between parent companies and subsidiaries or through either the cross-holding of shares or overlapping directorships. In practice, the commercial banks parted from their subsidiaries involved in securities transactions, whereas the vast majority of private banks opted for investment banking. The major exception was J. P. Morgan & Co., Wall Street's most famous bank, which chose to become a commercial bank, a decision that led several partners to resign and to found an investment bank, Morgan, Stanley & Co.[47] The Glass–Steagall Act also introduced federal deposit insurance, compulsory for banks that were members of the Federal Reserve System, but optional and conditional for the others. The insured institutions paid a premium based on a percentage of their total assets, as a contribution to a guarantee fund intended to pay the depositors of a bankrupt bank. Six months after voting on the law, 14,000 banks had already decided to insure their clients, for a maximum sum of $5,000 per deposit. Another federal regulation—Regulation Q—set a maximum interest rate that the banks could pay on savings deposits. Other laws completed this New Deal legislation, in particular the Securities Exchange Act of 1934, which created the Securities and Exchange Commission (SEC); the Investment Companies Act of 1940, which codified the rules governing investment companies; and the Banking Act of 1935, which reformed the Federal Reserve System, centralizing the conduct of monetary policy with the seven members of the Board of Governors in Washington.

Financial regulation did not go so far in the major European economies, including Germany, where universal banking managed to survive. Even so, owing to the particularly close links between banking and industry, its abolition was debated in a tense mood marked by populist anti-capitalism, rampant anti-Semitism, and politicians' paranoid fear of banking power. The banking law of December 1934, enacted under the Nazis, attributed the crisis to individual failings rather than to any shortcoming of the system; and it made do with strengthening bank supervision and introducing some restrictions on long-term deposits and on banks' representation on the supervisory boards of other companies. But, even though universal banking survived, the government considerably strengthened its hold over financial institutions, whose role in the economy grew weaker as a result of state subsidies granted to companies, the expansion of the savings banks,[48] and the more or less automatic financing of growing public deficits through bank deposits.[49] In France, things were left unchanged until 1941, when the Vichy government introduced a law, upheld and completed in 1944, which controlled and regulated banking activities that until then had been open to any newcomers. Henceforth, banks had to be registered according to their type of activity. The law made a clear distinction between an investment bank and a deposit bank. It also defined a number of specialized institutions, according to their operations or clientele, including finance companies and discount houses.[50] Britain, for its part, steered clear of the trend towards greater regulation of the banks, probably because there had not been any bank bankruptcies during the 1930s, the financial system was more specialized than elsewhere, and the Bank of England effectively monitored it to ensure that it was working properly. Among other European countries, Italy and Belgium opted for abolishing universal banking, Switzerland for maintaining it. In Switzerland, the federal banking law of 1934, apart from setting some general rules and entrusting the supervision of the banking system to an independent commission, has above all been famous for its article 47 relating to banking secrecy—a measure that undoubtedly increased the competitive advantage of Swiss banks.[51]

With the exception of the United States, the measures of financial regulation taken in the wake of the Great Depression appear relatively mild and barely intrusive. As far as European countries were concerned, state intervention in banking affairs was as much a result of the Depression as a consequence of the economic and political context of the 1930s and, even more, the Second World War. Britain is a case in point. From an informal regulatory framework, based mainly on the personal suasion of the Bank of England's Governor, it emerged from the war with a nationalized central bank, though its governing structure at first remained virtually unchanged; and clearing banks were still in the private sector but under the Treasury's and the Bank of England's strict control—as Keynes put it, in no need to be nationalized, as in actual fact they had already been so. Not only was the London Stock Exchange tightly regulated by the authorities, but its dealings were regarded with suspicion—options, considered highly speculative, were reintroduced only in May 1958 after an interruption of nineteen years. In effect, the London Stock Exchange set itself up as the regulator of the securities market, with all the caution and conservatism that that implies.[52] In France, most of the financial sector came under state control after Liberation. The Bank of France was nationalized, together with the four big deposit banks[53] and all major insurance companies—though the *banques d'affaires* remained in private hands.[54] The state's grip ended up stifling the Parisian capital market, not only when it came to foreign issues, but also for issues by French companies. The Paris Bourse became pretty sluggish. Having lost two-thirds of the nominal value of its securities through nationalizations, it went through a 'long depression' that lasted until the 1980s.[55]

The 'lessons' from the Great Depression must, then, be put in their proper context. The regulations that characterized the third quarter of the twentieth century were the result of an exceptional historical period marked by two world wars, the redrawing of international boundaries, a devastating economic crisis, massive political upheavals, and shifts in ideological outlooks—the 'Thirty Years War' of the twentieth century. This led to an ideological shift that, combined with a generational change, favoured state intervention and a more organized form of capitalism. Even in the United States, where the regulatory framework was essentially set up in the wake of the crisis, the Glass–Steagall Act appears to have been more ideological than pragmatic and was rooted in Americans' instinctive distrust of financial concentration and power, already denounced by the Pujo Commission of Enquiry at the beginning of the century.[56] In particular, the separation between commercial and investment banking did not really address the main cause of the banking crises: most of the small banks that failed between 1930 and 1933 were only commercial banks, and they failed because of the Depression, their fragility, and the failure of the Federal Reserve to come to their aid. Conversely, the large New York and major city banks, which had securities affiliates, survived the crisis. And, while there might have been conflicts of interests between commercial and investment banking, there is no evidence that the banks engaged in the two activities took more risks in the sort of securities they underwrote and marketed than specialized investment banks.[57] On the other hand, the introduction of deposit insurance—in other words, the government commitment to make banks safer to depositors—could justify a measure limiting risk taking.

The Finanacial Instability of the early 1970s did not give rise to wide-ranging regulatory reforms, but led to a closer supervision of a number of activities. In the United States, foreign-exchange trading began to be monitored: the Federal Reserve imposed stricter capital and liquidity requirements on American banks expanding abroad, while foreign banks operating in the United States were brought under federal control, with the International Banking Act in 1978. In Germany, the federal authorities established limits to foreign-exchange transactions by German banks and, in 1976, the Lex Herstatt put limits on loans as a percentage of bank capital and increased the powers of the Federal Supervisory Office and the Bundesbank.[58] In Britain, where the crisis had been most acute, the Bank of England strengthened its supervisory organization and gave it a much more formal basis. This was complemented by the Banking Act of 1979, which put stricter conditions on the recognition of institutions as banks by the Bank of England. As Margaret Reid, a highly respected financial journalist, commented at the time: 'The Bank of England is indeed justified in insisting that the banking community should not again risk running into crisis through excessive mismatching and scarcity of liquidity.'[59] Everywhere, central banks extended their prerogative to prudential supervision.[60]

But it was the need for an international form of financial regulation that was most strongly felt, forty years after the Great Depression. In December 1974, the central banks' governors created the Committee on Banking Regulation and Supervisory Practices, better known as the Basle Committee. The concordat it issued the following year advocated sharing supervisory responsibility for banks' foreign activities between host and home-country authorities. It took another crisis, the International Debt Crisis of 1982, for practical recommendations to emerge, in 1988, in the form of capital requirements, known as the Basle Agreement, or Basle I; it was followed by a revised agreement, known as Basle II, in 2004. This, however, is mainly a matter of international financial cooperation, which will be discussed in the next chapter.

In the meantime, while progress was being made towards some form of international regulation of the financial system, financial deregulation was the order of the day at national level from the late 1970s onwards, including in the wake of the shock waves of 1974 and 1982. This was part of a much broader trend: the growing influence, first in the Anglo-Saxon countries, and then elsewhere in the world, of a neo-liberal view of the economy and society, symbolically marked by the coming-to-power of Margaret Thatcher in Britain in 1979 and Ronald Reagan in the United States in 1981. Whatever the shifts in policies and attitudes, the fundamental dispensation—the smaller state and the strengthening of market mechanisms—was not really challenged until the Financial Debacle of 2007–8.

The movement started in the United States, with a liberalization of the financial markets. From 1 May 1975, the Securities and Exchange Commission abolished fixed commissions on the New York Stock Exchange, making competition there keener and leading to numerous small brokers disappearing, and the largest ones, along with investment banks, which henceforth had far greater equity capital at their disposal, being transformed into joint stock companies. The City of London followed with 'Big Bang' on 27 October 1986, also a reform of the stock exchange abolishing fixed commissions and also the separation, unique to the London Stock Exchange, between the functions of brokers and jobbers.[61] Banks were also permitted to buy member firms, hitherto banned, bringing about the disappearance of almost all the leading brokerage houses, which were taken over by merchant banks, as well as the main commercial banks, both British and foreign. In Paris, the stockbrokers' monopoly was abolished in 1992. In Germany, the Bundesbank authorized certificates of deposits and floating-rate issues in 1984–5, despite its distrust of financial innovation, and allowed foreign banks to act as lead banks for foreign issues in Deutschmarks.

Banking legislation was also relaxed in the United States. In 1980, Regulation Q was abolished by the Depository Institutions Deregulation and Monetary Control Act; in 1982, the Garn–St Germain Depository Institutions Act deregulated the savings and loans association—ushering in a crisis that devastated the industry; in 1994, with the Riegle–Neal Interstate Banking and Efficiency Act, banks were able to set up a network of branches throughout the country. Deregulation culminated in 1999 when the Glass–Steagall Act of 1933 was repealed by the Financial Modernization Act. Commercial banking and investment banking could again be brought together on the grounds that new financial instruments justified greater concentration among the various intermediaries in the world of finance.

Deregulation was also the answer to the Japanese Banking Crisis, through a series of measures dubbed the 'Big Bang' and implemented between 1998 and 2001. They abolished, among others, barriers separating banking activities, securities transactions and insurance, and liberalized foreign-exchange transactions, bringing the international system into line with international standards. However, the powers of the bodies monitoring the financial system were strength-ened, while more autonomy was granted to the Bank of Japan.

The Financial Debacle of 2007–8 is unlikely to be followed by further deregulations of the financial system. The trend has clearly run its course, and the 'never-again' factor calls for stronger regula-tion. Controlling rather than liberating financial institutions and markets is the order of the day. The question is how far the reverse trend is likely to go. At the time of writing, in early 2010, the picture was not yet clear. It is tempting to look back to the 1930s for historical pointers, especially in the light of the determination of the Obama administration to rein in commercial banks. Yet this would be a mistake. Not only the actual regulatory measures, but also the reg-ulatory framework, will have to be different—because of the complex-ity of financial operations, the economic weight of the financial sector, and the global character of financial activities, all far more pronounced than in any previous major crisis, and, because it is likely to be, at least to a certain extent, the outcome of international cooperation.

6

International Cooperation

International cooperation has rightly been credited for helping to prevent a collapse of the international financial system. The high point was the decision on 12 October 2008 by France, Germany, and the other members of the Eurozone to follow Britain's rescue plan and simultaneously announce measures to recapitalize their banks and guarantee loans, and then the adoption of similar measures by the United States. Global coordination was clearly the order of the day, with the G20 replacing the G7 as the key forum for discussing the economic crisis and meetings held in Washington in November 2008 and London in April 2009. On the other hand, international cooperation has been blamed for its inability radically to address the shortcomings of a system unable to prevent a financial catastrophe, with persistent disagreements about, among other things, global regulation, financial transaction taxes, or bonus taxes. International cooperation has been one of the hallmarks of the post-war era, in sharp contrast to its failure in the inter-war years, often seen as one of the causes of the severity of the Great Depression. Yet all financial crises since the late nineteenth century have required the intervention of actors from more than a single country. This chapter will consider the nature of these interventions and the extent of their success in both a short- and long-term perspective.

CENTRAL BANK COOPERATION

Despite its international implications, the Baring Crisis of 1890 remained very much a British affair. A major crisis affecting all the leading financial centres was avoided by the intervention of the Bank of England with the banking community of London. The bank took account of the fact that a panic could have erupted, though it did not, and made sure that it had sufficient gold reserves to face heavy withdrawals. With £10,815,000 considered 'quite inadequate', the Governor, William Lidderdale, arranged through the Rothschilds to borrow from the Banque de France £2 million of gold on Monday, 10 November, followed by another million two days later. The Bank of England also bought £1.5 million outright from Russia, and Lidderdale was further guaranteed that the Russian government would not withdraw a deposit of about £2.4 million that it had with Barings.[1] The Bank of England could probably have managed to attract gold anyway 'by measures more or less stringent', as Lidderdale put it to the Governor of the Bank of France, but this time they would have been 'too severe' and, having raised the bank rate to 6 per cent a couple of days earlier, he did not want to alarm the City. For his part, the French finance minister considered that such help was necessary in order to prevent harmful repercussions for France of a deeper crisis in London.[2]

In the same way, the Panic of 1907 was an American affair. The situation was re-established by the intervention of J. P. Morgan, acting in lieu of a central bank, with the leaders of the New York banking community. However, New York was still dependent on the City of London for obtaining liquid assets and, ultimately, gold. Despite having become the world's leading economic power, the United States was still a country that basically exported agricultural products, with a markedly seasonal demand for credit from rural regions. Yet the American banking system, the bulk of whose resources was concentrated in New York, had great difficulty in coping with these fluctuations, because of its fragmentation, the persistence of rudimentary banking habits, and the absence of a central bank. The inevitable tightening of the New York money market resulting from the panic occurred at the height of demand for credit from cereal exporters, demand that could be met only by purchasing huge quantities of gold from London. The Bank of England did not check the flow of gold to the United States but raised its discount rate to 6 and then 7 per cent at the beginning of November, attracting gold from twenty-four countries, including the Bank of France, which was persuaded once again to help and lend it £3 million worth of gold.[3]

The primary aim of international financial cooperation was thus monetary stability—in other words, the maintenance of the gold standard—rather than the avoidance of a financial crisis. The two were, of course, interrelated, as a banking crisis could lead to a currency crisis, and vice versa, though the latter did not occur in the core industrial countries during the classical gold standard—the quarter of a century preceding the First World War. The stability of the international monetary system was in great part due to the cooperation between central banks. To use Keynes's metaphor, the Bank of England was the 'conductor' whose leadership the other central banks were prepared to follow and to which they provided assistance in times of crisis. Their motives were not altruistic, but guided by self-interest—not least on the part of the Bank of France, whose huge gold reserves enabled it to maintain regulation and stability by allowing its gold to flow to Britain when the need arose or by voluntarily making it available to the Bank of England on a temporary basis. This enabled it to maintain a low and stable discount rate, and to make a profitable operation.[4] International cooperation thus functioned efficiently in the two most severe financial crises of the pre-1914 era.

The financial crises of July–August 1914 were overcome, separately in each country, by the exceptional measures taken in order to wage a total war. However, international financial cooperation resumed during the war. Loans totalling nearly $20 billion were contracted among the Allies, mainly in the form of government loans granted by the United States and the United Kingdom.[5] Economic and financial cooperation between the Allies, in particular the United States, Britain, and France, laid the ground for future common work. With the war over, international cooperation was indeed the order of the day, not least with the creation of the League of Nations, decided by the Treaty of Versailles in 1919. The economic and financial problems inherited from the war were also addressed within an international collective framework. The International Financial Conference held in Brussels in 1920 at the initiative of the League of Nations made a series of recommendations regarding the necessity to balance budgets, to restore exchange-rate stability, and to issue international loans for reconstruction, including a Belgian proposal for an international bank of issue—though they were not followed by any specific action. A major outcome of the conference, however, was the call for the creation of what would soon become the Economic and Financial Organization of the League of Nations, which was to play a major role in international financial cooperation.[6] Two years later, the proposals of the Genoa Conference, in 1922, called by Britain and France with a view to restoring the gold standard, stressed the importance of central bank cooperation, and proposed the adoption of a gold-exchange standard, with central countries holding their reserves entirely in gold and others partly in gold and partly in foreign exchange.[7]

Monetary stability thus remained the main objective of international financial cooperation in the 1920s, but it required a far higher degree of concerted intervention than before the war. The first task was to restore the gold standard, a prime objective for both political and economic leaders; the second was to ensure that it worked properly. Central bank cooperation was relatively successful in the former, less so in the latter. And it proved totally powerless in the face of the Great Depression.[8]

The gold standard was suspended, whether officially or unofficially, during the conflict, and the United States was the first to re-establish the convertibility of the dollar, at its pre-war parity, in 1919. Other countries stabilized their currency in the following years (Britain in 1925, France de facto in 1926, de jure in 1928), at pre-war parity for the countries that managed to bring inflation under control (Britain and the former neutrals); with a new currency for the countries that were ravaged by hyperinflation (Germany, Austria, Hungary, Poland); and a depreciated currency for those in between (France, Belgium). There was no coordinated return to gold, but the central banks cooperated in monetary stabilizations.

The functioning of the inter-war gold standard was beset with difficulties and was unable to achieve its main objective— namely to permit balance-of-payments adjustments. Surpluses persisted in surplus countries (the United States and France) and deficits in deficit countries (Britain)—a problem stemming partly from the overvaluation of the pound sterling and the undervaluation of the French franc.[9] But the problems were compounded by the uneasy cooperation between central banks, in particular insufficient expansionary policy in the surplus countries and the burden of adjustment falling on the deficit countries, especially Britain, whose position remained central to the working of the system.[10] Some actions, nonetheless, took place in order to smooth over the working of the system. The most notable was the July 1927 meeting in Long Island between Montagu Norman (Governor of the Bank of England), Benjamin Strong (president of the Federal Reserve Bank of New York), Hjalmar Schacht (president of the Reichsbank), and Charles Rist (Deputy Governor of the Bank of France, replacing the

Governor, Émile Moreau). The meeting had been planned for some time, and cooperation worked successfully. The Federal Reserve agreed to loosen its policy, reducing its discount rate by half a point to 3½ per cent and buying $200 million of government securities in open-market operations, thus easing the pressure on London to tighten its monetary policy, a pressure coming mainly from France, through the conversion of part of its huge claims on London. This was also alleviated by the Fed's agreement to exchange gold for sterling with France.

International cooperation, on the other hand, had clear limits. Throughout the 1920s and early 1930s, disagreements over German reparations[11] and Allied debts had stood in the way of all international negotiations, whether economic and political, and caused many a near agreement to collapse. National rivalries, especially between the Bank of England and the Bank of France, were a further obstacle. While the French authorities did not wish to force Britain to abandon the gold standard and thus provoke a crisis in the international monetary system, they were determined to take full advantage of the country's restored financial power after the 1926 stabilization to achieve a certain number of political and economic goals. In this way, the Bank of France's international influence strengthened considerably in the three or four years that preceded the Great Depression, especially over the central banks of central Europe, an objective that corresponded to the broad lines of French diplomacy, whereas until then it had been obliged to leave the initiative to the Bank of England.[12] The pound's fragility and the franc's strength therefore altered temporarily the balance of power between Paris and London and put the Bank of England on the defensive. The fact that Norman and Moreau did not get on well personally did not improve matters.

More generally, and not surprisingly, central banks' interventions were dictated by national economic interests rather than the imperatives of the gold standard, even when international cooperation worked best. The Federal Reserve's concessions in the summer of 1927 might have neatly met the needs of the international monetary system, but the decision to ease its monetary policy met just as neatly those of a contracting American economy. In any case, American enthusiasm for central bank cooperation waned thereafter. And, were a conflict of interest to arise, national economic considerations came first. This was clearly the case a few months later, in April 1928, when the Federal Reserve raised its interest rate in order to curb the wave of speculation on the New York Stock Exchange, ushering in a chain of events that would lead to the Great Depression.

In the meantime, international cooperation became more structured with the creation in 1930 of the Bank for International Settlements (BIS).[13] A proposal for an international bank might have been made at the Brussels conference, and in 1925 Montagu Norman, the Governor of the Bank of England and high priest of monetary orthodoxy, had floated the idea of a central bankers' club. However, it was in the discussions for the settlement of the German reparations by the members of the Young Committee, in 1929, that the setting-up of such a bank was seriously envisaged. The Young Plan not only proposed a rescheduling of the reparations payments but established a financial institution charged with the transfer of Germany's payments. However, the BIS, which was officially born on 27 February 1930, was more than a simple 'reparations bank'. Its objective was also 'to promote the co-operation of central banks and to provide additional facilities for international financial operations'. With the end of reparations and the collapse of the gold standard, the role of the BIS was considerably reduced before it had even had a chance to make a real impact. Still, the creation of the first international financial organization was in itself an achievement—even if the United States was not officially represented, though the first president, Gates W. McGarrah, was American. And one of its most significant contributions was to bring together, at the board of directors' monthly meetings, the governors of the leading central banks. It was an occasion they rarely missed and that enabled them to get to know each other, meet informally, and discuss monetary policy away from political pressure.

Despite undoubted progress achieved during the 1920s, international cooperation failed when confronted with the Great Depression. There has been much debate as to why it failed and whether coordinated policies would have prevented the Depression from being so deep and from lasting so long. Given that the severity of the Depression was primarily caused by the deflationary policies dictated by the adhesion to the gold standard and the defence of the currency's parity, the question of international financial cooperation is, of course, of upmost importance. Attachment to the gold standard prevailed everywhere until the system's collapse in September 1931, when the pound went off gold. Until then, international cooperation was primarily directed at preserving the existing monetary order.

Coordinated actions took place in times of acute crisis—the Austrian schilling in May 1931, the Reichsmark in June and July, and the pound in September—and ended in failure. Political conflicts stood in the way, but the huge scale of the difficulties and the sheer magnitude and unprecedented character of the required collective effort rendered the task almost impossible.[14]

Austria was granted a $14 million loan on 31 May 1931 by the BIS, the Bank of England, the Federal Reserve, the Bank of France, the Reichsbank, as well as the central banks of seven other countries. This was nearly three weeks after the outbreak of the crisis[15] and the amount was clearly insufficient, given that the foreign claims of the Credit-Anstalt were $100 million in early May and perhaps $20 million were withdrawn during the first two weeks of the crisis. The loan had been exhausted by 5 June and a second $14 million credit was requested by the Austrian National Bank on 8 June. It was granted on the 14th for a further three months on the condition that the Austrian government should negotiate a $21 million foreign loan in order to strengthen the position of the Credit-Anstalt. Negotiations proceeded but soon stumbled on France's requirement that Austria should renounce any change in its existing political and economic relations. The Bank of England then stepped in and on 18 June offered a £5 million advance for a week, renewable, to give Austria some time. Austrian banks could thus remain open until a $40.5 million international loan was eventually sponsored by the BIS in July 1932, though exchange controls had been introduced by then, on 9 October 1931.[16]

Germany required far larger amounts. On 19 June, Hans Luther, the president of the Reichsbank, and former Reich Chancellor, approached Montagu Norman for a credit from the Bank of England, the Federal Reserve, and possibly the BIS, in the order of £80 million to $100 million. By 24 June, a $100 million credit to the Reichsbank had been put together, with the Bank of England, the Federal Reserve, the Bank of France, and the BIS taking $25 million each. However, the credit had been exhausted by 4 July. Hectic efforts were then made to raise a new loan, with Luther asking for an unlimited amount and Norman estimating the credit needed at something between $500 million and $1 billion. Luther travelled to London, Paris, and Basle between 9 and 13 July, but negotiations soon arrived at a deadlock. France demanded, in particular, that Germany should unconditionally resume payment of reparations at the end of the one-year moratorium and renounce a custom union with Austria; George Harrison, the Governor of the Federal Reserve bank of New York, was convinced that Congress would never sanction a government loan; and Montagu Norman was of the view that the German problem had become too big for the central banks and should be handled by governments. In the meantime, the German banking crisis had been met by a two-day bank holiday and the installation of exchange controls when banks reopened on 16 July. A conference held in London between 20 and 23 July failed to achieve anything apart from the appointment of a committee of experts chaired by Albert Wiggin, the president of Chase National Bank, charged to 'inquire into Germany's immediate further credit needs and to study the possibilities of converting a portion of short-term credits into long-term credits'.[17]

Britain was different. There was no banking crisis and the sterling crisis was that of a currency that retained a dominant position worldwide and played, with the dollar, the main role as reserve currency within the gold-exchange standard. International cooperation to support the pound came up against both Britain's economic and political difficulties—balance-of-payment and budget deficits, and divisions within the Labour Party, then in power, about the measures to be taken to tackle the situation. The support provided by the United States and France proved wholly inadequate. On 30 July, the Bank of England was granted a $125 million credit by the Federal Reserve and the same amount by the Bank of France—an amount inferior to the reserves lost by the bank in the second half of July. Made available on 7 August, it was exhausted within three weeks.[18] The British government then negotiated loans of $200 million each in Paris and New York,[19] announced on 28 August. But it was again too little. The credibility in Britain's unconditional adherence to the gold standard had been lost, and the sums required for its maintenance would have been astronomic.[20] Britain left the gold standard on 19 September 1931.

The world depression reached its nadir in 1932 with still no progress towards collective action. Nothing symbolizes more vividly the failure of international cooperation than the World Monetary and Economic Conference that started in London on 12 June 1933. The gathering was impressive, with representatives from sixty-five countries and six international organizations, and the declared objectives were ambitious on both financial and economic fronts. The questions to be tackled included monetary and credit policy, exchange difficulties, and movements of capital, as well as tariff policy and other restrictions to production and trade. In the end, and although it was not on the agenda, currency stabilization dominated the debates, and eventually killed the conference.[21] Discussions on the matter took place between Britain, France, and the United States outside the official conference, in order to stabilize, for the duration of the conference, the floating (pound and dollar) and gold (French franc) currencies. Roosevelt first refused, on 17 July, the rate agreed by the delegates ($4 to the pound); and then sent, on 3 July, his 'infamous' telegram, rejecting in deliberately chosen strong words 'the specious fallacy of achieving a temporary and probably an artificial stability in foreign exchange on the part of a few large countries only'. The move was applauded by Keynes and other economists, though many blamed the Americans for the conference's failure. In fact, all countries were giving priority to their domestic recovery programmes. Roosevelt was determined to reflate the American economy, Britain and the other members of the sterling area had no intention of returning to gold, while France wanted exchange-rate stabilization without reflation.

INTERNATIONAL ORGANIZATIONS

The post-war years were marked by political stability and cooperation among states, with the founding of the United Nations in 1945 and the setting-up of a series of multilateral organizations. The opening-up of borders, especially in the field of international trade once the GATT had come into force in 1947, and for Europe the establishment of the European Coal and Steel Community (ECSC) in 1951, then the Common Market in 1958, were also important steps in this direction. In financial affairs, international cooperation remained primarily concerned with monetary stability. However, this was no longer solely a matter for central banks, as governments gained the upper hand in financial policy; and it increasingly took place within the framework of international organizations, in the first place the institutions set up in 1944 as part of the Bretton Woods agreements, the International Monetary Fund (IMF), and the World Bank. While the World Bank's main task was to promote economic growth in developing countries, the IMF's function was to ensure exchange-rate stability by providing support to currencies whose parity with the dollar might be endangered by temporary external payments difficulties.[22] As for the BIS, its very existence was questioned at Bretton Woods, mainly because of its controversial relationships with Germany during the war,[23] and a resolution in favour of its dissolution was actually voted. However, a combination of factors enabled it to survive—persistent hesitation about its fate, difficulty of winding it up, unconditional support on the part of European central banks, as well as its technical usefulness in the early stages of post-war reconstruction. It soon became an essential cog in the new financial order, providing a forum for monetary cooperation, hosting the regular meetings of central banks' governors, and serving as a research centre on economic and monetary questions interesting central banks.[24]

The Bretton Woods regime really came into force only in January 1959, after the European currencies' return to convertibility. It was almost immediately confronted by growing American balance-of-payments deficits, leading to a glut of dollars in the world, which came to swell the reserves of the central European banks and threatened to destabilize the system. Faced with these risks, various forms of monetary cooperation were devised in the early 1960s under the aegis of the United States, in particular the *gold pool* to stabilize the price of gold at $35 per ounce, the *swap network* quickly to bring the collective assistance of the central banks to any that found itself short of currency reserves, and *the general arrangement to borrow*, through which ten countries (which would later form the Group of Ten and which Switzerland would join de facto) made additional medium-term resources available to the IMF in the event of an emergency. In 1967 the latter created a new international reserve unit, the Special Drawing Right (SDR), which was supposed to act partially as a substitute for the dollar.[25] Despite these efforts to prop it up, the regime did not survive. The dollar's gold convertibility was suspended on 15 August 1971, and the greenback was devalued de facto in December through a revaluation, at different rates, of the other main currencies. The attempt to maintain fixed exchange rates came to an end in March 1973, when currencies started to float, ushering in a new era in international monetary and financial relations.

The return of financial crises in the mid-1970s called for a new kind of international financial cooperation—one concerned with the failures of financial institutions rather than the failings of the monetary system. The secondary banking crisis, the failure of the Franklin National Bank and the closure of Herstatt Bank, required some degree of collective action—an unprecedented step, as banking crises had so far been dealt with at national level. The level of financial interconnection created by the growth of Eurodollar transactions, mainly consisting in inter-bank deposits, involved the intervention of more than a single authority.

The closure of the Herstatt Bank on 26 June 1974, in particular, carried serious systemic risks, with heavy debts being owed to a large number of banks across the world. The problem was tackled at the July meeting of the central banks' governors in Basle. The Bank of England, with its recent experience of the 'Lifeboat' rescue of secondary banks and its historical experience of international finance, provided leadership on this occasion. Its Governor, Gordon Richardson, put forward the principle that parent banks should take responsibility for their subsidiaries' losses, with their central bank acting as lender of last resort. Despite some reservations, not least from the Bundesbank, about the principle of 'parental responsibility', central bank governors let it be known, in order to bolster confidence, that they were prepared to assist sound banks within their own country that were facing difficulties through losses in the foreign-exchange markets.[26]

International cooperation took a more practical form in the orderly liquidation of the Franklin National Bank. From 11 May 1974, the Federal Reserve Bank of New York informed all major central banks about the bank's alarming situation so they could be prepared in case of a crisis. Foreign central banks were consulted about a possible buyer for Franklin National Bank, as Federal Law prevented the latter from being bought by a non-New York State bank; and they cooperated with the Federal Reserve in its support of Franklin's foreign-exchange trading during the crisis and after taking over its business later in the year. The Bank of England assisted the Federal Reserve in its loans to Franklin National, making the substantial assets of Franklin's London branch available as collateral.[27]

The extent of the collective action was commensurate to the severity of the crisis. But it proved efficient, and central bankers and policy-makers were better aware of the dangers posed by the internationalization of the financial system in a floating exchange-rate regime. More importantly, international cooperation moved to another uncharted territory: international financial regulation. There were, admittedly, some precedents. In the inter-war years, the Economic and Financial Organization of the League of Nations studied such questions as double taxation and the harmonization of international loan contracts.[28] At the BIS, prudential issues were occasionally discussed from the early 1960s at central banks governors' meetings largely dominated by monetary issues. The rise of the Euromarkets raised questions about the excessive exposure of some participants, the mismatch between short-term deposits and medium-term credits, the size of short-term international capital flows, and the lack of supervision, but no initiative was taken in the matter.[29] The Financial Instability of the early 1970s thus marks a turning point—the beginning of international cooperation in the field of financial regulation, a domain whose significance was to assume paramount importance in the following decades.

A first step was the formation later in 1974 of the Standing Committee on Banking Regulation and Supervisory Practices—later known as the Basle Committee. Its was formed by the Group of Ten, plus Switzerland and Luxembourg, on the proposition of Gordon Richardson, with the BIS as its secretariat, and held its first meeting in February 1975. The main purpose of the committee was to prevent international financial crises resulting from bank failures. Significantly, it did not seek to establish a supranational supervisory authority, but rather to improve national supervisory systems and develop cooperation between national authorities.[30] Particular attention was paid to the supervision of banks' foreign establishments, and recommendations on the matter were made to the governors in September 1975. This led to the so-called Basle Concordat, which laid down the principles that no foreign bank should escape supervision, host and home supervisory authorities should cooperate, and restraints on transfer of information should be removed. These principles were extended in the following years. In 1983, the revised Basle Concordat established the principle of consolidated supervision, and confirmed that host authorities should be responsible for subsidiaries.

In the meantime, however, international cooperation had reached new heights, with the actions taken in the autumn of 1982 to prevent a collapse of the world banking system. The risks posed by the Mexican default in August 1982 required measures that were at once well tried at national level, especially in Britain, and innovative at international level. As Jeremy Morse, chairman of Lloyds Bank and a former director of the Bank of England, put it:

Gordon Richardson played a very big part originally and that was in a totally British tradition. It was consciously modelled on the Baring crisis and the secondary banking crisis—the idea that, when you have widespread debt, the central bank organises a lifeboat. That was *the* model, transferred to the international stage. Larosière is, I think, the real long-term hero of this story, because he assumed internationally the job that the Governor of the Bank of England would take in a domestic crisis.[31]

Jacques de Larosière was the managing director of the IMF and clearly played the leading role in the rescue operation, together with Paul Volcker, the chairman of the Federal Reserve Board. Yet, at the outbreak of the crisis, the IMF was ill prepared to handle an international financial crisis. It had been mainly concerned with monetary policy rather than banking stability, and its decision-making process tended to be slow and thus not really adequate for a potential international lender of last resort. On the other hand, the IMF had started reinventing itself after Bretton Woods, providing loans to developing countries and helping them make structural adjustments. And there was a need for an international organization to coordinate the response to the crisis and Jacques de Larosière carried the Fund's executive board with him.[32] International cooperation involved the debtor countries, the creditors, in other words hundreds of commercial banks, the monetary authorities of the rich countries, in particular the Federal Reserve, and the BIS. Preventing a collapse of the international banking system meant extending new loans to Mexico, Argentina, and Brazil, in order to avoid a general default. These loans came from the IMF itself, from the leading industrial countries, and from the banks. The task of the IMF consisted in negotiating adjustment programmes with the debtor countries as a condition for its own loans and as a seal of good housekeeping for the loans granted by the other parties. It also consisted in convincing the banks, which were already overexposed in Latin America, to consent to further advances.

Negotiations with Mexico led, on 10 November 1982, to an agreement on the extension of three years' credit facilities, involving 450 per cent of Mexico's IMF quota (around $3.7 billion); the budget deficit was to be reduced, in stages, from 16.5 per cent in 1981 to 3.5 per cent in 1983, and the current account deficit from $13 billion in 1981 to $4.25 billion in 1983.[33] Six days later, on 16 November, at a meeting at the New York Federal Reserve, de Larosière told the banks' representatives that the stabilization plan required a $8.3 billion advance for 1983: $1.3 billion would come from the IMF, $2 billion from the US and other governments, and the $5 billion balance, representing about 7 per cent of their exposure, should be provided, within a month, by the banks. The banks were left with little choice: the IMF executive board would approve the credit to Mexico only if they accepted the plan, the alternative being a default on the payment of both interest and principal. A certain amount of pressure, not least by the leading central banks, was necessary to obtain the agreement of the hundreds of creditor banks, especially the smaller among them, but the plan was approved on 30 November. Similar negotiations were held more or less at the same time with Argentina and Brazil in the following weeks. By May 1983, as Donald Regan, the US Treasury Secretary put it at the G7 summit, the debt situation was still 'dangerous', but it had 'lost some of its urgency'.

International cooperation tends to work efficiently in times of acute crisis—when the 'instinct of self-preservation', in Paul Volcker's words, is at work.[34] In 1982, the banks did not need to be recapitalized, but the risks of financial meltdown were sufficiently high to convince them to consent to further advances. In any case, the IMF plan, including its own loans and those of the various governments, effectively amounted to a bailout of the banks, as its prime objective was to prevent a collapse of the world's banking system. International cooperation can prove more problematic once danger has receded and discussions about building a new financial order, or improving the existing one, get under way. Such a situation was fairly new after the International Debt Crisis. Institutional reforms following the Baring Crisis and, more significantly, the American Panic of 1907 were carried out at national level. The restoration of the gold standard in the early 1920s and Bretton Woods in 1944 were monetary programmes, and both resulted from economic and financial upheavals caused by world wars. International cooperation in the wake of a banking crisis started timidly in 1974 and more purposely in 1982. Two problems had to be solved: one was concerned with global imbalances, which concerned mainly debtor countries, the other with global regulation, which concerned mainly creditor banks. On both fronts, cooperation was not an unqualified success.

Dealing with the Debt Crisis proved difficult after the initial breakthrough. Agreements between debtors and creditors became harder to reach, as the adjustment programmes fell heavily on the debtor countries, whose economic condition had badly deteriorated. The banks, on their part, were reluctant to reschedule their loans and provide new credit—even though they were earning more in interest than they were lending. The IMF was accused in some quarters of siding with the banks, but the general feeling was that the banks should make some concessions, through interest rates or even debt reduction. On both sides, there were increasing signs of what has been described as 'debt fatigue'. An attempt at moving forward was made in 1985 by James Baker, the Treasury Secretary. The plan required the banks to provide new funds ($20 billion) to fifteen developing and indebted countries to pursue a series of economic reforms, mainly liberalization, together with a rescheduling of the debt. Multilateral agencies would contribute an additional $9 billion and a greater role was given to the World Bank, which had so far remained in the sidelines. The Baker Plan was essentially a failure. Under the pressure of the commercial banks, it confined itself to rescheduling and did not address the crucial issue of debt relief. The Brady Plan, launched in 1989 by Nicholas Brady, Baker's successor as Treasury Secretary, while continuing on the path of liberalization, recognized the importance of reducing the debt burden and mobilized more than $30 billion to allow debtor countries to buy back their debt or to convert it into discount bonds. The largest deal was concluded with Mexico. The banks could swap old debt either for fifteen years 'discount bonds' (at 65 per cent) or for par bonds with a reduced interest rate. The new bonds would be transferable, they could not be rescheduled by the debtor, and the principal was collateralized with US zero-coupon bonds. The Brady Plan succeeded in tackling the phenomenon of debt overhang that discouraged new loans and took developing countries back to the financial markets.[35]

While the Debt Crisis undoubtedly gave the IMF a new role at the centre of international financial cooperation, the threat to the international banking system called for greater international supervision.[36] Following the International Lending Supervision Act passed in the United States in 1983, the Basle Committee turned its attention to the issue of capital adequacy, with the aim of creating a level playing field for competition among international banks. The Basle Agreement—more formally 'The International Convergence of Capital Measurements and Capital Standards'—was the result of the cooperation between the members of the G10, forming the committee, plus Spain. It was adopted in 1988 and was to be implemented in 1992. It rested on three pillars: one measuring capital; a second weighting risk; and a third, with which Basle I is readily associated, setting a capital ratio of 8 per cent of risk-weighted assets. The accord had weaknesses: harmonizing various national practices proved difficult and the ratio of 8 per cent had no objective basis; risk-weighting also left a lot to be desired; and, more importantly from the perspective of international financial cooperation, it was not binding.

In the face of criticisms, the evolution of the financial markets, and the financial crises of the 1990s, the Basle Committee undertook in 1998 to develop a 'Revised Framework on International Convergences of Capital Measurement and Capital Standards', known as Basle II, which was agreed in 2004, after six years of complex negotiations, still between the members of the G10, despite the growing number of countries adopting its standards. Basle II also rested on three pillars: the first, 'Minimum Capital Requirements', offered a more comprehensive approach to risk-weighting; it also included capital to back operational risks and market risks in addition to credit risks on which Basle I was exclusively focused. The second pillar, 'Supervisory Review Process', addressed the relationships between regulator and bank, with extended rights for the former. And the third pillar, 'Market Discipline', prescribed greater disclosure of capital and risk-taking positions to empower shareholders. Basle II has also been the object of criticism, in particular its excessive reliance on rating agencies and on the banks' internal ratings models. The latter, in particular, was judged pro-cyclical and thus likely to make matters worse during a downturn, with all firms behaving in the same manner and facing increasing risks of illiquidity. The Financial Debacle of 2007–8 seems to have confirmed these doubts.

International cooperation in the field of financial regulation has not been confined to the Basle Committee. A number of other organizations have been established, in particular the International Organization of Securities Commission (IOSCO) for the securities industry, the International Association of Insurance Supervisors (IAIS) for the insurance industry, the Financial Action Task Force (FATF) for money laundering, and several others for accounting and auditing standards. Following the Asian crisis in 1997, proposals were made for the creation of a new international financial authority, leading to the creation in 1999 by the G7 countries of the Financial Stability Forum (FSF). The FSF brought together the financial authorities of the leading financial powers as well as the various international and regional supervisory agencies, but was devoid of proper regulatory authority.

When the credit crunch started in the summer of 2007, the institutionalization of international financial cooperation had thus made great strides since the Financial Instability of the early 1970s and the International Debt Crisis of 1982. Admittedly, no collective rescue of the world banking system had had to be undertaken since the early 1980s, but coordination and cooperation had taken place within the resolution of bank failures at national level, such as the Bank of Commerce and Credit International (BCCI) in London in 1991, with discussions about the timing of the bank's shutdown in order to minimize disruption to the financial markets; or the Long-Term Capital Management (LTCM) in New York in 1998, when the well-tried formula first used to rescue Baring Brothers in 1890 was once again used successfully. The authority of the IMF had grown, though somewhat controversially, during the Asian Crisis of 1997–8. Consultation between heads of state and government, finance ministers, central bankers, and other officials had been common practice for several decades and had intensified since the end of Bretton Woods, not only within international organizations, but also in regular and highly publicized meetings—inaugurated in 1975 with the G7 'summit' in Rambouillet hosted by the French president Valéry Giscard d'Estaing. Closer cooperation worked at regional level, especially within the European Union and even more closely within the Eurozone.

The extent to which international financial cooperation played a positive role during the credit crunch can be assessed at three levels: first, its capacity to prevent the outbreak of a major financial crisis; second, if faced with an acute crisis, its capacity to avoid a global financial catastrophe; and, third, after the crisis, its capacity to improve the existing international financial architecture. International consultation and coordination proved successful on one of these three counts: avoiding disaster. Banks were rescued by their own government, but the coordination of national efforts was essential to restore some confidence in the financial system. On the other hand, the various existing international organizations proved totally unable to prevent the outbreak of the most severe financial crisis in history— the regulation of the financial system, whether at national or international level, proved woefully inadequate. In the aftermath of the crisis, a number of steps were promptly taken in order to strengthen the stability of the global financial system. At the Washington meeting in November 2008, the leaders of the G20 countries called for a larger membership of the Financial Stability Forum, which was reestablished as the Financial Stability Board (FSB) at the next G20 meeting in London in April 2009, with a broadened mandate to promote financial stability.[37] At the same London meeting it was agreed to increase the resources available to the IMF by up to $500 billion—which would triple the total pre-crisis lending resources of about $250 billion—to support growth in emerging market and developing countries. At the BIS, the Basle Committee has made proposals 'to strengthen global capital and liquidity regulations with the goal of promoting a more resilient banking sector'.[38]

However, despite unanimous declarations about the importance of international cooperation to exit the financial crisis, agreements have often proved difficult to reach. The extent, depth, and level of regulation inevitably posed problems. Within the European Union, for example, dissensions appeared as early as February 2009, with Britain's opposition to one of the main planks of the de Larosière report on financial supervision—the concentration of banking supervision at European level.[39] In December 2009, Gordon Brown, the British Prime Minister, approved the principle of a tax on financial transactions, the so-called Tobin tax,[40] which received a cool reception from the Obama administration in the United States. Bankers' bonuses for 2009 have been condemned universally but dealt with nationally, with Britain and France deciding to levy a 50 per cent super-tax and the United States limiting pay restrictions to banks benefiting from the Troubled Assets Relief Program (TARP). The reforms of the banking systems, to the extent that they have proceeded, have done so along national rather than international lines.

International financial cooperation has been one of the main advances of the second half of the twentieth century, especially since the opening-up of the world economy in the early 1970s. Each shock led to closer cooperation in order, first, to prevent an imminent disaster, and then to improve the existing system and avoid the recurrence of financial crises. If the first goal was regularly achieved, not least because of the instinct of self-preservation, the second, without systematically failing, was never an outright success—because of the complexity of the issues, the prevailing ideology of deregulation, and the weight of national interests, in particular the shifting balance of power within international finance.

7

———

Balance of Power

Has the centre of gravity of international finance irreversibly started to shift from the Atlantic to the Pacific since the Financial Debacle of 2007–8? There has been no lack of forecasts predicting the end of New York's and London's world dominance and their replacement by Hong Kong, Singapore, Shanghai, or Dubai. The quasi-immediate replacement of the G8 by the G20 as the international forum to deal with the crisis has been a clear signal of a new balance of power in the world economy. And yet the move had been underway well before the credit crunch—the term 'Brics' was forged in 2001[1]—and such major changes are very slow processes. Moreover, London and New York remained, a year after the fall of Lehman Brothers, the world's two leading global financial centres.[2] There can be little doubt that the financial landscape is changing. But to what extent? And at which rhythm? This chapter looks at previous changes in the balance of power in international finance and the role played by financial crises in these changes.

FINANCIAL POWER

Financial power is an elusive concept. It can refer to single financial firms, especially banks—the Rothschilds, or J. P. Morgan were indeed financial powers, if there ever were any. It can refer to clusters of financial services—Wall Street, the City of London. It can refer to nations—usually in their capacity to use public and/or private finance in order to achieve political objectives. There is, of course, a close connection between the three: no country can reasonably claim to be a financial power without being the home of major financial institutions and a financial centre of international proportions. In the same way, big banks and international financial centres have been the attributes of large industrialized countries, though there have been exceptions to the rule, most notably the top three (then two) Swiss banks since the 1960s, and Zurich and Geneva, Singapore, or Hong Kong (even after its return to China) as financial centres.

Financial power is not only difficult to define, it is also difficult to measure. As far as individual firms are concerned, size is of course an essential though not always the determining factor. In Britain, the London clearing banks (Barclays, Lloyds, Midland, National Westminster) remained sleeping giants well beyond the First World War. The most influential players—especially in international finance—remained the much smaller merchant banks (Rothschild, Baring, Schroders, Morgan Grenfell). The same applies, though to a lesser extent, especially in the 1920s, to the respective roles of the commercial banks (Citibank, Chase National, Bank of America, Bank of Manhattan, Central Hanover, Manufacturers Trust) and the investment banks (J. P. Morgan, later Morgan Stanley, Kuhn Loeb, Dillon Read, Kidder Peabody, Lehman Brothers, Goldman Sachs) in the United States. Conversely, the big credit banks—commercial in France (Crédit Lyonnais, Société Générale), universal in Germany (Deutsche, Dresdner)—dominated the field in continental Europe from the turn of the twentieth century. However, with the spread of the universal-type of banks in the later part of the twentieth century, financial power has primarily become a matter of size (balance sheet, market capitalization) and presence (range of activities, multinational expansion). Financial centres are best compared in terms of international influence. For most, relations with other centres are essentially of a bilateral nature; some cater to the needs of one region of the world; a few play a wider international role; and one or two (London around 1900, London and New York a century later) are truly global.[3] They also differ in the range of services they offer (international banking, capital market, assets management, foreign exchange, derivatives, professional services, and so on), with the leading centres performing generalist functions, the lesser ones specializing in niches.[4]

Economic power, as measured by GNP, is a necessary though not a sufficient condition of a country's financial power. Admittedly, the dominant financial power of the day—the Netherlands in the eighteenth century, Britain in the nineteenth and early twentieth, the United States since the mid-twentieth—has also been the leading economic power, and, further down the line, only the world's largest economies have wielded financial power. However, there has always been a time lag between the rise of an economic giant and its emergence as a financial powerhouse, as witnessed by the United States in the late nineteenth and early twentieth centuries; and occasional discrepancy between financial and industrial might, as witnessed by France's financial prominence and Germany's industrial might during the same period. Financial power depends less on financial resources than on the way these resources are used. From this perspective, foreign lending is a good indicator of a country's international financial influence. Another one is the strength of the national currency, especially the status of reserve currency— pound sterling, French franc, German mark, US dollar, Japanese yen, and euro, depending on the period. And there is, of course, state power, the will to direct public funds towards foreign-policy objectives.

The balance of power has been shifting between banks, financial centres, and countries since the late nineteenth century, at the top and near the top of the international financial hierarchy. Financial crises, however, have played only a limited part in these processes.

THE FIRST GLOBALIZATION

The pre-1914 order was centred on a dominant economy: Great Britain. By the late nineteenth century, Britain was no longer the world's premier economy: it had been overtaken by the United States in terms of total national income by 1870 and in terms of per capita income shortly before 1914.[5] Nor was Britain the world's foremost industrial power any longer: it had been overtaken by the United States towards 1880 and by Germany towards 1905. Britain's dominant position was ensured mainly by its leadership in trade and finance. British foreign trade still represented some 14 per cent of world trade in 1913, and the British merchant navy was the world's foremost, with one-third of world tonnage, operating most of the traffic between non-British ports. Britain was at the centre of the system of multilateral settlements, on account of its trade deficit with the major industrial countries, from which it purchased mainly manufactured goods, and its surplus with its colonial empire, which absorbed more than a third of its exports, especially with India—the main outlet for the English cotton industry.[6] Britain was also the world's leading exporter of capital, with 42 per cent of the stock of foreign investment in 1913, spread worldwide, though with a distinct preference for the two Americas.[7] The pound sterling was the main international trading and reserve currency and formed the cornerstone of the international monetary system in force at that time, the gold standard. Finally, the City of London was the undisputed financial centre of the world, with a dominant position in a uniquely broad range of financial services—the issue of foreign loans and securities, international trade finance, money market, financial market, insurance market, commodity markets, auditing, legal advice, and others.[8]

Despite the City's pre-eminence, Britain's financial institutions were not the most powerful in the world—whatever the clout of the London merchant banks in international finance. British banks were not the world's largest, though they were among the largest,[9] and remained confined to commercial banking with hardly any foray into the issuing, accepting, or investing business. French banks were far from being fully fledged universal banks, but they had opened branches abroad and were active in the issuing and placing of foreign loans, not least on behalf of the Russian government. More than their British counterparts, they contributed to France's financial power, the world's number two. France's strengths lay in its foreign lending (20 per cent of the stock of foreign investment in 1913), more closely connected to foreign policy's objectives than that of Britain. The franc was a reserve currency and the Bank of France, with its huge gold reserves, was the bedrock of the international monetary system. And, as a financial centre, Paris was a 'brilliant second', with its main strengths lying in its long-term capital market, the Paris Bourse (second only to the London Stock Exchange) and powerful banks.[10] Imperial Germany emerged as an industrial rather than a financial power during the thirty years preceding the First World War. However, its financial presence was being increasingly felt as a result of its foreign investment (in third position behind Britain and France with 13 per cent of the world's total in 1913) and the expansion of its big universal banks, with which German financial might was readily associated. On the other hand, despite its impressive rise, Berlin remained a fairly provincial financial centre compared with London and Paris with, in particular, fewer foreign issues and a Börse hampered by anti-speculation regulations.[11]

Outside Britain, France, and Germany, only the United States could claim to be a financial power before 1914—Belgium, the Netherlands, and Switzerland, despite being large exporters of capital, were too small to enjoy such a status. The United States was an emerging, albeit fast-rising, financial power, fuelled by the dynamism of its economy. Essentially a capital-importing country—the top destination for overseas investment—before the war, it started investing abroad from the closing years of the nineteenth century. By 1913, it had become the fourth largest holder of foreign securities (with 8 per cent of the total), though it remained a net debtor, with private liabilities in excess of $3 billion.[12] And, significantly, New York became a major financial centre as an entry point into a capital-importing country, rather than as an exit point from a capital-exporting country, and mostly kept this status until 1914.

This did not happen to other capital-importing countries at the periphery. A possible contender was Russia, a fast-growing economy, the second destination (with Canada) for overseas investment, and a financial centre (St Petersburg) that was home to three of the world's top thirty banks[13] and a stock exchange with a market capitalization nearly as high as that of the Berlin Börse.[14] But Russia was heavily dependent on foreign capital, both economically—most Russian banks were controlled by foreign banking groups—and diplomatically—with France making full use of its financial leverage to strengthen the military alliance between the two countries.[15] Other countries were financial minnows, whether measured by the size of their financial institutions or by the development of their financial market. However, trade finance led to the emergence of dynamic international financial centres in Asia, especially Hong Kong, Shanghai, Yokohama, Bombay, and Calcutta, thanks to the presence of powerful merchant houses, mostly though not exclusively British, and overseas banks; some of them, especially Shanghai, started to play a regional role and to develop domestically owned and controlled financial institutions.[16]

Neither the Baring Crisis of 1890 nor the American Panic of 1907 led to any change in the balance of power in international finance. The City was shaken by the Baring Crisis, but the shock was not strong enough to jeopardize its supremacy, which, in any case, no other centre was in a position to challenge. Paris had harboured such ambition earlier, in the 1850s and 1860s. There was a strong rivalry between the two centres over foreign lending, with France actually exporting more capital than Britain, but London remaining the main issuing centre.[17] One of the most striking signs of Paris's new ambitions was the proposal made by France in December 1866 to introduce a universal currency, based on the franc, a year after establishing the Latin Monetary Union, with Italy, Belgium, and Switzerland. But it came to nothing, as Britain and Prussia refused the plan. And France's defeat by Prussia in 1871 put an end to Parisian ambitions.[18] Three decades later, London sensed for the first time a foretaste of New York's competition. In August 1900, half the £10 million British loan aimed at financing the Boer War was placed in the United States through J. P. Morgan. The issue was a resounding success, and the American public subscribed for part of the four subsequent British war loans, but caused fear and resentment in the City, even though its position was for the time being secure.[19] But for how long? The American Panic of 1907 did not enhance Wall Street's international standing, but the subsequent determination to go ahead with a central bank, eventually formed in 1913, enabled it fully to seize the opportunities presented by the outbreak of the war.

THE LEGACY OF THE WAR

The repercussions of the Financial Crisis of July–August 1914 were limited if compared with the upheaval created by the First World War itself. Yet the first steps towards a change in the balance of power were taken during the first months of the conflict, as the United States saw an opportunity to overtake Britain as the world's leading financial power. The emergency measures taken by Treasury Secretary William McAdoo to halt the dollar crisis were clearly made with this objective in mind.[20] Maintaining the gold standard, if only nominally, when all countries bar Britain had suspended it, was seen as paramount in order to restore American financial credibility and to establish the dollar as a reserve currency. The New York Stock Exchange was closed on 31 July, as a way to stem the massive selling of American securities by Europeans and the ensuing outflow of gold, and did not reopen until 12 December; the issue of currency notes was stepped up to the level required to meet demand; the already delayed opening of the Federal Reserve banks was hastened to take place on 16 November; and exports of agricultural products to Europe were promoted to reverse the gold drain. By early November the pound-to-dollar exchange rate stabilized before decidedly moving in the dollar's favour in 1915. And, with China and Japan drawing bills on New York rather than exclusively on London, a Washington Post headline announced in January 1915 'the Eventual Shift of the World's Financial Center from the English Capital to New York'.[21]

By then, what was expected to be a short war ending by Christmas was turning into a total war that was profoundly to alter the pre-1914 order. In most respects, financial power shifted from Europe to the United States. Within a few years, the US position changed from that of a debtor to that of a creditor country—from having net liabilities in excess of $3 billion in 1913 to having net assets of $4.5 billion in 1919. Europe, on the other hand, was no longer the world's banker. Britain, France, and Germany together lost more than a third of their foreign investment—in other words, some $12 billion. However, while Germany lost nearly all its foreign assets and France most of them (80 per cent, following sales and, especially, the default by the Russian and Ottoman borrowers), Britain was mainly obliged to sell $3 billion of American securities—just over 15 per cent of its foreign assets.[22]

This resulted in a new balance of power within Europe and between Europe and the United States. Germany paid the price of defeat. Burdened with reparations, it became a huge importer of capital; and it was mainly in this capacity that Berlin remained an international financial centre of some significance. The German universal banks were weakened by hyperinflation, losing nearly half of their capital and reserves between 1913 and 1924; moreover, their international sphere of influence was considerably reduced by the confiscation or sale of a considerable part of their foreign assets.[23] France was crippled until 1926 by the weakness of the franc, capital flight, and reconstruction requirements. The big banks suffered from war and inflation, and their assets decreased, not only in real terms compared with their 1913 levels, but also against those of their foreign competitors, especially the English 'Big Five'. Things changed with the stabilization of the franc by Raymond Poincaré in December 1926: the French currency inspired confidence once more, capital returned to France, and foreign issues picked up again. As a financial centre, Paris recovered part of its pre-war vitality, rekindling ambitions to compete with London and New York. Its main asset was the amount of gold and foreign claims, mainly in pounds, held by the Bank of France as a result of the French current-account surplus. While this strengthened France's position in international financial diplomacy, it left Paris far behind London and New York in terms of financial capacity.[24]

Britain was in a different position. Despite the constraints weighing down its balance of payments, especially because of the loss of competitiveness of its staple industries, it was far from being obliterated as a force in international finance. The 1920s were at once a period of close cooperation and intense rivalry between the old and the new financial power, especially between London and New York.[25] Overall, London still ranked first in the hierarchy of international financial centres on account of the unrivalled range of services it was able to offer, its unique expertise, its solid and well-established networks and client bases, its considerable openness to the world, and also, though to a lesser extent than New York, its far from insignificant financial capabilities, especially in relation to the size of its banks and its stock of capital invested abroad, still the world's largest. New York's decisive advantage lay in foreign lending. If expertise remained in London, capital was henceforth in New York and, during the second half of the 1920s, foreign issues placed in New York generally exceeded those offered in London by 50 per cent.[26] New York's other strength was that of the American economy. In spite of its new world role, New York remained as much an American as an international financial centre.[27] Foreign issues (15 per cent of the total) played a secondary role to domestic issues, which enjoyed an incredible boom in the 1920s. Foreign capital continued to be invested in the US economy, not only long-term investment, but also short-term funds attracted by American stocks, especially with the bullish trend that marked the decade. This interaction between national and international business was one of the main characteristics of New York when compared to London.

The Great Depression had a far smaller impact than the First World War on the balance of power in international finance. New York was certainly wounded, but not sufficiently for London to regain its undisputed dominance or for Paris to overtake it. As international capital flows declined rapidly, national, or imperial, withdrawal prevailed over world influence. Foreign loans issued in New York fell from a peak of $1.3 billion in 1927 to less than $300 million in 1931 and less than $100 million in 1932 and 1933—that was less than the foreign issues offered in London. The City, for its part, retreated into the British Empire, which enabled it to continue to play, within the framework of the sterling area, the role that it had previously played at world level.[28] Its significance was evident in the field of issues. Whereas foreign loans outside the empire ceased almost completely after September 1931, imperial issues continued throughout the decade, reaching £187 million between 1932 and 1938.[29] At the same time, short-term capital flows took a different direction after 1931, no longer starting out from the traditional capital-exporting countries and ending up in the less-developed economies or, as in the 1920s, in central Europe. Instead, they followed the opposite trend—primarily towards the United States and Britain, and also towards small neutral countries such as the Netherlands and Switzerland. This was partly due to the economic situation, which drove creditor countries to repatriate their assets, and partly due to political troubles, which brought about capital flight in numerous countries—especially France, Germany, and, to a lesser extent, Belgium.[30]

PAX AMERICANA

It took another world war radically to transform the nineteenth-century financial order and definitely to shift the balance of power in favour of the United States: in 1950 its GDP was more than double that of Britain, France, and West Germany combined, up from being about 20 per cent larger in 1938[31]—a reflection of the devastation of Europe at the end of the Second World War. America's financial supremacy was based on the dollar, the linchpin of the Bretton Woods system and the only convertible currency (with the Swiss franc). The United States held about 60 per cent of the official stocks of gold and was the great purveyor of capital, starting during the war with Lend-Lease. The programme was adopted in 1941 and provided, without reimbursement terms, to countries at war with Germany and Japan the goods and services needed for their military effort. The transfers totalled nearly $50 billion at the end of the war, from which thirty-eight countries, including the Soviet Union, benefited, with two-thirds going to Britain. American aid continued after the war, especially with the Marshall Plan, a programme for European recon-struction: $13 billion worth of donations, mainly in kind, were trans-ferred to Europe between 1948 and 1952, solving one of the major post-war imbalances, the shortage of dollars needed to import capital goods and raw materials from across the Atlantic.[32]

Throughout the 1950s and 1960s, international capital flows mainly originated from the United States—though carried out by public bodies rather than private institutions or markets: between 1955 and 1962, foreign issues floated in New York reached $4.2 billion, as against $98 billion in economic and military aid granted by the United States to foreign countries between 1945 and 1952.[33] However, international issues offered in New York exceeded nearly fourfold those offered in London, and nearly fivefold those offered in Zurich.[34] New York became the undisputed financial centre of the world, with the financial institutions and markets befitting this status. The Federal Reserve of New York played a key role in international finance, as the correspondent bank in the United States for the main foreign central banks. The New York commercial banks had become, as a group, the world's largest, ahead of London's 'Big Five', all with well-organized departments for international business and most with a direct presence overseas.[35] The New York Stock Exchange was still a market where mostly American stock was traded, but in which traders from all over the world took part, giving it a truly international dimension. And New York had an extensive range of specialist firms, typical of a large international financial centre—brokers and foreign-exchange dealers, custom brokers, accepting houses, investment banks, and many others.

London could no longer compete—despite the institutions, mechanisms, and expertise, all still in place and all in many respects ahead of New York. Britain was no longer in a position to support a financial centre of world dimension, and the sterling area was a poor substitute. The British economy was not only too small; it was also too weak, with, in particular, severe balance-of-payments constraints, and the need to impose exchange controls and restrictions on capital movements.[36] The Thirty Years War of the twentieth century brought about the first change in the world's financial leadership in 150 years—when London supplanted Amsterdam during the French wars, at the turn of the nineteenth century.[37]

AFTER BRETTON WOODS

The end of Bretton Woods marked the end of the United States' financial supremacy—though not of its dominant position. The changed balance of power was the result not of any specific monetary or banking crisis, but of changes taking place in the world economy in the 1950s and 1960s. Western Europe's and, especially, Japan's faster economic growth meant that, by the early 1970s, they had closed much of the gap separating them from the leader at the end of the war. In 1973, Europe's GDP per head was, on average, 71 per cent that of the United States, and Japan's 65 per cent, up respectively from 51 per cent and 18 per cent in 1950.[38] In many respects, this was a natural catching-up process, especially as the gap was artificially large at the end of the war, but it led to a number of readjustments. The US share of world industrial output, for example, fell from 45 per cent in 1950 to 33 per cent in 1970; its share of world's exports fell from 17 per cent to 14 per cent, and it was overtaken by West Germany in manufactured goods; its share of the stock of gold and foreign exchange fell from 50 per cent to 16 per cent.[39] Similar trends could be found across the board. And there were, of course, the increasing pressures on the dollar, because of the widening deficit of the American balance of payments, the attempts at propping it up, the eventual devaluation and suspension of convertibility, and the end of its role as the key currency of the Bretton system of fixed exchange rates.

Financial crises played little role in whatever changes happened in the balance of power in international finance. The collapse of the Bretton Woods system, marked by the dollar crisis and the announcement of the closure of the gold window by Richard Nixon on 15 August 1971, was the expected outcome of a process starting in the 1950s. The oil shocks and the petrodollars did not turn the oil-producing countries into fully-fledged financial powers, and the banking crises of the early 1970s were not deep enough to have a significant impact. American banks were the most exposed in the International Debt Crisis of 1982, but West European and Japanese banks were also affected. In any case, whatever its relative decline, the United States remained the dominant financial power after Bretton Woods, with varying encroachments to what was once an unassailable position. The dollar continued to be held as the reserve currency of choice—making up 65–70 per cent of the world's foreign reserves, after dropping from over 80 per cent under Bretton Woods. The United States' share of the foreign direct investment stock fell from 50 per cent in 1970 to 40 per cent in 1980, and 26 per cent in 1995—still far ahead of Japan and Britain, with respectively 13 and 12 per cent.[40] American banks faced increased foreign competition: eight of them were in the world's twenty largest in 1970, including the top three (Bank of America, Chase Manhattan, and Citibank), only three in 1980, with the Bank of America still in the top spot, but Citicorp down to nine and Chase Manhattan to seventeen.[41]

As an international financial centre, New York had to cede first place to London, as the Euromarkets made the City their natural home. The City was well equipped for this task, with its bankers' age-old experience, their expertise in international finance, and the size and diversity of its institutions and markets. But the positive attitude of the British monetary authorities also played a decisive role, in contrast to their more cautious counterparts in continental Europe.[42] They were helped by the regulations in place or newly introduced in America—Regulation Q, dating back to the New Deal, for Eurodollars, and the Interest Equalization Act, introduced in 1963, for Euro-bond issues.[43] The issue of Eurobonds, 70 per cent of which took place in London, soon overtook that of classic foreign bonds (issued in local currency on behalf of a non-resident), primarily offered in New York since the late 1940s.[44] The number of foreign banks attracted to the City went from 69 in 1955 to 159 in 1970 and 261 in 1975—that is to say, twice the corresponding number for New York.[45] Several of them were consortium banks, particularly active in the field of syndicated Eurocredits, which swelled to reach four times the amount of Eurobonds by 1973.[46] However, London's advantage should not be overstated. On the one hand, domestic financial activities have always prevailed in New York, limiting the impact of any loss of international business. On the other hand, American banks actually took control of the Euromarkets—their share of Eurocurrency deposits reached a maximum of 54 per cent in 1960 and eight of the top twenty intermediaries in the Eurobond market were American—and integrated the City in their global strategy.

Competition from Japan appeared more serious. By the early 1970s, Japan had become the world's second largest economy, and its growth continued to outpace that of the United States and Western Europe during the 1970s and 1980s. From being about a third of the size of the American economy, measured in terms of GDP, in 1973 (and just over a tenth in 1950), the Japanese economy had become 40 per cent as large by 1989.[47] Japan first emerged as an industrial giant, with particular strength in electronic products, cameras, motorcycles and later motor cars, iron and steel, and shipbuilding; and a huge surplus in its manufactured goods trade balance, overtaking West Germany in the 1970s. The rise of Japan as a financial power, and of Tokyo as an international financial centre, was thus above all due to Japan's rise to the rank of economic superpower. However, it was not before the late 1970s that the impact of the phenomenal Japanese industrial growth was translated into financial terms. Until then, the country's financial resources had been devoted entirely to the reconstruction effort and to fostering national economic growth, through a banking system that was almost autarchic and tightly regulated by the Ministry of Finance and the Bank of Japan. Capital flows entering and leaving the country were tightly controlled, including banking transactions in Eurocurrency and inflows of short-term bank funds.[48] As a result, Japan was kept out of the international financial system. In 1975, less than 1 per cent of international bonds were denominated in yen, compared with 51 per cent in dollars, 17 per cent in Swiss francs, and 16 per cent in marks.[49]

Economic conditions in the 1970s, marked by inflation, the end of the fixed exchange-rate regime, and the slowdown in economic growth, practically forced the Japanese authorities to open up the economy to the world. This was brought about by the simultaneous development of the Tokyo capital market and the liberalization of international financial operations. By volume of national transactions, Tokyo was already the world's second financial centre at the end of the 1970s: domestic issues on the Japanese capital market, for example, amounted to $161 billion in 1980, behind the United States ($272 billion), but ahead of Germany ($79 billion) and Britain ($36 billion). The Tokyo Stock Exchange was the world's second, in terms of market capitalization, in 1981, with $418 billion, behind New York ($1,100 billion), but way ahead of London ($190 billion) and Frankfurt ($56 billion). But its influence started to make itself felt on an international level. Japanese capital outflows went from an average of some $5.1 billion per year between 1973 and 1977 to $18.4 billion between 1978 and 1982; inflows went from $1.5 billion to $8.9 billion. The percentage of yen-denominated issues exceeded 5 per cent of total foreign issues in 1980, the number of branches of non-Japanese banks in Tokyo increased from forty-five to seventy-six between 1970 and 1980, and the country's five big commercial banks all came among the top twenty in the world in 1980.

By the late 1980s, the possibility that Tokyo might overtake New York and become the world's leading financial centre was increasingly mooted. The 'Japanese model' was at its height, while the United States was showing signs of 'decline'. The world's top ten banks, measured by total assets, were all Japanese, and in the spring of 1987 Tokyo's market capitalization exceeded that of the New York Stock Exchange. Long-term analyses were indicating that the world's financial leadership was in the process of switching from New York to Tokyo, just as it had started to switch from London to New York at the beginning of the twentieth century.[50] Such judgements proved far too hasty. First, the strength of the yen skewed rankings and international comparisons expressed in dollars in Japan's favour. Second, the American economy, far from declining, experienced spectacular growth in the 1990s. And, third, the Japanese slump and banking crisis had serious repercussions on the country's and Tokyo's international position.

While the International Debt Crisis of 1982 hardly had any effect on the balance of power in international finance, the Japanese Banking Crisis of 1997–8 clearly diminished Japan's international influence. Of course, as the financial capital of the world's second economic power, Tokyo continued to play a far from insignificant role—the yen remained the third international currency after the dollar and the euro, the Tokyo Stock Exchange the second after New York in terms of capitalization, and Japanese bank loans overseas were still in second or third place worldwide, depending on the year. Nevertheless, the erosion suffered by Tokyo was one of the most serious ever observed in a period of less than a decade and in peacetime: the use of the yen dropped sharply (from 13.5 per cent to 10.5 per cent of world currency turnover between 1989 and 1998); market capitalization fell by half; and the steady level of bank credit to non-residents was more apparent than real, as it was made up almost entirely of loans to the subsidiaries of Japanese enterprises established abroad, mainly in Asia. Moreover, the Japanese banks withdrew en masse from the international markets; and foreign banks' presence in Tokyo decreased, some having considerably scaled back their activities and others having completely abandoned their operations in Japan. This disappearance of numerous international players in fact greatly contributed to reducing the activity and, above all, the international influence of Tokyo.

While remaining the leading centre in Asia, Tokyo had to face growing competition from two rapidly rising financial stars: Singapore and Hong Kong. Singapore's development, which preceded Hong Kong's, was the result of the systematic effort made on the part of the authorities, immediately upon the country's independence in 1965, to turn it into an international financial centre.[51] The Eurodollar market, known as the Asian dollar market, from the outset established itself in Singapore following the authorization given in

1968 to the Bank of America to collect deposits and grant loans in dollars to Asian clients. The market expanded quickly to reach $86 billion in 1982, helped by a whole series of government measures and orchestrated by the Monetary Authority of Singapore, Singapore's central bank, established in 1971.[52] The government also intervened more directly to encourage the emergence of a bond market.[53] Singapore's financial markets really took on an international dimension from the 1980s: the Asian dollar market went from $86 million in 1982 to more than $350 million in 1990; the foreign-exchange market grew in its wake, from a daily average of some $12 billion in 1985 to $139 billion in 1998—in fourth position in the world behind London, New York, and Tokyo; derivatives started being traded in 1984, with the foundation of the SIMEX (Singapore International Monetary Exchange), the first organized market in Asia; and the number of foreign banks setting up there reached 185 in 1995.[54]

While Singapore became the main centre in Asia for the Eurodollar and Eurobond markets, syndicated Eurocredits found a home in Hong Kong. The British colony was able to use Eurocurrencies redirected from Singapore to set up syndicated Eurocredit operations on behalf of enterprises and governments in the region's main economies: Japan, Taiwan, South Korea, and even Australia and New Zealand, joined by Thailand, the Philippines, and, above all, China. In the space of about twelve years, Hong Kong established itself as the world's third centre for Eurocredits, behind London and New York.[55] Hong Kong benefited from a number of competitive advantages: its liberal standpoint towards hosting foreign bankers and businessmen; a non-interventionist stance by the authorities; a favourable tax system and modern infrastructure; the absence of exchange control, as well as free circulation of capital; a robust legal system; the existence of the rule of law; and, especially, its position as the door for a China that began to open up to the world at the end of the 1970s. Hong Kong's other prominent activities included international banking, the gold market, and the financial market, where its market capitalization was second only to that of Tokyo, serving particularly as a financing bridge for the whole region, and first and foremost for China. Hong Kong's international status was mirrored in the presence of foreign banks, numbering 357 in 1995—that is to say, more than in any other financial centre except for London.[56]

A MULTIPOLAR FINANCIAL WORLD

One view of the balance of power in international finance at the turn of the twenty-first century is provided by the world's leading financial centres.[57] Three global centres stood at the top of the hierarchy: New York, London, and Tokyo, though Tokyo could be seen as having slipped behind the two Anglo-Saxon cities, followed by five international centres, three in Europe (Frankfurt, Paris, and Zurich) and two in Asia (Hong Kong and Singapore). These were themselves followed by centres on a lesser scale, but whose importance should not be underestimated, including Amsterdam, Chicago, Geneva, Hamburg, Luxembourg, Toronto, and Sydney. The top five centres were the financial capitals of the world's five leading economies: the United States, Japan, Germany, Britain, and France. London's ranking was higher than that of Britain because of the City's far greater level of internationalization—London actually ranked first for international financial activities, though it dropped back to third place, behind New York and Tokyo, if national financial activities were included. Zurich and Singapore were the exceptions that confirmed the rule—a favourable position at a particular moment in history and increased specialization in niche markets. And Hong Kong owed, indirectly at least, its rise to the growing weight of a China opening up to the world economy. A similar picture emerged from other indicators of financial power. In 2000, the United States held 26 per cent of the stock of foreign investment, ahead of Britain (15 per cent), Japan (10 per cent), Germany (9 per cent), and France (8 per cent);[58] four of the five largest commercial banks, measured by market capitalization, including the top one (Citigroup) were American, and one was British (HSBC, ranked number two); and four of the top five investment banks were also American.[59] And, perhaps most significantly, the nerve centre of world finance was the New York–London axis—in terms of innovation, business strategy, and model of capitalism.

At the same time, the balance of power in international finance started to be affected by the arrival of a new economic giant: China. Following the economic reforms introduced by Deng Xiaoping in 1978, China experienced spectacular growth, with GDP rising at an average annual rate of more than 9 per cent. Measured at purchasing power parity, China's GDP was already the world's second largest, ahead of Japan's, by the early 1990s—though it was hardly more than a tenth of its size at market exchange rates. On this latter measure, it was not before the turn of the twenty-first century that China reached the level of the largest European economies, overtaking Britain and France in 2005, and Germany in 2007.[60] Until then, the impact of Chinese economic growth on the international financial scene remained fairly limited. China, whose export capability was partly built by foreign firms, was the world's second recipient of foreign direct investment after the United States, but its own investment abroad remained limited. The big four state-owned banks were plagued with non-performing loans amounting to about a quarter of their total lending in 2002. And no financial centre of any significance had emerged in China, though the return of Hong Kong in 1997, with an autonomous status, provided it with powerful international links.

The situation changed rapidly from the turn of the century. In particular, the growth of China's current-account surplus started to accelerate, increasing more than twentyfold between 2001 and 2007—from about \$17 billion to \$370 billion—becoming larger than that of other surplus countries: Japan, the emerging East Asian countries, and the oil-exporting countries, as well as Germany. As a result, China accumulated huge foreign-exchange reserves, which increased more than sevenfold during the same period—from about \$220 billion to some \$1,500 billion—becoming the world's largest, with over two-thirds of them being held in US dollars. In 2007, the China Investment Corporation, a sovereign wealth fund, was established to manage part of these reserves, with some \$200 billion of assets, which had grown to \$298 billion a year later, making it the world's third largest, behind the Abu Dhabi Investment Authority and the Norwegian government pension fund. China's big commercial banks rose to the top of the world's rankings following their part privatization process launched in 2005: in 2007, three were in the top ten: the Industrial and Commercial Bank of China, in third position, the Bank of China in sixth, and the China Construction Bank in seventh.

The Financial Debacle of 2007–8 has reinforced these trends, as China has emerged relatively unscathed from the turmoil. One of the main implications of China's phenomenal growth has been the exacerbation of its imbalance with the United States—as China's surplus has financed, through its massive holdings of dollar assets, the US debt. More generally, the imbalances between surplus and deficit countries have deepened, as emerging economies have run current-account surpluses and accumulated foreign reserves since the Asian crisis of 1997 in order to protect themselves against the effects of financial crises. These imbalances have had deeply destabilizing effects on the world economy, contributing to the subprime crisis and leading to the aberration of capital exports from poor to rich countries. And their long- or even medium-term unsustainability has been made all the more apparent by the financial crisis and the probable reduction of debt and consumption levels in the United States and other Anglo-Saxon economies.[61] Rectifying them is part of the challenge of rebuilding the global financial system.[62]

On the other hand, the Financial Debacle of 2007–8 is unlikely, in the medium term, to alter the balance of power in international finance. Past financial crises have not led to a change in international financial leadership, and there are no signs that the latest should prove any different. Such shifts have resulted from long-term changes in the world economy. Brutal shocks, especially a major war, have tended to hasten the process, but the effects of financial crises have been marginal. Whatever damage has been caused to its financial system and the model it represented, the United States remains, by a long distance, the world's leading financial power, and China is in no position to challenge it. Some historical parallels are revealing. When the United States started challenging Britain before 1914, its GDP was already two-and-a-half times as large, and its GDP per head 20 per cent higher—and it took thirty years, including two world wars, for the transition to be finally completed. In 1989, at the height of Japan's apparently unstoppable rise, its GDP was 40 per cent that of the United States and its GDP per head 80 per cent—and the challenge soon petered out. In 2008, China's GDP was a third of that of the United States, and its GDP per head less than a tenth. Its foreign-exchange reserves provide it with leverage over the United States, but primarily in matters of policy, including monetary policy, such as the debates over a diminished international role for the dollar—a position reminiscent of that of France in the late 1920s, when its current-account surplus, generated by an undervalued franc, enabled it to amass a vast amount of sterling claims and to put pressure on the Bank of England. China's huge size and the absence of another credible challenger play in its favour, but it will take time before the conditions enabling it to become the centre of gravity of world finance are met.

In the meantime, the growing weight of a number of emerging economies, above all China, but also the other members of the so-called BRICs (Brazil, Russia, and India) will enable them to be part of an increasingly multipolar financial world and, in particular, to host a financial centre of world significance—as did Germany with Berlin and the United States with New York in the nineteenth century, and Japan with Tokyo in the twentieth. So Shanghai, Mumbai, Moscow, and Sao Paulo should in due course, though not necessarily at the same time, rank alongside New York, London, Tokyo, Frankfurt, and Paris in the international financial hierarchy.

Conclusion

The Financial Debacle of 2007–8 was the most severe financial crisis in modern history. Never before, even in the 1930s, did so many of the leading banks—in terms of both size and reputation—in so many advanced countries find themselves, at almost exactly the same moment, requiring state intervention to save them from failing. However, a financial catastrophe was avoided. Banks were bailed out by their governments in various ways, usually through loans or by buying a stake in their capital. The governments' intervention proved effective and the worst of the financial crisis appeared to be over by the start of 2009.

THE FINANCIAL DEBACLE OF 2007–2008

The unprecedented severity and global scale of the crisis can be attributed to three main factors. In the first place, the structure of the advanced economies at the start of the twenty-first century was not the same as it had been during most of the twentieth century. The transition to a post-industrial society from the 1980s onwards has gone hand in hand with the tremendous growth of the tertiary sector in general and financial services in particular. Banking and finance have always played a central role in the functioning of the economy, now they have themselves become a significant part of the economy, whether in terms of employment or of share of GDP. The globalization of the world economy has also reached new heights, even compared with the pre-First World War period, leading to a hitherto unequalled degree of interdependence between financial institutions. Secondly, the very business of banking had changed radically during the twenty to thirty years preceding the crisis, through the inexorable trend towards securitization, the continuous flow of innovations, and the devising of new financial products, the most important of which may be grouped under the generic title of derivatives. A far from insignificant feature of these new products was their extreme complexity and opacity. Few bankers really understood them and therefore few were able to assess the risks involved. They heralded in a new financial era. The packaging of structured products incorporating a number of mortgages with different levels of risk, the price of which is fixed by mathematical formulae, was something radically new and radically different from previous innovations, including the Euromarkets, which ultimately remained traditional financial operations. Nevertheless, it is not financial innovation per se but the way it is used and regulated that can be dangerous. This was the third factor explaining the exceptional severity of the crisis of 2007–8. Derivatives and securitization were supposed to have reduced if not eliminated risk by spreading it more widely and assessing it through highly sophisticated models. This illusion was reinforced by the widely held belief in the self-regulatory power of the market, leading to ever more deregulation and lighter supervision by the authorities, and the total failure of the credit-rating agencies properly to assess risks.

The combination of these factors set the Financial Debacle of 2007–8 apart from previous financial collapses, even if the crisis itself erupted in a more familiar context—a culture of greed marked by sky-high remunerations and excessive bank leverage and, at macroeconomic level, low interest rates and the oversupply of capital on the financial markets. Of course, the history of financial crises can be approached from this latter perspective, underlining their common characteristics and identifying the conditions in which they are likely to occur in order to draw lessons from the past. However, the lessons of history involve observing not just similarities, but also, and perhaps above all, differences. They must help to avoid repeating past mistakes, but also not to fight the previous war.

THE GREAT DEPRESSION OF THE 1930s

Comparisons with 1929 have been a prerequisite for the discussion of all post-war financial crises; 2008 has been no exception—on the contrary. Yet the two crises are different. First, the financial crisis that broke out in October 1929 following the burst of a bubble was a stock-market crisis, not a banking crisis. The New York Stock Exchange lost 12.8 per cent on Monday, the 28th, and 11.7 per cent on Tuesday, the 29th. By comparison, it lost 22 per cent in a single day nearly sixty years later, on 19 October 1987, with talk of a repeat of 1929. More importantly, the Wall Street crash of October 1929 was not the cause of the Great Depression, whereas the banking crisis of September 2008 was very clearly the cause of what has come to be known as the Great Recession. The length and depth of the Great Depression were primarily due to the constraints imposed by the international monetary system of the time, the gold standard, forcing monetary authorities to face a downturn with restrictive monetary policies in order to defend their currency's parity. The banking crises in the early 1930s were the consequence and not the cause, as in 2008, of the economic crisis, even though they helped to exacerbate the situation. Despite the global nature of the Great Depression, the banking crises did not affect all countries simultaneously and with the same degree of intensity. Significantly, the most serious banking crises occurred in the two countries where the Depression was most severe, Germany, where nearly all the big banks were on the verge of collapse in July 1931; and the USA, where, following three crises since 1930, the banking system came to a complete standstill in March 1933. On the other hand, Britain was not affected by any banking crisis, while France experienced a protracted but never an acute one.

The parallels between 1929 and 2008 are thus not obvious, particularly in how the various crises—in the banking sector, on the stock markets, in the economy—were linked. In some respects, clearer parallels can be established with the other banking crises that affected the advanced economies since the late nineteenth century. The panic during the Financial Crisis of late July and early August 1914 had similar symptoms to the panic in September 2008. Never before, or indeed until then, had the international financial system been so near collapsing. But its causes were different: the war, not an uncontrolled financial boom. And so were its effects: a total war, not an economic crisis. The chance that the financial system might implode was also very real during the International Debt Crisis that followed the Mexican default in August 1982. However, the risks of collapse were more potential than immediate, a financial crisis was avoided, and the panic was not followed by an economic crisis in the core industrial countries—though the Third World countries were heavily penalized, with their standard of living taking a decade to return to pre-crisis levels.

Yet 1929 retains much of its significance for comparative purposes: because it remains the most severe economic crisis in modern history and as such the benchmark by which to measure the intensity of all subsequent downturns; because of the persisting strength of the 'never-again' feeling—it all seems as if we have been anxiously but resignedly expecting a repeat of 1929 since the end of the Second World War, or at least since the end of Bretton Woods and the opening-up of the world economy in the early 1970s; and because some of the 'lessons' of 1929 seem to have been learned, at any rate as far as macroeconomic policy is concerned. The expansionary fiscal policies pursued by the political and monetary authorities in the face of the 2008 crisis, in contrast to the deflationist policies of those in charge in the early 1930s, seemed, in early 2010, to have had a positive effect and prevented the recession from turning into a depression. However, these should by now be seen as economics prescriptions rather than history lessons, for even if Keynesianism has been shaped by the experience of the Great Depression, it is above all an advance in economic theory.

Perhaps even more significantly, 1929 is perceived as a turning point in the history of capitalism and, closer to our purpose, of banking and finance, not so much in terms of banking practices as in terms of state intervention and regulation. Banking legislation was introduced in most countries, defining the frontiers of the banking profession and instituting supervisory authorities. Some went further and decreed the separation of investment banking from commercial banking—in Italy, Belgium, France, and, of course, the United States with the Glass–Steagall Act of 1933. State intervention in banking and finance remained in force until the early 1970s and included, with variations depending on countries and periods, controls over interest rates, credit distribution, foreign exchange, and international capital flows. The Bretton Woods system of fixed exchange rates based on the dollar, established in 1944, has been seen by later generations as the showpiece of the reforms adopted in the wake of the collapse of international order, with repeated calls, since the 1970s, for a 'new Bretton Woods'. However, these changes in the financial order are not entirely attributable to the lessons drawn from the Great Depression. In particular, the scale of the state intervention was part of a much wider phenomenon, the 'Thirty Years War' of the twentieth century—the years 1914–45, which saw two world wars and the worst economic crisis in history.

CRISES AND OPPORTUNITIES

This raises the question of the extent to which the opportunities for change presented by financial crises have actually been seized by bankers and policy-makers. The record is mixed and distinctly marked by the interaction between finance and politics. Private banks declined and the forward march of the big banks gathered pace after the Baring Crisis, but the more intricate problem of the Britain's gold reserves was not solved until the First World War. The opportunity to improve the US banking system with the creation of a central bank was not missed after the American Panic of 1907. The Federal Reserve System was duly put in place in 1913, yet political compromises impaired its efficiency; and a wider-ranging reform allowing branch banking and interstate banking was not contemplated. The Financial Crisis of July–August 1914 can be understood only within the context of the First World War and its consequences. Monetary rather than strictly banking matters were paramount here. But the restoration of the gold standard in the early 1920s was the main cause of instability during the inter-war years, despite the—ultimately failed—attempts at closer central bank cooperation.

If the banking system was in need of a major overhaul after the shocks of the early 1930s, it did not really happen—at any rate in the leading West European economies. State intervention, in various guises, was the main outcome. The changes to the financial system were of little consequence. None took place in Britain, Germany did not abolish universal banking, and the separation between commercial and investment banking had a long tradition in France before being enacted by the Vichy government in 1941. The nationalization of the Bank of England and the Banque de France were to a great extent politically motivated, and they took place after the war, the real boundary as far as state intervention is concerned. The United States was different. The Glass–Steagall Act did change the shape of American banking. And yet it was dictated by political as much as by economic reasons, and it is doubtful that it addressed the main causes of the banking crises that broke out between 1930 and 1933. The introduction of the federal deposit insurance did, but the fragmentation of the banking system remained a major weakness, which could not be remedied.

The impact of later crises—1974 and 1982—does not entirely pale in comparison with that of the banking crises of the 1930s. They set in motion the establishment of a system of international financial regulation, which considerably developed over the years, though not always in the most satisfactory way. On the other hand, they did not prevent the process of deregulation from sweeping aside any resistance—nor did more circumscribed crises. Interestingly, the Japanese Banking Crisis of 1997–8 led to more drastic changes in the banking system than any previous one bar the American crises of the 1930s. They included not only further liberalization of the financial system, but also the modernization of the banking sector through decartelization, mergers, and changes in ownership structures. There thus seems to be a correlation between the severity of an economic and financial crisis and the readiness to seize the opportunity for changes.

Has the Financial Debacle of 2007–8 been severe enough to be followed by a fundamental reform of the financial system, at both national and international levels? As events had unfolded by early 2010, there were good reasons to be sceptical: a financial catastrophe had been avoided, and, however serious, the downturn had not been on the same scale as the Great Depression or the Japanese slump. On the other hand, there are reasons to believe that significant changes could take place. One is the severity and the global scale of the financial crisis itself, without precedent in history, and the factors that made it different from previous historical experiences—the stage of economic development in which it occurred, the transformation of the business of banking, the political and ideological context. Economic and political leaders have been well aware of the seismic nature of the shock and have attempted to provide adequate answers, especially in the United States with the possible implementation of the 'Volcker rule'. Another reason is that financial crises should not be considered in isolation from other defining events. Two major turning points took place in the history of world capitalism in the twentieth century: one, during the Great Depression and the Second World War, led to a marked level of state intervention; the other, during the 1970s, led, in far less dramatic circumstances, to a reversal of this trend. Financial crises were only one aspect of a wave of economic, political, socio-cultural, and geo-political changes. There are signs of a turning point of similar proportions happening, not least with the rise of new economic powers and the neo-liberal model reaching its limits. This, however, is no longer the territory of the historian, though it can be safely predicted that we are unlikely simply to witness a swing of the pendulum back to state intervention and regulation. History never repeats itself in such a simplistic way.

THE SHAPING OF MODERN FINANCE

In the end, modern finance has been shaped by the long-term development of the world economy, within the peculiarities of each national financial system. But this linear course has, on occasions, been inflected, in a decisive way, by the effects of financial crises. The growth of the big banks is a case in point. Their rise from the mid-nineteenth century to the 1930s was concomitant with the advent of the second industrial revolution, the opening-up of the world economy, the increase in world trade and international capital flows, and the rise of big business. Financial crises marginally favoured this development, as big banks tended to strengthen their position by taking over smaller and weaker competitors. The Great Depression put a temporary halt to this advance. Being deemed from an early stage too big to fail, the big banks weathered the storm, but were overtaken, in overall size or in terms of growth rate, by partly state-owned or state-guaranteed institutions such as savings banks. Growth resumed after the war, with increased internationalization from the 1970s, hardly affected by financial crises, and accelerated from the 1990s, with the huge development of financial services in the post-industrial economies.

The banks' larger size went hand in hand with a growing separation between ownership and control, in line with the development of the corporate economy. In the same way, institutional shareholders became dominant from the 1960s. The specific features of banks' governance have not been shaped by the effects of financial crises—despite the very nature of the banking business, which is to work with other people's money. Banking legislations in the 1930s emphasized bankers' responsibility, but the question of their remuneration was only a side issue. In effect, well until the Second World War, powerful private banks retained a dominant position at the very heart of international finance, in Wall Street and the City of London. The financial elite then made money with its own money. The disappearance of these private banks or their conversion into public companies did not entirely eradicate the partnership form of organization, which has persisted in the governance of the world's leading banks—a characteristic of a triumphant financial world, enabling top-salaried managers and star traders to enjoy a level of remuneration previously attained only by risking one's own capital.

Regulation has in many ways been the result of financial crises. This is the time when the authorities are expected to provide long-term solutions to existing problems, and regulation is the domain where they can best attempt to alter the shape of things to come. The Great Depression constitutes the defining moment in that respect. However, regulation is not only an upshot of financial crises. Regulated financial systems have a dynamic of their own, with constant adaptation of existing rules to the changing nature of the markets. Such adaptations can in fact be measures of deregulation, as was the case from the 1980s onwards. Regulation has also often missed important targets. This has especially been the case with financial innovation, one of the main forces shaping the financial system. Few of them have been regulated before destabilizing the existing order. Moreover, financial innovations, especially in the United States, have often been motivated by the constraints imposed by existing regulations and attempts at circumventing them. Regulators have thus rarely been ahead of the game since the Great Depression, though they might regain the upper hand in the wake of the recent crisis.

Financial crises, perhaps surprisingly, did not lead to clear changes in the balance of power in international finance. The only change at the very top, the replacement of London by New York and Washington as nerve centres of the world's finance, was the result of the United States becoming the world's dominant economic superpower. It was a slow process, taking place between 1914 and 1945, at once hastened by the First World War and slowed down by the Great Depression. The rise and fall of international financial centres has primarily been dictated by long-term economic development and, in the shorter run, by world wars rather than financial crises. The financial centres of the leading emerging economies are more likely, in the short to medium term, to rank alongside rather than topple those of the established powers.

Financial crises are unavoidable; they are an integral part of the functioning of the financial markets. However, their severity has varied greatly, and, in the advanced economies, major crises presenting a real risk of collapse of the international financial system have been a fairly rare occurrence. These are the crises that can and must be prevented. The lessons of 1929 are not so much the actual regulatory measures adopted at the time as the determination to prevent the repetition of a similar cataclysm. It took nearly eighty years to happen again—in similar but also, and mainly, in very different ways. We will have done very well if the changes introduced in the wake of 2008 achieve comparable results.

Notes

INTRODUCTION

1. The *Financial Times*, for example, which provided a penetrating coverage of the crisis, ran a series of articles on this topic in early 2009.
2. Revealing quantitative comparisons of the first year of the two crises are provided by B. Eichengreen and K. O'Rourke, 'A Tale of Two Depressions', VoxEU.org, 6 Apr. 2009, 4 June 2009, and later updates.
3. J. K. Galbraith, *The Great Crash 1929* (Boston, 1929); C. P. Kindleberger, *Manias, Panics, and Crashes: A History of Financial Crises* (London, 1978).
4. See, e.g., C. Goodhart and P. J. R. Delargy, 'Financial Crises: Plus ça change, plus c'est la meme chose', *International Finance*, 1 (1998), 261–87; B. Eichengreen and M. Bordo, '*Crises Now and Then: What Lessons from the Last Era of Financial Globalization*', NBER Working Paper 8716 (Jan. 2002); M. Bordo, B. Eichengreen, D. Klingebiel, and M. S. Martinez-Peria, 'Is the Crisis Problem Growing More Severe?', *Economic Policy*, 16/32 (Apr. 2001).
5. C. Reinhart and K. Rogoff, *This Time is Different: Eight Centuries of Financial Folly* (Princeton and Oxford, 2009).
6. Eichengreen and Bordo, '*Crises Now and Then*', for example, have identified 258 financial crises in 21 countries (56 after 1973) between 1880 and 1997.
7. Bordo et al., 'Is the Crisis Problem Growing More Severe?', 56–7.
8. Technically speaking, Overend, Gurney & Co. was a discount house, a financial institution specializing in discounting bills of exchange by borrowing short term from the commercial banks. Once a highly reputable house, it became involved, under new management, in increasingly dubious business from 1859, taking poor-quality bills and locking up investment in all sorts of speculative ventures. It was converted into a joint stock company, with £5 million capital, in 1865.
9. W. Bagehot, *Lombard Street: A Description of the Money Market* (London, 1873), 162–75; J. Clapham, *The Bank of England: A History*, ii. 1797–1914 (Cambridge, 1944), 260–70; D. Kynaston, *The City of London*, i. *A World of its Own 1815–1890* (London, 1994), 235–43.
10. The Union Générale, a catholic and legitimist bank with headquarters in Lyons, expanded extremely rapidly from 1878, recklessly investing in risky ventures and takeovers and stock-market speculations in France and abroad. Its collapse in 1882 was followed by a long and severe recession.

11. Kindleberger, *Manias, Panics, and Crashes*.
12. Reinhart and Rogoff, *This Time is Different*.

CHAPTER 1

1. Figures from P. Bairoch, *Victoires et déboires: Histoire économique et sociale du mode du XVIe siècle à nos jours*, 3 vols. (Paris, 1997), ii. 123–7, 175–9, 317.
2. See C. H. Feinstein, P. Temin, and G. Toniolo, *The European Economy between the Wars* (Oxford, 1997); H. James, *The End of Globalization: Lessons from the Great Depression* (Cambridge, Mass., 2002).
3. See Y. Cassis, *City Bankers 1890–1914* (Cambridge, 1994).
4. C. Marichal, *A Century of Debt Crises in Latin America* (Princeton, 1989), 131.
5. A. G. Ford, 'Argentina and the Baring Crisis of 1890', *Oxford Economic Papers*, 8 (1956), 127–60.
6. Marichal, *Debt Crises*, 152.
7. See the analysis of the financial press in J. Flores Zendejas, 'Lorsque le leader suit la foule: La Crise Baring dans une perspective macroéconomique, 1880–1890' (Ph.D. dissertation, Institut d'Études Politiques de Paris, 2004), 21–43.
8. I. Stone, *The Global Export of Capital from Great Britain, 1865–1914: A Statistical Survey* (New York, 1999), 66–7, 378–80.
9. *Marichal*, Debt Crises, 153.
10. P. Ziegler, *The Sixth Great Power: Barings, 1762–1929* (London, 1988), 243.
11. *The Economist*, 22 Nov. 1890, quoted in J. Clapham, *The Bank of England: A History*, ii. *1797–1914* (Cambridge, 1944; repr. 1970), 327.
12. J. Orbell, *Baring Brothers & Co., Ltd, A History to 1939* (London, 1985), 51; Marichal, *Debt Crises*, 247–8.
13. Western Railway of Santa Fé (£1 million, 1887–9), Curamalan Land Company (£500,000, 1888), and the Buenos Aires Water Supply and Drainage Company (£3.5 million in 1888, to be followed by a further £6.5 million) (Orbell, *Baring Brothers*, 51).
14. According to some estimates, Baring Brothers held some £5.7 million in Argentine securities in November 1890, and another hardly more valuable £2.1 million Uruguayan bond (*South African Journal*, 13 June 1891, quoted in *Marichal, Debt* Crises, 150).
15. Orbell, *Baring Brothers*, 58.
16. A total of £17 million was raised for the fund. The Bank of England put in £1 million, Glyn, Mills, Currie & Co., the City's leading private bank, and N. M. Rothschild & Sons £500,000 each, followed by most leading merchant and private banks with £100,000–£250,000. The joint stock

banks joined in with £750,000 each for National Provincial, London & County, and London & Westminster, and lower sums for the others (Clapham, The Bank of England, ii. 333).

17. Stone, *Global Export of Capital*, 378–80.

18. M. Lévy-Leboyer, 'La Balance des paiements et l'exportation des capitaux français', in M. Lévy-Leboyer (ed.), *La Position internationale de la France: Aspects économiques et financiers XIXe–XXe siècles* (Paris, 1977), 120.

19. G. Jones, *British Multinational Banking 1830–1990* (Oxford, 1993), 63.

20. K. J. Mitchener and M. D. Weidenmier, 'The Baring Crisis and the Great Latin American Meltdown of the 1890s', *Journal of Economic History*, 68/2 (2008), 462–500.

21. A. Maddison, *The World Economy: A Millennial Perspective* (Paris, 2006).

22. L. E. Davis and R. J. Cull, *International Capital Markets and American Economic Growth 1820–1914* (Cambridge, 1994), 8. Between 1897 and 1908, foreign direct investment increased more than two and a half times (from $634.5 to $1,638.5 million) and portfolio investment almost eighteenfold (from $50 million to $886.3 million).

23. See Y. Cassis, *Capitals of Capital: A History of International Financial Centres, 1780–2005* (Cambridge, 2006), 114–24.

24. See the recent account of the crisis by R. F. Bruner and S. D. Carr, *The Panic of 1907: Lessons Learned from the Market's Perfect Storm* (Hoboken, NJ, 2007).

25. The New York Clearing House was created in October 1853 for daily settlements of net balances arising among the city's fifty-two banks. The clearing house loan certificate, used for the first time in 1860, provided banks needing aid with loans of up to 75% of the face value of the bonds and bills deposited with the New York Clearing House as collateral. The large denomination certificates received in exchange were the joint liability of the members of the clearing house and could be used in local settlements or balances due (B. J. Klebaner, *American Commercial Banking: A History* (Washington, 1990), 27, 93).

26. J. Moen and E. W. Tallman, 'The Bank Panic of 1907: The Role of Trust Companies', *Journal of Economic History*, 52/3 (1992), 612.

27. Trust companies could own shares directly, they had a higher proportion of collateralized loans than national banks, and capital–asset ratio was lower than for national banks (Moen and Tallman, 'The Bank Panic of 1907', 616).

28. By comparison, National City Bank, the country's largest bank, had $231.5 million in assets in 1907.

29. Moore & Schley had borrowed $30 million from New York banks, using shares of the Tennessee Coal, Iron and Railroad Company as collateral.

With the banks likely to call in their loans, Moore & Schley would have to liquidate these shares, causing a catastrophe on the stock market (Bruner and Carr, *The Panic of 1907*, 115–19).

30. L. Neal, 'Trust Companies and Financial Innovation, 1897–1914', *Business History*, 45/1 (1971), 35–51.

31. Damages were estimated at between $350 million and $500 million, or 1.2–1.7% of the US GNP; share prices fell on the London and New York Stock Exchange.

32. Moen and Tallman, 'The Bank Panic of 1907', 617–20. Moen and Tallman suggest that unequal regulation of banks resulted in a concentration of riskier assets in trust companies.

33. See M. Friedman and A. J. Schwartz, *A Monetary History of the United States 1867–1960* (Princeton, 1963), 156–68.

34. Bruner and Carr, *The Panic of 1907*, 142–3.

35. R. S. Sayers, *The Bank of England 1891–1944* (Cambridge, 1976), 58–60.

36. E. Wicker, *Banking Panics of the Gilded Age* (Cambridge, 2000), 84, 111–13.

37. E. White, *The Regulation and Reform of the American Banking System, 1920–1929* (Princeton, 1983), 79.

38. O. M. W. Sprague, 'The American Crisis of 1907', *Economic Journal*, 18/71 (Sept. 1908), 354–5.

39. *Journal of the Institute of Bankers*, 33/2 (1912), 82.

40. Quoted in Cassis, *City Bankers*, 309.

41. Germany declared war on Russia on 1 August and on France on 3 August. Following the invasion of Belgium, Britain declared war on Germany on 4 August.

42. Quoted in D. Kynaston, *The City of London*, ii. *Golden Years 1890–1914* (London, 1995), 610.

43. See B. Brown, *Monetary Chaos in Europe: The End of an Era* (London, 1988), 1–34, for a good account of how the markets reacted after Sarajevo.

44. See T. Seabourne, 'The Summer of 1914', in F. Capie and G. E. Wood (eds.), *Financial Crises and the World Banking System* (London, 1986), 77–116; R. Roberts, 'Then', in R. Roberts, B. Reading, and L. Skene, *Sovereign Rescues: How the Forgotten Financial Crisis of 1914 Compares with 2008–2009* (Lombard Street Research; London, New York, Hong Kong, n.d. [2009]).

45. R. Michie, *The London Stock Exchange: A History* (Oxford, 1999), 165.

46. According to a senior banker, seven-eighths of the banks' assets were 'frozen up' and potentially unrecoverable; supposedly liquid assets amounted to 2.5 times capital and reserves (Roberts, 'Then', 5).

47. J. M. Keynes, 'War and the Financial System, August 1914', *Economic Journal*, 24/95, (Sept. 1914), 460–86, was particularly scathing about

their behaviour. See also M. de Cecco, *Money and Empire: The International Gold Standard, 1890–1914* (Oxford, 1974).

48. R. Roberts, *Schroders: Merchants & Bankers* (London, 1992), 153–4. The bank also undertook to lend the necessary amounts, at 2% above the official discount rate, to acceptors who were unable to repay any bills presented that had fallen due.

49. G. D. Feldman, *The Great Disorder: Politics, Economics, and Society in the German Inflation, 1914–1924* (Oxford, 1997), 34–5.

50. W. L. Silber, *When Washington Shut Down Wall Street: The Great Financial Crisis of 1914 and the Origins of America's Monetary Supremacy* (Princeton, 2007), 9–41.

51. See, e.g., O. Feiertag, 'Le Crédit Lyonnais et le Trésor public dans l'entre-deux-guerres: Les Ressorts de l'économie d'endettement du XXe siècle', in B. Desjardins et al.(eds.), *Le Crédit Lyonnais 1863–1986* (Geneva, 2003), 805–32; G. D. Feldman, 'The Deutsche Bank from World War to World Economic Crisis 1914–1933', in L. Gall et al., *The Deutsche Bank 1870–1995* (London, 1995), 130.

52. They exceeded 30% of the securities quoted on the London Stock Exchange in 1920, compared with 11.5% in 1913 (Michie, *The London Stock Exchange*, 184).

53. In 1920, the national debt reached 169 per cent of GDP in France and 155 per cent in Britain, though only 33 per cent in the United States; figures from M. Obstfeld and A. Taylor, 'Sovereign Risk, Credibility and the Gold Standard: 1870–1913 versus 1925–1931', *Economic Journal*, 13 (Apr. 2003), 241–75.

54. Statistics from the League of Nations cited in Feinstein et al., *The European Economy between the Wars*, 104–7.

55. Bairoch, *Victoires et déboires*, iii. 80.

56. J. K. Galbraith, *The Great Crash, 1929* (Boston, 1954). For Galbraith, the raging bull market from early 1928 was conditioned by a popular belief in the market's perpetual rise, by the forming of investment trusts and holding companies, and by the tremendous leverage caused by the increasingly widespread practice of margin buying.

57. See P. Rappoport and E. White, 'Was the Crash of 1929 Expected?', *American Economic Review*, 84/1 (1994), 271–81.

58. E. White, 'The Stock Market Boom and Crash of 1929 Revisited', *Journal of Economic Perspectives*, 4/2 (1990), 81.

59. B. Eichengreen, *Golden Fetters: The Gold Standard and the Great Depression 1919–1939* (Oxford, 1992).

60. M. Friedman and A. J. Schwartz, *The Great Contraction, 1929–1933* (Princeton and Oxford, 1963), 25.

61. E. Wicker, *The Banking Panics of the Great Depression* (Cambridge, 1996), 28.

62. By comparison, the deposits of National City Bank, the United States' largest bank, reached $1,500 million in 1930.

63. Wicker, *Banking Panics of the Great Depression*, 55–9; E. White, 'A Reinterpretation of the Banking Crisis of 1930', *Journal of Economic History*, 44/1 (1984), 119–38.

64. See H. James, *The Creation and Destruction of Value: The Globalization Cycle* (Cambridge, Mass., 2009), for a comparative discussion of 1929 and 1931 in connection with 2008.

65. A. Schubert, *The Credit-Anstalt Crisis of 1931* (Cambridge, 1991), 7.

66. Schubert, *Credit-Anstalt Crisis*, 12–18.

67. On the German banking crisis, see, in particular, K. E. Born, *Die Deutsche Bankenkrise 1931* (Munich, 1967); H. James, 'The Causes of the German Banking Crisis of 1931', *Economic History Review*, 38/1 (1984), 68–87; T. Balderston, 'The Banks and the Gold Standard in the German Financial Crisis of 1931', *Financial History Review*, 1/1 (1994), 43–68; I. Schnabel, 'The German Twin Crisis of 1931', *Journal of Economic History*, 64/3 (2004), 822–71, and the ensuing discussion with T. Ferguson and P. Temin in the same volume.

68. The two others were the Dresdner Bank and, by far the largest, the newly merged De-Di Bank (Deutsche Bank und Disconto-Gesellschaft).

69. H. Wixforth, 'German Banks and their Business Strategies in the Weimar Republic: New Findings and Preliminary Results', in M. Kasuya (ed.), *Coping with Crisis: International Financial Institutions in the Interwar Period* (Oxford, 2003), 138.

70. T. Balderston, 'German Banking between the Wars: The Crisis of the Credit Banks', *Business History Review*, 65/3 (1991), 564–5.

71. The Chancellor, Heinrich Brüning, declared that 'the limits of what the German people can tolerate have been reached'.

72. H. James, *The German Slump: Politics and Economics, 1924–1936* (Oxford, 1986), 302–3.

73. G. Hardach, 'Banking in Germany, 1918–1939', in C. H. Feinstein, *Banking, Currency and Finance in Europe between the Wars* (Oxford, 1995).

74. See Sayers, *Bank of England*, 387–415; A. Cairncross and B. Eichengreen, *Sterling in Decline: The Devaluations of 1931, 1949 and 1967* (Oxford, 1983); D. B. Kunz, *The Battle for Britain's Gold Standard in 1931* (London, 1987); P. Williamson, *National Crisis and National Government: British Politics, the Economy and Empire, 1926–1932* (Cambridge, 1992).

75. Wicker, *Banking Panics of the Great Depression*, 66–8. The crisis in Chicago was mainly a sequel of a property boom.

76. Wicker, *Banking Panics of the Great Depression*, 67, 86–97.

77. See S. E. Kennedy, *The Banking Crisis of 1933* (Lexington, 1973).

78. H. van B. Cleveland and T. F. Huertas, *Citibank 1812–1970* (Cambridge, Mass., 1985), 172.

79. Wicker, *Banking Panics of the Great Depression*, 145–6.

80. H. Bonin, *La Banque nationale de crédit: Histoire de la quatrième banque de dépôts française en 1913–1932* (Paris, 2002), 165–77. From about Fr.3,700 million in August 1931, its deposits had fallen to under Fr.1,000 million by the end of the year.

81. H. Bonin, *La Banque de l'union parisienne (1874/1904–1974): Histoire de la deuxième banque d'affaires française* (Paris, 2002).

CHAPTER 2

1. As explained in the Introduction, financial crises that took place in less-developed economies, and that have received much attention on the part of economists, politicians, and international organizations, are not discussed in this book, because they represent a different reality, in terms of severity, socio-political consequences, and effects on the international financial system.

2. M. Obstfeld and A. M. Taylor, *Global Capital Markets: Integration, Crisis and Growth* (Cambridge, 2004), 53.

3. A. Maddison, *The World Economy: A Millennial Perspective* (Paris, 2006), 132. Growth rates varied between European countries. In particular, expansion was more pronounced in Germany (5%) and France (4.1%) than in the United Kingdom (2.4%), where, however, the level of income was higher at the start of the period.

4. A European's average income, which barely exceeded half an American's in 1950, was getting on for three-quarters in 1973 (G. Toniolo, 'Europe's Golden Age, 1950–1973: Speculations from a Long-Run Perspective', *Economic History Review*, 51/2 (1998), 256).

5. H. Van der Wee, *Prosperity and Upheaval: The World Economy 1945–80* (Harmondsworth, 1986), 62–3. In Europe, negative growth occurred only in some countries and in some years—for example, Britain in 1952, Belgium in 1958, or Switzerland in 1949 and 1958.

6. The Bretton Woods Agreements, signed in 1944, made the dollar, a currency convertible to gold at the rate of $35 to the ounce, the system's reference currency against which the other currencies defined their parity. Exchange rates were fixed (with a fluctuation margin of ±1%) but adaptable in the event of a fundamental imbalance in the balance of payments. And the International Monetary Fund (IMF) was established to make it easier for the system to function properly by providing support to currencies whose parity with the dollar might be endangered by temporary external payments difficulties.

7. See below, Chapter 5, pp. 106–9.

8. See S. Battilossi and Y. Cassis (eds.), *European Banks and the American Challenge: Competition and Cooperation in International Banking under Bretton Woods* (Oxford, 2002); C. Schenk, 'The Origins of the Eurodollar Market in London, 1955–1963', *Explorations in Economic History*, 35/2 (1998), 221–38; I. M. Kerr, *A History of the Eurobond Market: The First 21 Years* (London, 1984).

9. OECD, *International Capital Markets Statistics, 1950–1995* (Paris, 1996).

10. Maddison, *World Economy*, 129.

11. See M. Reid, *The Secondary Banking Crisis, 1973–75* (London, 1982).

12. Cedar Holdings was backed by Phoenix Assurance, the pension funds of the electricity supply industry, the National Coal Board, and Unilever, with Barclays Bank as main bankers.

13. A number of banks suffered heavy losses, including the Union Bank of Switzerland, Westdeutsche Landesbank, and Lloyds Bank, through a Swiss branch (Reid, *Secondary Banking Crisis*, 114).

14. In 1973, its return on assets was just over two-fifths of that achieved by other large banks while its bad loans reached 177% of equity in June 1974 (M. H. Wolfson, *Financial Crises: Understanding the Postwar US Experience*, 2nd edn. (New York, 1994), 56).

15. On the Franklin National bank's failure, see J. E. Spero, *The Failure of the Franklin National Bank: Challenge to the International Banking System* (New York, 1979). See also the *Banker* (June 1974).

16. 'The Herstatt Crisis in Germany', in Basle Committee on Banking Supervision, 'Bank Failures in Mature Economies', Working Paper No. 13, Bank for International Settlements (Apr. 2004), 4–6.

17. Spero, *Failure of the Franklin National Bank*, 115–16; Reid, *Secondary Banking Crisis*, 115–16.

18. On the origins and development of the Eurobond market, see Kerr, *History of the Eurobond Market*; 'Witness Seminar on the Origins and Early Development of the Eurobond Market', introduced and edited by Kathleen Burk, *Contemporary European History*, 1/1 (1992), 65–87; D. Kynaston, *The City of London*, iv. *A Club No More, 1945–2000* (London, 2001). Eurobonds benefited from the introduction, from 18 July 1963, of the Interest Equalization Tax, a tax on foreign loans issued in the United States. But they also offered advantages to investors, as they were issued to the bearer, so were anonymous and exempt from withholding tax.

19. The reference rate of these loans is the famous LIBOR (London Interbank Overnight Rate).

20. A secondary market was set up at the same time by the American firm White Weld & Co.

21. R. Roberts, *Take your Partners: Orion, the Consortium Banks and the Transformation of the Euromarkets* (Basingstoke, 2001), 13.

22. G. Jones, *British Multinational Banking 1830–1990* (Oxford, 1993), 550.

23. G. Bird, *Commercial Bank Lending and Third World Debt* (London, 1989), 2–3.

24. R. Devlin, *Debt and Crisis in Latin America: The Supply Side of the Story* (Princeton, 1989), 23–4.

25. Usually calculated in basis points above the LIBOR.

26. Wolfson, *Financial Crises*, 89.

27. See, e.g., D. Delamaide, *Debt Shock: The Inside Story of the Crisis that Threatens the World's Banks and Stock Markets* (London, 1984), 17–24.

28. *Wall Street Journal*, 31 Dec. 1982, quoted in Wolfson, *Financial Crises*, 91.

29. Devlin, *Debt and Crisis*, 53–4.

30. Devlin, *Debt and Crisis*, 38. The top ten banks were Citicorp, Chase Manhattan, Bank of America, Manufacturers Hanover, J. P. Morgan, Chemical Bank, Bankers Trust, First Chicago, Continental Illinois, and Security Pacific.

31. Devlin, *Debt and Crisis*, 95. For Latin America alone, the figures were respectively 59% and $5.3 billion for the top nine, and 79% and $6.4 billion for the top twenty-four.

32. A. Sampson, *The Money Lenders: Bankers in a Dangerous World* (London, 1981), 128.

33. Devlin, *Debt and Crisis*, 75–6, 100–12.

34. Ezra Vogel's book, *Japan as Number One* (Cambridge, Mass., 1979), was a bestseller.

35. Comparative measures are available in C. Reinhart and K. Rogoff, *This Time is Different: Eight Centuries of Financial Folly* (Princeton and Oxford, 2009), 141–73.

36. See J. Amyx, *Japan's Financial Crisis: Institutional Rigidity and Reluctant Change* (Princeton, 2004).

37. The *keiretsu* was an enterprise group organized around a leading company, such as Toyota, Nissan, Honda, Toshiba, Sony, Hitachi, to name but a few, with cross-shareholding linking these companies. See H. Morikawa, 'Japan: Increasing Organizational Capabilities of Large Industrial Enterprises, 1880s–1980s', in A. D. Chandler, F. Amatori, and T. Hikino (eds.), *Big Business and the Wealth of Nations* (Cambridge, 1997).

38. Y. Shimizu, 'Convoy Regulation, Bank Management, and the Financial Crisis in Japan', in A. S. Posen and R. Mikitani (eds.), *Japan's Financial Crisis and its Parallels to US Experience* (Washington, 2000), 58.

39. K. Hosono, K. Sakai, and K. Tsuru, 'Consolidation of Banks in Japan: Causes and Consequences', NBER Working Paper 13399 (Sept. 2007), 10–11.

40. H. Miyajima and A. Hidetaka, 'Changes in the J-Type Firm', in J. Maswood, J. Graham, and H. Miyajima (eds.), *Japan: Change and Continuity* (London, 2002), 76.

41. Banks were limited in their possibilities to turn to more profitable activities, such as offering new financial products or investment banking services, because of the costs implied by a change in business model, and because they were still regulated as deposit banks (A. K. Kashyap, 'Discussion of the Financial Crisis', in Posen and Mikitani (eds.), *Japan's Financial Crisis and its Parallels to US Experience*, 107).

42. The Bank of Japan created an ad hoc company, Tokyo Kyodo Bank, to provide it with ¥20 million and raised the same amount from private financial institutions (Basle Committee on Banking Supervision, 'The Japanese Financial Crisis during the 1990s', in 'Banking Failures in Mature Economies', Working Paper 13, BIS (Basle, 2004), 7–9).

43. H. Nakaso, 'The Financial Crisis in Japan during the 1990s: How the Bank of Japan Responded and the Lessons Learnt', BIS Papers 6 (2001), 11.

44. Nakaso, 'The Financial Crisis in Japan', 10–11.

45. See G. Tett, *Saving the Sun: Shinsei and the Battle for Japan's Future* (London, 2004).

46. In 2001, Goldman Sachs's estimate was ¥237 trillion, over twenty times the estimate published the same year by the Financial Service Agency (A. Kashyap, 'Sorting Out Japan's Financial Crisis', NBER Working Paper 9384 (2002); Financial Services Agency, *Status of Non-Performing Loans* (various issues)).

47. Shimizu, 'Convoy Regulation, Bank Management, and the Financial Crisis in Japan', 71–4.

48. On the wave of deregulations and innovations starting in the late 1970s, see below, Chapter 5, pp. 110–11.

49. Foreign-exchange transactions, for example, increased from $60 billion per day in 1982 to $1,880 billion in 2004, Eurocurrency bank lending from $983 billion to $9,900 billion during the same period, derivatives from $3,500 billion in 1990 to $184,000 billion in 2004 (IMF; BIS, International Swaps and Derivatives Association).

50. See, e.g., B. Eichengreen and M. Bordo, '*Crises Now and Then: What Lessons from the Last Era of Financial Globalization*', NBER Working Paper 8716 (Jan. 2002).

51. On securitization, MBS and other structured products, see below, Chapter 5, pp. 101–4.

52. *Bloomberg*, 19 May 2008.

53. The Dow Jones fell from 13,366 on 28 Dec. 2007 to 12,099 on 25 Jan. 2008, and from 12,480 on 23 May 2008 to 11,101 on 11 July 2008; the FTSE fell from 6,500 on 4 Jan. 2008 to 5,700 on 21 Jan. 2008, and from 6,054 on 27 May 2008 to 5,172 on 15 July 2008.

54. In particular, between the Federal Reserve, the European Central Bank, the Bank of England, the Bank of Canada, and the Swiss National Bank.
55. Such an initiative was taken by the Federal Reserve in Mar. 2008 and by the Bank of England in Apr. 2008.
56. The Federal Reserve cut its primary rate eight times between 17 Aug. 2007 and 1 May 2008, from 5.75% to 2.25%; the European Central Bank twice between 9 July 2007 and 9 Oct. 2009, from 5.25% to 4.25%.
57. They had reached more than $500 billion by Aug. 2008 (*Bloomberg*, 12 Aug. 2008).
58. In particular, Abu Dhabi Investment Authority (Citigroup), Kuwait Investment Authority (Citigroup, Merrill Lynch), Qatar Investment Authority (Barclays Bank, Crédit Suisse), Government of Singapore Investment Corporation (Citigroup, UBS), Temasek Holdings (Merrill Lynch), China Investment Corporation (Morgan Stanley).
59. *Bloomberg*, 12 Aug. 2008.
60. AIG had insured structured products held by banks in the form of default credit swaps for several hundred billion of dollars, and the consequences of its collapse were deemed as potentially catastrophic.
61. OECD Quarterly National Accounts, 25 May 2009; OECD Harmonized Unemployment Rates, 8 June 2009.
62. See a regularly updated comparison between the two crises in B. Eichengreen and K. O'Rourke, 'A Tale of Two Depressions', VoxEU.org.
63. For a recent update and discussion, see M. Wolf, *Fixing Global Finance: How to Curb Financial Crisis in the 21st Century* (New Haven and London, 2009).
64. A. Schroeder, *The Snowball: Warren Buffet and the Business of Life* (London, 2008), 733.

CHAPTER 3

1. Continental Illinois suffered heavy losses after the failure of Penn Square Bank, in Oklahoma, in 1982, being the largest participant in its very speculative oil and gas exploration loans. Following rumours about Continental's condition, European, Japanese, and American investors started withdrawing their deposits, thus increasing the bank's problems. The Bank was provided with interim assistance by the supervisory authorities, with, in particular, an explicit and controversial guarantee that all depositors, whether insured or uninsured, and other general creditors would be fully protected—even though $30 billion of deposits were uninsured. See Basle Committee on Banking Supervision, 'Bank Failures in Mature Economies', Working Paper No. 13 (Apr. 2004), 62–3.
2. In 1891, the National Provincial Bank of England had a total balance sheet of £45 million, London and County Banking Company £43

million, and London and Westminster Bank £32 million (*Bankers'
Magazine* (1890)).

3. N. Ferguson, *The World's Banker: The History of the House of Rothschild*
   (London, 1998).
4. See above, Chapter 1, pp. 12–13.
5. P. Ziegler, *The Sixth Great Power: Barings, 1762–1929* (London, 1988),
   256. The main shareholder, with £210,000, and senior director was
   Thomas Charles Baring, who had recently retired from the firm.
6. Deutsche Bank und Disconto-Gesellschaft; Dresdner Bank; Darmstädter
   und National Bank; Commerz-und-Privat Bank; Reichs Kredit-Gesell-
   schaft; and Berliner Handels-Gesellschaft.
7. The Deutsche Bank und Disconto-Gesellschaft was formed in 1929 by
   the merger of these two banks. The name was shortened to Deutsche
   Bank in 1937.
8. K. E. Born, *International Banking in the 19th and 20th Centuries* (Leam-
   ington Spa, 1983), 267.
9. G. Tett, *Saving the Sun: Shinsei and the Battle for Japan's Future*
   (London, 2004).
10. Figures from E. Wicker, *The Banking Panics of the Great Depression*
    (Cambridge, 1996), 29.
11. In September and October 1931, 827 banks suspended payments with $705
    million deposits (Wicker, *Banking Panics of the Great Depression*, 64).
12. The Union Guardian Trust and the First National Bank of Detroit. The
    latter was the country's third largest bank outside New York.
13. Wicker, *Banking Panics of the Great Depression*, 132–4.
14. H. Wixforth and D. Ziegler, 'The Niche in the Universal Banking
    System: The Role and Significance of Private Bankers within German
    Industry', *Financial History Review*, 1/2 (1994), 102.
15. H. Laufenburger, *Les Banques françaises* (Paris, 1940), 237.
16. For an attempt at defining a medium-sized bank at various points in the
    twentieth century, see Y. Cassis, 'Small and Medium Sized Companies in
    the Financial Sector in Europe, 19th–20th Centuries', in M. Müller (ed.),
    *Structure and Strategy of Small and Medium-Sized Enterprises since the
    Industrial Revolution* (Stuttgart, 1994), 39–58. Assets of around $20 mil-
    lion in 1900, $60 million in 1920, $300 million in 1960, and $3 billion in
    1980 can be taken as a rough indication of the size of a typical medium-
    sized bank.
17. A few banks were officially nationalized, in particular Northern Rock in
    the United Kingdom. However, the taxpayers' stake in such banks as
    RBS and Lloyds TSB, also in the UK, has been seen as a nationalization
    in all but name.
18. This was in particular the case with the takeover of Merrill Lynch by the
    Bank of America and HBOS by Lloyds TSB.

19. McKinsey Global Institute, quoted in H. Davies and D. Green, *Global Financial Regulation: The Essential Guide* (London, 2008), 5.

20. *Financial Times*, 17 Feb. 2010.

21. The savings and loans crisis in the United States in the 1980s, which is not discussed in this study, could be added to the list.

22. C. de Murrieta & Co., an old Anglo-Spanish house involved in Argentine issues, slipped into bankruptcy in early 1892 (S. Chapman, *The Rise of Merchant Banking* (London, 1984), 80).

23. According to J. Sykes, *The Amalgamation Movement in English Banking* (London, 1926), 97, an annual average of over eleven mergers took place between 1890 and 1902, compared with over seven for the years 1862–89.

24. The London *private banks* were deposit banks whose legal form was that of a partnership. Thirteen of them were still members of the London Clearing House in 1870 and ten in 1890, but only five in 1891 and two in 1900 (*Banking Almanac, Yearbook and Directory* (London, various years)). Low interest rates in the early 1890s, complaints about the inadequacy of their reserves, and tempting offers from expanding joint stock banks encouraged them to sell. By contrast, the London *merchant banks*, which specialized in the accepting and issuing of business, survived as private banks in the legal sense (partnerships, limited partnerships, or even limited companies whose directors held a majority stake in the company) until after the Second World War.

25. In 1910, the share in total deposits in England and Wales was 43% for the top five and 64.7% for the top 10, up from respectively 26.5% and 38% in 1890 (F. Capie and G. Rodrik-Bali, 'Concentration in British Banking, 1870–1920', *Business History*, 29/3 (1982), 287).

26. Y. Cassis, *City Bankers, 1890–1914* (Cambridge, 1994), 46–52. Other significant mergers included the formation of Barclays Bank in 1896 by the simultaneous amalgamation of eighteen private banks all linked by family ties; and the merger of the two leading London joint stock banks, the London and County Bank and the London and Westminster Bank, into what became known as the Westminster Bank.

27. Capie and Rodrik-Bali, 'Concentration in British Banking', 290–1.

28. See M. Pohl, *Konzentration im deutschen Bankwesen, 1848–1980* (Frankfurt am Main, 1982). The Deutsche Bank, for example, had links with fourteen provincial banks, with the entire group's capital and reserves reaching 700 million marks in 1904, more than twice those of the parent company (J. Riesser, *Zur Entwicklungsgeschichte der deutschen Grossbanken mit besonderer Rücksicht auf die Konzentrationbestrebungen* (Jena, 1906), 228).

29. Y. Cassis, *Capitals of Capital: A History of International Financial Centres, 1780–2005* (Cambridge, 2006), 92.

30. B. J. Klebaner, *American Commercial Banking: A History* (Washington, 1990), 102.

31. The National Banking Act of 1864 made New York the central reserve city, where all banks were required to keep 25% of their reserves; Chicago and St Louis also obtained that status in 1887. See J. A. James, *Money and Capital Markets in Postbellum America* (Princeton, 1978).

32. H. van B. Cleveland and T. Huertas, *Citibank, 1812–1970* (Cambridge, Mass., 1985), 32–53.

33. The Deutsche Bank, for example, took over seven banks between 1920 and 1924, extending its network of branches from 15 in 1913 to 142 in 1924.

34. M. Friedman and A. J. Schwartz, *The Great Contraction, 1929–1933* (Princeton, 1963), 105.

35. C. Kopper, *Zwischen Markwirtschaft und Dirigismus: Bankenpolitik im 'Dritten Reich' 1933–1939* (Bonn, 1995), 224–39. Significantly, he was not opposed to the Nuremberg Laws of 1935, which forbade marriages between Jews and non-Jews and deprived German Jews from their citizenship.

36. There were an estimated 485 Jewish private banks in 1930 and still more than 400 in 1935; their number dropped to 275 in mid-December 1937 and to 209 in March 1938, when the 'aryanization' measures started in earnest (Kopper, *Zwischen Markwirtschaft und Dirigismus*, 220, 255–6).

37. See C. Andrieu, *La Banque sous l'occupation: Paradoxes de l'histoire d'une profession* (Paris, 1990), 232–5.

38. Andrieu, *La Banque sous l'occupation*, 268–79.

39. G. Hardach, 'Banking in Germany, 1918–1939', in C. Feinstein, *Banking, Currency, and Finance in Europe between the Wars* (Oxford, 1995).

40. A. Gueslin, 'Banks and State in France from the 1880s to the 1930s: The Impossible Advance of the Banks', in Y. Cassis (ed.), *Finance and Financiers in European History, 1880–1960* (Cambridge, 1992), 78.

41. E. White, 'Banking and Finance in the Twentieth Century', in S. L. Engerman and R. E. Gallman (eds.), *The Cambridge Economic History of the United States*, iii. *The Twentieth Century* (Cambridge, 2000), 762.

42. M. Collins, *Money and Banking in the UK: A History* (London, 1922), 215.

43. M. Reid, *The Secondary Banking Crisis, 1973–75* (London, 1982), 150–61; J. Coakley and L. Harris, *The City of Capital* (London, 1983), 72–3.

44. Reid, *Secondary Banking Crisis*, 147–9, 162–9.

45. By 1960, the largest American banks had become the largest in the world: the Bank of America was in the lead, with a balance-sheet total reaching $11.23 billion, followed by Chase Manhattan ($8.42 billion) and First National City ($8.16 billion); the largest British bank, Barclays, was in fourth position with $7.44 billion. See Y. Cassis, 'Before the Storm: European Banks in the 1950s', in S. Battilossi and Y. Cassis (eds.), *European Banks and the American Challenge: Competition and Cooperation in International Banking under Bretton Woods* (Oxford, 2002), 39–42.

46. See Cleveland and Huertas, *Citibank*, 239–42.

47. K. Hosono, K. Sakai, and K. Tsuru, 'Consolidation of Banks in Japan: Causes and Consequences', NBER Working Paper 13399 (Sept. 2007), 17.

48. Hosono et al., 'Consolidation of Banks in Japan', 11–12.

49. T. Beck, A. Demirguc-Kunt, and R. Levine, 'Bank Concentration, Competition, and Crises: First Results', *Journal of Banking and Finance*, 30/5 (May 2006), 1581–603.

50. The Swiss National Bank, for example, has advocated such a move. Others do not see size as the problem. Josef Ackermann, for example, head of Deutsche Bank, has argued that interconnectedness rather than size was the main factor of systemic risk (*Financial Times*, 30 July 2009).

51. F. Capie, 'Structure and Performance in British Banking, 1870–1939', in P. L. Cottrell and D. E. Moggridge, *Money and Power* (London, 1988), 90–1. Return of equity was 9–10% in the 1920s.

52. M. Ackrill and L. Hannah, *Barclays: The Business of Banking 1690–1996* (Cambridge, 2001), 437.

53. Percentage calculated from J. Rivoire, *Le Crédit lyonnais: Histoire d'une banque* (Paris, 1989), annexe IV, pp. 195–201.

54. Historische Gesellschaft der Deutschen Bank e.V., Geschäftsberichte, 1931–1938, Deutsche Bank Aktie, 31.12. 1931–1938, www.bank-geschichte.de/index_02_05.html.

55. Percentages calculated from Cleveland and Huertas, *Citibank*, appendix B, p. 121.

56. B. Wigmore, *The Crash and its Aftermath: A History of Securities Markets in the United States 1929–1933* (London, 1985), 354–7, 361, 468.

57. D. Gros, 'Banking during the Great Depression: The Good News', VoxEU.org, 1 May 2009.

58. 'Top 100: The Development of the World's Largest Banks during the 1970s', *A Banker Research Unit Survey* (1981). The growth has been calculated in local currency. In dollars, both German and British banks grew at the compound rate of 500%.

59. *The Banker* (May 1977), 111. See also R. Devlin, *Debt and Crisis in Latin America: The Supply Side of the Story* (Princeton, 1989), 35–8.

60. With some variations depending on individual banks, the ratio of pre-tax profits to total assets remained at around 1% for the leading American and British banks, and 0.5% for the leading German and Japanese banks between 1982 and 1985; figures from *The Banker*, various issues.

61. The capital requirements imposed on commercial banks, for example, gave investment banks the possibility to offer loans with a lower spread, further increasing their competitive advantage (E. P. M Gardener and P. Molyneux, *Changes in Western European Banking* (London, 1990); *The Banker* (Jan. 1988), 7).

62. *The Banker* (Jan. 1986), 36.

63. IMF, *Global Financial Stability Report* (Oct. 2009).
64. Average monthly close price adjusted for dividends and splits.
65. NYSE Euronext; London Stock Exchange.

CHAPTER 4

1. Interestingly, these issues have rarely been discussed in connection with financial institutions as such, though some recent studies have emphasized how some features of banks, especially opaqueness and regulation, can make it harder to discipline managers; see, in particular, G. Caprio and R. Levine, 'Corporate Governance in Finance: Concepts and International Observations', in R. E. Litan, M. Pomerlano, and V. Sundarajan (eds.), *Financial Sector Governance: The Role of the Public and Private Sectors* (Washington, 2002), 17–50. The main debates on the topic have been concerned with how different banking systems, especially market-oriented and bank-oriented ones, have affected different models of corporate governance, especially those advocating shareholders' value and those advocating stakeholders' value.
2. Quoted in P. Ziegler, *The Sixth Great Power: Barings, 1762–1929* (London, 1988), 252.
3. See D. Kynaston, *The City of London*, i. *A World of its Own, 1815–1890* (London, 1994), 435–6.
4. R. F. Brunner and S. D. Carr, *The Panic of 1907: Lessons Learned from the Market's Perfect Storm* (Hoboken, NJ, 2007), ix–xiii, 64–76.
5. Steven Fraser, *Wall Street: A Cultural History* (London, 2005), 234.
6. V. Carosso, *Investment Banking in America: A History* (Cambridge, Mass., 1970), 137–55.
7. J. M. Keynes, 'War and the Financial System, August 1914', *Economic Journal*, 24/95 (Sept. 1914), 472.
8. See R. S. Sayers, *The Bank of England 1891–1944* (Cambridge, 1976), 72–3; T. Seabourne, 'The Summer of 1914', in F. Capie and G. Wood (eds.), *Financial Crises and the World Banking System* (London, 1986); D. Kynaston, *The City of London*, ii. *Golden Age, 1890–1914* (London, 1995), 608.
9. See Carosso, *Investment Banking*, 330–48; Fraser, *Wall Street*, 381–4; R. Chernow, *The House of Morgan: An American Banking Dynasty and the Rise of Modern Finance* (London, 1990), 360–74; H. van B. Cleveland and T. Huertas, *Citibank 1812–1970* (Cambridge, Mass., 1985), 172–85.
10. See Carosso, *Investment Banking*, 330–48.
11. K. Hardach, 'Banking in Germany, 1918–1939', in C. Feinstein (ed.), *Banking, Currency and Finance in Europe between the Wars* (Oxford, 1995), 286.
12. H. James, *The German Slump* (Oxford, 1986), 317, 323.

13. H. James, 'The Deutsche Bank and the Dictatorship 1933–1945', in L. Gall et al., *The Deutsche Bank, 1870–1995* (London, 1995), 283–4.

14. See W. Mosse, *Jews in the German Economy: The German Jewish Economic Elite, 1820–1935* (Oxford, 1987); James, 'The Deutsche Bank and the Dictatorship'; C. Kopper, *Zwischen Markwirtschaft und Dirigismus: Bankenpolitik im 'Dritten Reich', 1933–1939* (Bonn, 1995).

15. See P. Williamson, 'A "Bankers' Ramp"? Financiers and the British Political Crisis of August 1931', *English Historical Review*, 99/303 (1984), 770–806.

16. On 8 Jan. 1934, the body of Alexandre Stavisky, a Ukrainian-born businessman with connections in political and media circles, was discovered in a chalet at Chamonix. Despite being charged for fraud and forgery, Stavisky was not being tried, thanks to support in high places involving the left of centre Radical Party in power. On 6 Feb. 1934, a demonstration against 'the thieves', organized by the extreme right parties, ended with sixteen deaths after the guard fired at the crowd, and led to the resignation of Édouard Daladier, the radical Prime Minister, intensifying political tensions in France.

17. See A. Plessis, *La Banque de France et ses deux cents actionnaires sous le Second Empire* (Geneva, 1982); R. Sédillot, *Les Deux Cents Familles* (Paris, 1988).

18. M. Reid, *The Secondary Banking Crisis, 1973–75* (London, 1982), 200.

19. J. Spero, *The Failure of the Franklin National Bank: Challenge to the International Banking System* (New York, 1979), 120.

20. Reid, *Secondary Banking Crisis*, 151–61.

21. R. Devlin, *Debt Crisis in Latin America: The Supply Side of the Story* (Princeton, 1989), 74–5.

22. G. Jones, *British Multinational Banking 1830–1990* (Oxford, 1993), 352.

23. Although acquitted by a first-instance court, they were found guilty on appeal, and the Supreme Court upheld the sentence in 2009.

24. They were convicted in 2002 and acquitted on second appeal in 2008, the judges ruling that their conduct had been licit and standard practice at the time.

25. Deposit Insurance Corporation of Japan, 'Record of Debt Recovery and Pursuit of Liabilities' (www.dic.go.jp/english/e_katsudou/e_katsudou5.html).

26. J. Amyx, 'Reforming Japanese Banks and the Financial System', in J. Maswood, J. Graham, and H. Miyajima (eds.), *Japan: Change and Continuity* (London, 2002), 55–71.

27. Lloyd C. Blankfein, chairman and CEO of Goldman Sachs, James Dimon, chairman and CEO of J. P. Morgan Chase, John J. Mack, chairman of the board of Morgan Stanley, and Brian T. Moynihan, CEO and president of Bank of America (http://fcic.gov).

28. *Washington Post*, 14 Jan. 2010.
29. *Financial Times*, 24 Dec. 2009.
30. See P. L. Cottrell, 'Aspects of Commercial Banking in Northern and Central Europe, 1880–1931', in S. Kinsey and L. Newton (eds.), *International Banking in an Age of Transition* (Aldershot, 1998); Y. Cassis (ed.), *Finance and Financiers in European History, 1880–1960* (Cambridge, 1992).
31. In 1913, the largest European banks (Lloyds Bank, London City and Midland Bank, and London County and Westminster Bank in Britain, Crédit Lyonnais in France, and Deutsche Bank in Germany) all had assets in excess of £100 million. With £57 million, National City Bank, the United States' largest bank, did not rank in the world's top ten.
32. Banks, like other companies, were run by a single board in Britain, France, and the United States and by a dual board (executive board or *Vorstand* and supervisory board or *Aufsichtsrat*) in Germany.
33. See A. D. Chandler, Jr., *The Visible Hand: The Managerial Revolution in American Business* (Cambridge, Mass., 1977); 'The Emergence of Managerial Capitalism', *Business History Review*, 58/3 (1984), 473–503; *Scale and Scope: The Dynamics of Industrial Capitalism* (Cambridge, Mass., 1990).
34. For 1884, the deposits of 35 London private banks have been estimated at £68 million, as against £77 million for 21 London joint stock banks (W. F. Crick and J. E. Wadsworth, *A Hundred Years of Joint Stock Banking* (London, 1936), 34).
35. See above, Chapter 3, pp. 59–60.
36. Cleveland and Huertas, *Citibank*, 49.
37. See Y. Cassis, *City Bankers 1890–1914* (Cambridge, 1994), 43–73.
38. See A. R. Holmes and E. Green, *Midland: 150 Years of Banking Business* (London, 1986), 121–52.
39. See M. Reitmayer, *Bankiers im Kaiserreich: Sozialprofil und Habitus der deutschen Hochfinanz* (Göttingen, 1999), 83–162.
40. See C. Ronzon-Belot, 'Banquiers de la Belle Epoque: Les Dirigeants des trois grands établissements de crédit en France au tournant du XXème siècle' (unpublished doctoral dissertation, University Paris X-Nanterre, 2000).
41. Percentage calculated from W. D. Rubinstein, *Men of Property: The Very Wealthy in Britain since the Industrial Revolution* (London, 1981), 62–5, and D. Augustine-Perez, *Patricians and Parvenus: Wealth and High Society in Wilhelmine Germany* (Oxford, 1994), 29. Amounts in dollars must be multiplied by about twenty to account for inflation.
42. In 1913, 212 managers earned over $10,000 a year, their average salary being $21,500 (G. Routh, *Occupation and Pay in Great Britain, 1906–*

1960 (Cambridge, 1965), 71). The general managers of the leading banks earned well over $25,000 a year (Cassis *City Bankers*, 131–2).

43. See T. Gourvish, 'A British Business Elite: The Chief Executive Managers of the Railway Industry, 1850–1922', *Business History Review*, 4/3 (1973), 289–316.

44. See E. Glovka-Spencer, *Management and Labor in Imperial Germany: Ruhr Industrialists as Employers, 1896–1914* (New Brunswick, 1984), 33; Reitmayer, *Bankiers im Kaiserreich*, 114.

45. W. D. Rubinstein (ed.), *Wealth and the Wealthy in the Modern World* (London, 1980), 19.

46. Cassis, *City Bankers*, 197–200.

47. Reitmayer, *Bankiers im Kaiserreich*, 112–20.

48. M. Ackrill and L. Hannah, *Barclays: The Business of Banking 1690–1996* (Cambridge, 2001), 59. The bank was formed in 1896 through the merger of twenty private banks linked together by family and religious ties, and virtually all its directors were former partners in the constituent banks.

49. Cleveland and Huertas, *Citibank*, 111; J. K. Galbraith, *The Great Crash 1929* (2nd edn., London, 1975), 171; Carosso, *Investment Banking*, 333–4.

50. Bonuses were also part of bank executives' salary in Europe. At Barclays, for example, Goodenough's undisclosed total salary enabled him to accumulate wealth rivalling that of small private bankers (Ackrill and Hannah, *Barclays*, 68). At the Bank de Paris et des Pays-Bas, the salary of its all-powerful managing director, Horace Finaly, stood at a mere Fr.100,000 ($4,000 after the franc's post-war devaluation), plus 1% of the bank's net profits; with the addition of director's fees and participations in the bank's flotations, his total package probably reached Fr.1 million in the late 1920s (E. Bussière, *Horace Finaly, banquier 1871–1945* (Paris, 1996), 260–1).

51. Quoted in Carosso, *Investment Banking*, 333–4; 347.

52. Chernow, House of Morgan, 469, 586, 600; E. Perkins, *Wall Street to Main Street: Charles Merrill and the Middle-Class Investors* (Cambridge, 1999), 199; Carosso, *Investment Banking*, 505–7.

53. Chernow, *House of Morgan*, 580, 598.

54. R. Roberts, *Schroders: Merchants and Bankers* (London, 1992), 426.

55. When Dillon Read was bought by Swiss Bank Corporation in 1997, management owned 75% of the firm's equity, and ING Baring the remaining 25%.

56. C. D. Ellis, *The Partnership: The Making of Goldman Sachs* (London, 2008).

57. See P. Augar, *The Death of Gentlemanly Capitalism* (London, 2000), 307–8.

58. See L. Galambos, 'Recasting the Organizational Synthesis; Structure and Process in the Twentieth and Twenty-First Centuries', *Business History Review*, 79 (Spring 2005).

59. See L. Bergeron, *Les Rothschild et les autres . . . La Gloire des banquiers* (Paris, 1991); S. Chapman, *The Rise of Merchant Banking* (London, 1984); B. Supple, 'A Business Elite: German–Jewish Financiers in Nineteenth Century New York', *Business History Review*, 31/2 (1957), 143–78; Y. Cassis, *Capitals of Capital: A History of International Financial Centres, 1780–2005* (Cambridge, 2006).

60. According to a recent study on the United States, wages in the financial sector, compared to the rest of the private sector, exhibit a U-shape pattern between 1909 and 2006, with a sharp decline from the 1930s to the 1950s and a moderate one from the 1950s to the 1980s; see T. Philippon and A. Reshef, 'Wages and Human Capital in the US Financial Industry', NBER Working Paper No. 14644 (Jan. 2009).

61. Between £5,000 and £10,000 could be taken as a basis for the yearly package of the senior manager of a major bank in the City of London in 1900. While comparisons between periods are difficult, the equivalent at the turn of the twentieth century would have been between £750,000 and £1,000,000.

62. See K. Z. Ho, *Liquidated: An Ethnography of Wall Street* (Durham, 2009).

63. See, e.g., an article by J. Fox, 'Cultural Change is Key to Banking Reform', *Financial Times*, 26 Mar. 2010.

CHAPTER 5

1. According to estimates by B. Eichengreen and M. Bordo, '*Crises Now and Then: What Lessons from the Last Era of Financial Globalization*', NBER Working Paper 8716 (Jan. 2002), 41, the number of banking crises in industrialized countries fell from 11 between 1919 and 1939 to 0 between 1945 and 1971, and then rose again to 9 between 1973 and 1997.

2. See, e.g., C. A. E. Goodhart, *The Regulatory Response to the Financial Crisis* (Cheltenham, 2009); E. Helleiner, S. Pagliari, and H. Zimmermann (eds.), *Global Finance in Crisis: The Politics of International Regulatory Change* (Abingdon, 2010).

3. The Argentine Funding Arrangement was in practice a moratorium that relieved the Buenos Aires authorities of having to make full payments on their debt during a period of three years in exchange for new bonds printed by the Argentine state (C. Marichal, *A Century of Debt Crises in Latin America: From Independence to the Great Depression, 1820–1930* (Princeton, 1989), 159–70).

4. See *Report of the Select Committee on Loans to Foreign States* (1875).
5. See M. Flandreau and J. Flores, 'Bonds and Brands: Foundations of Sovereign Debt Markets, 1820–1830', *Journal of Economic History*, 69/3 (2009), 646–84.
6. See R. S. Sayers, *The Bank of England 1891–1944* (Cambridge, 1976), 28–65.
7. Crises erupted in 1819, 1837, 1839, 1857, 1861, 1873, 1884, 1890, 1893, and 1896 (C. Calomiris, *US Bank Deregulation in Historical Perspective* (Cambridge, 2000), 3–4).
8. Quoted in J. Livingston, *The Origins of the Federal Reserve System: Money, Class and Corporate Capitalism, 1890–1913* (Ithaca, NY, and London, 1986), 172. Though the number of failed banks in 1907 was smaller than in 1893 (73 as against 503), their total liabilities were over 20% higher (E. Wicker, *Banking Panics of the Gilded Age* (Cambridge, 2000), 5, 87).
9. Experts included Hartley Whiters and Inglis Palgrave for England, Alfred Neymarck for France, and Jakob Riesser for Germany, among others. See National Monetary Commission, *Interviews on the Banking and Currency Systems of England, France, Germany, Switzerland and Italy*, under the direction of the Hon. Nelson W. Aldrich, chairman, Washington, NMC, 61st Congress, 2nd session, Senate Doc. No. 405, 1910.
10. Quoted in P. Ziegler, *The Sixth Great Power: Barings, 1762–1929* (London, 1988), 320.
11. Quoted in D. Kynaston, *The City of London*, iii. *Illusions of Gold, 1914–1945* (London, 1999), 7.
12. See B. Eichengreen, *Golden Fetters: The Gold Standard and the Great Depression 1919–1939* (Oxford, 1995).
13. B. Bernanke, *Essays on the Great Depression* (Princeton, 2000), 5.
14. See T. Balderston, 'The Banks and the Gold Standard in the German Financial Crisis of 1931', *Financial History Review*, 1/1 (1994), 43–68.
15. See S. Fraser, *Wall Street: A Cultural History* (London, 2005), 367–418.
16. C. Kindleberger, *Manias, Panics, and Crashes: A History of Financial Crises* (London, 1978); J. E. Spero, *The Failure of the Franklin National Bank: Challenge to the International Banking System* (New York, 1979); M. Reid, *The Secondary Banking Crisis, 1973–75* (London, 1982).
17. G. Bird, *Commercial Bank Lending and Third World Debt* (London, 1989).
18. R. Devlin, *Debt and Crisis in Latin America: The Supply Side of the Story* (Princeton, 1989).
19. See J. A. Amyx, *Japan's Financial Crisis: Institutional Rigidity and Reluctant Change* (Princeton, 2004).

20. T. Takeshita and M. Ida, 'An Empirical Study of Economic Reporting and Public Opinion', *Seiki ronsô* (Meiji University), 72/1 (2003), 1–42 (in Japanese, translated by M. Bourqui).

21. British Academy, 'Letter to Her Majesty the Queen', 22 July 2009.

22. Kindleberger, *Manias, Panics and Crashes*, 15–16.

23. See Y. Cassis, 'The Emergence of a New Financial Institution: Investment Trusts in Britain 1870–1939', in J. J. Van Helten and Y. Cassis (eds.), *Capitalism in a Mature Economy: Financial Institutions, Capital Exports and British Industry* (Aldershot, 1990), 139–58.

24. J. H. Busby, *London Trust Company Limited, 1889–1964* (London, 1964).

25. *Bankers' Magazine*, 56 (1893), 165–73.

26. *The Economist*, 6 Apr. 1889, pp. 433–4; 9 Aug. 1890, p. 1017.

27. P. L. Cottrell, *Industrial Finance, 1830–1914: The Finance and Organization of English Manufacturing Industry* (London, 1979), 64–75.

28. H. Bullock, *The Story of Investment Companies* (New York, 1959), 212.

29. Paul C. Cabot in the *Atlantic Monthly* (Mar. 1929), quoted in Bullock, *Investment Companies*, 30.

30. J. K. Galbraith, *The Great Crash 1929* (London, 1975 (1st edn. 1954)), 72, 82, 195, 203.

31. J. Rutterford, 'Learning from One Another's Mistakes: Investment Trusts In the UK and the US, 1868–1940', *Financial History Review*, 16/2 (2009), 170–2.

32. Bullock, *Investment Companies*, 45–7.

33. Bullock, *Investment Companies*, 78–9.

34. On the development of the Euromarkets, see above, Chapter 2, pp. 37–8, 42–3.

35. C. Schenk, 'International Financial Centres, 1958–1971: Competitiveness and Complementarity', in S. Battilossi and Y. Cassis (eds.), *European Banks and the American Challenge: Competition and Cooperation in International Banking under Bretton Woods* (Oxford, 2002), 86–7.

36. See G. Toniolo, *Central Bank Cooperation at the Bank for International Settlements, 1930–1973* (Cambridge, 2005), 452–71.

37. Technically speaking, one could add swaps (exchanges between maturity dates), which are used mainly by financial intermediaries themselves and thus have no direct influence on the bidders and primary seekers of funds.

38. There is a good overview in P. L. Bernstein, *Capital Ideas: The Improbable Origins of Modern Wall Street* (New York, 1992).

39. Founded in 1994, with two Nobel Prize winners in Economics (Merton and Scholes) among its directors, LTCM was hit with full force by the Russian government's default on part of its debt, after three extremely profitable years, and was on the brink of bankruptcy in September 1998.

It was saved only by the New York Federal Reserve, which set up a consortium of Wall Street's main banks that invested $3.65 billion in exchange for 90% of its capital.

40. A lively and highly perceptive account of the securitization revolution and its consequences can be found in G. Tett, *Fool's Gold: How Unrestrained Greed Corrupted a Dream, Shattered Markets and Unleashed a Catastrophe* (London, 2009).

41. The High Level Group on Financial Supervision in the EU chaired by Jacques de Larosière, Report, Brussels, 25 Feb. 2008, p. 8.

42. International Swaps and Derivatives Association, *Market Survey* (2008).

43. Figure from Tim Geithner, then President of the Federal Reserve Bank of New York, in a speech at the Economic Club of New York, quoted in P. Krugman, *The Return of Depression Economics and the Crisis of 2008* (London, 2008), 160–1.

44. See M. Anson, *Handbook of Alternative Investments* (Chichester, 2006).

45. E. White, *The Regulation and Reform of the American Banking System, 1900–1929* (Princeton, 1983). See also Calomiris, *US Bank Deregulation*.

46. See E. White, 'Banking and Finance in the Twentieth Century', in S. L. Engerman and R. E. Gallman (eds.), *The Cambridge Economic History of the United States*, iii. *The Twentieth Century* (Cambridge, 2000), 764–9.

47. R. Chernow, *The House of Morgan: An American Banking Dynasty and the Rise of Modern Finance* (London, 1990).

48. By 1938, savings banks had become the dominant element in the German banking system, with some 45% of total assets by 1938, compared with 15% for the commercial banks.

49. H. James, 'Banks and Bankers in the German Interwar Depression', in Y. Cassis (ed.), *Finance and Financiers in European History, 1880–1960* (Cambridge, 1992), 277–9.

50. C. Andrieu, *Les Banques sous l'occupation: Paradoxes de l'histoire d'une profession* (Paris, 1990), 201–37.

51. See S. Guex, 'The Origins of the Swiss Banking Secrecy Law and its Repercussions for Swiss Federal Policy', in *Business History Review*, 74 (2000), 237–66; R. Vogler, 'The Genesis of Swiss Banking Secrecy: Political and Economic Environment', *Financial History Review*, 8/1 (2001), 73–84.

52. R. Michie, *The London Stock Exchange: A History* (Oxford, 1999), 326–422.

53. Crédit Lyonnais, Société Générale, Comptoir National d'Escompte de Paris, and Banque Nationale pour le Commerce et l'Industrie.

54. The leading French *banque d'affaires*, or investment bank, was the Banque de Paris et des Pays-Bas, also known as Paribas.

55. See A. Straus, 'Structures financières et performances des entreprises industrielles en France dans la seconde moitié du XXe siècle', *Entreprises et histoire*, 2 (1992), 19–33; O. Feiertag, 'The International Opening-up

of the Paris Bourse: Overdraft-Economy Curbs and Market Dynamics', in Y. Cassis and E. Bussière (eds.), *London and Paris as International Financial Centres in the Twentieth Century* (Oxford, 2005), 229–46.

56. G. D. Smith and R. Sylla, 'Wall Street and the US Capital Markets in the Twentieth Century', *Financial Markets, Institutions and Instruments*, 1 (1993).

57. See E. N. White, 'Before the Glass–Steagall Act: An Analysis of the Investment Banking Activities of the National Banks', *Explorations in Economic History*, 23 (1986), 33–54; R. S. Kroszner and R. G. Rajan, 'Is the Glass–Steagall Act Justified? A Study of the US Experience with Universal Banking before 1933', *American Economic Review*, 84/4 (1994), 810–32.

58. Spero, *Failure of the Franklin National Bank*, 168–9.

59. Reid, *Secondary Banking Crisis*, 197.

60. Spero, *Failure of the Franklin National Bank*, 153 ff.

61. Jobbers were securities traders, but they could not buy or sell directly to the public, which did not have access to the stock exchange. For all its stock-market transactions, the public was obliged to go through a broker, who, in return for a commission, would negotiate with the jobber. A broker could speculate on his own account, but, when working for a client, stock-exchange rules did not allow him to sell a security for more than he had purchased it.

CHAPTER 6

1. J. Clapham, *The Bank of England: A History*, 2 vols. (Cambridge, 1944), ii. 329–36.

2. Quoted in M. Flandreau, 'Central Bank Cooperation in Historical Perspective: A Sceptical View', *Economic History Review*, 50/4 (1997), 756.

3. R. S. Sayers, *The Bank of England, 1891–1944* (Cambridge, 1976), 58–60.

4. See Flandreau, 'Central Bank Cooperation'; A. Plessis, 'La Banque de France et les relations monétaires internationales jusqu'en 1914', *Relations internationales*, 29 (1982), 3–23.

5. D. Artaud, *La Question des dettes interalliées et la reconstruction de l'Europe, 1919–1929* (Paris, 1978). The two main creditor countries were the United States ($9.2 billion) and the United Kingdom ($8.5 billion), with France ($1.7 billion) trailing far behind. But only the United States never needed to take out loans abroad. Britain had to borrow $4.2 billion and France $2.7 billion from the USA; France had to obtain loans for a more or less equivalent amount ($2.5 billion) from Britain. The other Allies merely borrowed: Italy $5.1 billion from the two Anglo-Saxon powers; Russia $4 billion, mainly from Britain and, to

a far lesser extent, from France; and the other small countries $1.5 billion, also shared among American, British, and French lenders.

6. Y. Decorzant, 'La Société des Nations et la naissance d'une conception de la régulation économique internationale' (unpublished doctoral dissertation, University of Geneva, 2008).

7. C. Fink, *The Genoa Conference: European Diplomacy, 1921–22* (Chapel Hill, NY, 1984).

8. S. V. O. Clarke, *Central Bank Cooperation: 1924–31* (New York, 1967), 220–1.

9. In 1925, the pound sterling returned to the gold standard at its pre-war parity, which was generally considered as overvalued, thus making British exports less competitive and putting pressure on the Bank of England to defend the pound's parity. The French franc, on the other hand, was de facto stabilized in 1926, after two severe crises, and de jure in 1928, at one-fifth of its pre-war value, a rate usually considered as undervalued. The overvaluation of the pound and the undervaluation of the franc were major sources of the global imbalances during the 1920s, in particular of a 'maldistribution of gold' between the major economies.

10. B. Eichengreen, *Golden Fetters: The Gold Standard and the Great Depression, 1919–1939* (Oxford, 1992), 187–221.

11. The Versailles Treaty attributed responsibility for the war to Germany and imposed reparation payments upon it. The amount was set by the Reparations Commission in April 1921 at 132 billion gold marks, or three times its GDP of the time: Germany would have to pay 2 billion gold marks per year from January 1922 plus 26% of its total exports over forty-two years. Germany initially accepted this programme, albeit unwillingly, but at the end of the year announced that it would not be able to pay the instalments scheduled for January 1922 and asked for a reduction in the amount set by the Commission. In response to the delayed payment of the instalments in kind, especially coal deliveries, Franco-Belgian troops invaded the Ruhr in January 1923, but in the face of passive resistance from the population scarcely obtained any results, apart from accelerating the hyperinflationary spiral on which the German government had embarked the previous year. A solution seemed to have been found with the Dawes Plan, which came into force in September 1924 and rescheduled reparations payments, with an annual amount of 1 billion gold marks until 1928, then 2.5 billion.

12. See O. Feiertag, 'La Banque de France et les problèmes monétaires européens de la Conférence de Gênes à la création de la B.R.I. (1922–1930)', in E. Bussière and M. Dumoulin (eds.), *Milieux économiques et intégration européenne en Europe occidentale au XXe siècle* (Arras, 1998).

13. On the BIS, see G. Toniolo, *Central Bank Cooperation at the Bank for International Settlements 1930–1973* (Cambridge, 2005).

14. Clarke, *Central Bank Cooperation*, 185.

15. A loan was agreed on 14 May 1931 with the BIS, the Bank of England, the National Bank of Belgium, and the Federal Reserve, but it took another two and half weeks to bring in the seven other banks, including the Bank of France, and to arrange standstill agreements with creditors in Berlin, London, New York, and Paris and to convince the Austrian government to guarantee the eventual repayment of the Credit-Anstalt's foreign obligations (Clarke, *Central Bank Cooperation*, 187).

16. Clarke, *Central Bank Cooperation*, 187–8; Toniolo, *Bank for International Settlements*, 88–97.

17. Clarke, *Central Bank Cooperation*, 189–201.

18. Eichengreen, *Golden Fetters*, 283.

19. Only half of the one-year French loan was provided by the banks, the other half being provided by a public issue made available on 14 September. The American loan was granted by a group of banks headed by J. P. Morgan & Co. (Clarke, *Central Bank Cooperation*, 213).

20. Eichengreen, *Golden Fetters*, 282–6.

21. See P. Clavin, *The Failure of Economic Diplomacy: Britain, Germany, France and the United States, 1931–36* (London, 1996); Eichengreen, *Golden Fetters*; C. Kindleberger, *The World in Depression, 1929–1939* (London, 1973).

22. The creation of the IMF, together with the introduction of pegged but adjustable exchange rates and controls over international capital flows within the Bretton Woods system, were meant to avoid reproducing the rigidities that had brought the gold standard to a standstill and had made economic problems worse during the inter-war period. See B. Eichengreen, *Globalizing Capital: A History of the International Monetary System* (Princeton, 1996), 93–5.

23. The BIS accepted looted gold from the Reichsbank.

24. See Toniolo, *Central Bank Cooperation*.

25. H. James, *International Monetary Cooperation since Bretton Woods* (New York and Oxford, 1996), 148–74.

26. M. Reid, *The Secondary Banking Crisis, 1973–75* (London, 1982), 115–16.

27. J. E. Spero, *The Failure of the Franklin National Bank: Challenge to the International Banking System* (New York, 1979), 147–9.

28. Decorzant, 'Société des Nations'; M. Hill, *The Economic and Financial Organization of the League of Nations* (Washington, 1946).

29. Toniolo, *Central Bank Cooperation*, 469–70.

30. G. Blunden, 'International Cooperation in Banking Supervision', *Bank of England Quarterly Bulletin*, 17/3 (1977). Blunden, executive director of the Bank of England, was the first president of the Committee.

31. Interview of Margaret Reid with Sir Jeremy Morse, 10 Nov. 1986, quoted in M. Reid, *All Change in the City: The Revolution in Britain's Financial Sector* (Basingstoke and London, 1988), 143.

32. James, *International Monetary Cooperation*, 367.

33. James, *International Monetary Cooperation*, 369.

34. P. Volcker and T. Gyohten, *Changing Fortunes: The World's Money and the Threat to American Leadership* (New York, 1992), 189.

35. James, *International Monetary Cooperation*; R. Devlin and R. Ffrench-Davis, 'The Great Latin America Debt Crisis: A Decade of Asymmetric Adjustments', *Revista de Economia Politica*, 15/3 (1995); I. Vazquez, 'The Brady Plan and Market-Based Solutions to Debt Crisis', *Cato Journal*, 16/2 (1996).

36. On this topic, see in particular K. Alexander, R. Dhumale, and J. Eatwell, *Global Governance of Financial Systems: The International Regulation of Systemic Risk* (Oxford, 2006); H. Davies and D. Green, *Global Financial Regulation: The Essential Guide* (Cambridge, 2008).

37. The objective was 'to strengthen its effectiveness as a mechanism for national authorities, standard setting bodies and international financial institutions to address vulnerabilities and to develop and implement strong regulatory, supervisory and other policies in the interest of financial stability'. See www.financialstabilityboard.org.

38. Basle Committee of Banking Supervision, Consultative Document, Strengthening the Resilience of the Banking Sector, issued for comments by 16 April 2010 (Dec. 2009).

39. The High-Level Group on Financial Supervision in the EU chaired by Jacques de Larosière, Report (Brussels, 25 Feb. 2008).

40. James Tobin, laureate of the Nobel Prize in economics in 1981, proposed a tax on foreign-exchange speculative dealings in 1973.

CHAPTER 7

1. The term 'Brics' was forged in 2001 by Jim O'Neil, chief economist at Goldman Sachs, to designate a group of four countries, Brazil, Russia, India, and China; they were predicted to overtake the six largest Western economies by 2040. See G. Tett, 'The Story of the Brics', *Financial Times*, 15 Jan. 2010.

2. *The Global Financial Centres Index*, 6 (Sept. 2009), produced by Z/Yen for the City of London,

3. On the ranking of international financial centres, see in particular H. C. Reed, *The Preeminence of International Financial Centers* (New York, 1981); G. Jones, 'International Financial Centres in Asia, the Middle East and Australia: A Historical Perspective', in Y. Cassis (ed.), *Finance and Financiers in European History 1880–1960* (Cambridge, 1992), 405–6.

4. See Y. Cassis, *Capitals of Capital: A History of International Financial Centres, 1780–2005* (Cambridge, 2006); R. Roberts (ed.), *International Financial Centres*, 4 vols. (Aldershot, 1994).

5. In 1870, the United Kingdom's GDP, measured in dollars of 1985, came to $82 billion and that of the United States to $90 billion. In 1913, the figures were $184 billion and $472 billion respectively. Even in terms of per capita income, while Britain retained a small lead over the United States in 1870 ($2,610 compared with $2,247), this was no longer the case on the eve of the war ($4,024 to $4,854) (A. Maddison, *Dynamic Forces in Capitalist Development* (Oxford, 1991), 6–7, 199).

6. See S. B. Saul, *Studies in British Overseas Trade, 1870–1914* (Liverpool, 1960), and F. Crouzet, 'Commerce extérieur et empire: L'Expérience britannique du libre-échange à la Première Guerre mondiale', *Annales ESC*, 19/2 (1964), 281–310.

7. United Nations, *International Capital Movements during the Interwar Period* (New York, 1949); M. Simon, 'The Pattern of New British Portfolio Investment, 1865–1914', in A. R. Hall (ed.), *The Export of Capital from Britain 1870–1914* (London, 1968).

8. Cassis, *Capitals of Capital*; D. Kynaston, *The City of London*, ii. *Golden Age 1890–1914* (London, 1995); R. Michie, *The City of London: Continuity and Change, 1850–1990* (Basingstoke and London, 1992).

9. See above, Chapter 3, p. 60.

10. A. Plessis, 'When Paris Dreamt of Competing with the City...', in Y. Cassis and E. Bussière (eds.), *London and Paris as International Financial Centres in the Twentieth Century* (Oxford, 2005).

11. The law of 1896 (*Börsengesetz*) put in place new supervisory bodies, including a government commissioner, a stock-exchange board, and a tribunal, and considerably limited forward transactions, prohibiting them on securities in mining and manufacturing companies and authorizing them in other sectors on shares only in companies whose capital exceeded 20 million marks (R. Gömmel, 'Entstehung und Entwicklung der Effektenbörse im 19. Jahrhundert bis 1914', in H. Pohl (ed.), *Deutsche Börsengeschichte* (Frankfurt am Main, 1992), 135–210).

12. See L. E. Davis and R. J. Cull, *International Capital Markets and American Economic Growth 1820–1914* (Cambridge, 1994).

13. The Banque russo-asiatique (7th), the Russian Bank for Foreign Trade (14th), and the Russian Commercial and Industrial Bank (24th) (*Banking Almanac*, 1913).

14. R. Michie, *The Global Securities Market: A History* (Oxford, 2006).

15. V. I. Bovykin and V. Anan'ich, 'The Role of International Factors in the Formation of the Banking System in Russia', in R. Cameron and V. I. Bovykin (eds.), *International Banking 1870–1914* (Oxford, 1991), 157–8;

R. Girault, *Emprunts russes et investissements français en Russie, 1887–1914*, (Paris, 1973), 497–503.

16. M.-C. Bergère, *L'Âge d'or de la bourgeoisie chinoise, 1911–1937* (Paris, 1986), R. Brown, 'Chinese Business and Banking in South-East Asia since 1870', in G. Jones (ed.), *Banks as Multinationals* (London, 1990).

17. See Cassis, *Capitals of Capital*, 60–5.

18. See L. Einaudi, *Money and Politics: European Monetary Unification and the International Gold Standard (1865–1873)* (Cambridge, 2001).

19. See K. Burk, *Morgan Grenfell 1838–1988: The Biography of a Merchant Bank* (Oxford, 1989), 111–23; Kynaston, *City of London*, ii. 222.

20. See W. L. Silber, *When Washington Shut Down Wall Street: The Great Financial Crisis of 1914 and the Origins of America's Monetary Supremacy* (Princeton, 2007).

21. Quoted in Silber, *When Washington Shut Down Wall Street*, 160.

22. C. Feinstein and K. Watson, 'Private International Capital Flows in Europe in the Inter-War Period', in C. Feinstein (ed.), *Banking, Currency and Finance in Europe between the Wars* (Oxford, 1995), 98.

23. H. Wixforth, 'German Banks and their Business Strategies in the Weimar Republic: New Findings and Preliminary Results', in M. Kasuya (ed.), *Coping with Crisis: International Financial Institutions in the Interwar Period* (Oxford, 2003), 138.

24. M. Myers, *Paris as a Financial Centre* (London, 1936); E. Moreau, *Souvenirs d'un gouverneur de la Banque de France: Histoire de la stabilisation du franc (1926–1928)* (Paris, 1954); K. Mouré, *Managing the Franc Poincaré: Economic Understanding and Political Constraints in French Monetary Policy, 1928–1936* (Cambridge, 1991).

25. See Cassis, *Capitals of Capital*, 154–67.

26. The foreign issues floated in New York and London amounted to $969 million and $592 million respectively in 1924, to $1,337 million and $676 million in 1927, and to $671 million and $457 million in 1929 (K. Burk, 'Money and Power: The Shift from Great Britain to the United States', in Y. Cassis (ed.), *Finance and Financiers in European History, 1880–1960* (Cambridge, 1992), 364).

27. See M. Wilkins, 'Cosmopolitan Finance in the 1920s: New York's Emergence as an International Financial Centre', in R. Sylla, R. Tilly, and G. Tortella (eds.), *The State, the Financial System and Economic Modernization* (Cambridge, 1999).

28. The sterling area was made up of a certain number of economies with political and/or economic ties to Britain whose governments decided to maintain a fixed exchange rate with the pound, even at the cost of exchange control. At the outset, it comprised the Commonwealth countries (except for Canada), which were joined in 1933 by the Scandinavian countries and Siam, as well as by associate members such as

Argentina, Bolivia, Greece, Japan, and Yugoslavia. The sterling zone also constituted a trade block after Britain's changeover to protectionism at the end of 1931 and the adoption of a preferential imperial tariff in 1932.

29. Imperial issues represented 17% of the total amount of issues placed in London between 1932 and 1938, as against 3% for the foreign loans outside the empire (£28.5 million) (T. Balogh, *Studies in Financial Organization* (Cambridge, 1947), 250).

30. Some $5.5 billion worth of short-term capital was transferred to the United States between 1934 and 1937; around $4 billion to the United Kingdom between 1931 and 1937; and respectively $340 million and $290 million to Switzerland and the Netherlands (C. Feinstein and K. Watson, 'Private International Capital Flows in Europe in the Inter-war Period' in C. Feinstein (ed.), *Banking, Currency and Finance in Europe between the Wars* (Oxford, 1995), 116–18).

31. Figures from A. Maddison, *Dynamic Forces in Capitalist Development: A Long-Run Comparative View* (Oxford, 1991), 198–9.

32. See, in particular, M. J. Hogan, *The Marshall Plan: America, Britain, and the reconstruction of Western Europe, 1947–1952* (Cambridge, 1987); R. Girault and M. Lévy-Leboyer (ed.), *Le Plan Marshall et le relèvement économique de l'Europe* (Paris, 1993).

33. M. Nadler, S. Heller, and S. Shipman, 'New York as an International Financial Center', in *The Money Market and Its Institutions* (New York, 1955), 290–1; R. Orsingher, *Les Banques dans le monde* (Paris, 1964), 140–1.

34. International issues amounted to $1,064 million in London and $882 million in Zurich between 1955 and 1962, as against $4,171 in New York (J. Mensbrugghe, 'Foreign Issues in Europe', *International Monetary Fund Staff Papers*, 11 (1964), 327–35).

35. Nadler et al., 'New York as an International Financial Center', 294–5; Cassis, *Capitals of Capital*, 205–8.

36. See Cassis, *Capitals of Capital*, 209–13; D. Kynaston, The City of London, iv. A *Club No More 1945–2000* (London, 2001); R. Michie, *The City of London: Continuity and Change, 1850–1990* (Basingstoke and London, 1992); C. Schenk, *The Decline of Sterling: Managing the Retreat of an International Currency 1945–1992* (Cambridge, 2010).

37. See J. Jonker, *Merchants, Bankers, Middlemen: The Amsterdam Money Market during the First Half of the 19th Century* (Amsterdam, 1996).

38. Figures from Maddison, *Dynamic Forces in Capitalist Development*, 6–7.

39. P. Bairoch, *Victoires et déboires: Histoire économique et sociale du monde du XVIe siècle à nos jours*, 3 vols. (Paris, 1997), iii. 414–18.

40. Bairoch, *Victoires et déboires*, iii. 420–1; G. Jones, *The Evolution of International Business: An Introduction* (London, 1996), 46–58.

41. *The Banker* (June 1971, June 1981).

42. C. Schenk, 'The Origins of the Eurodollar Market in London, 1955–1963', *Explorations in Economic History*, 35/2 (1998), 221–38.

43. Regulation Q limited the interest rates paid on bank deposits within the United States. British banks, which were able to offer higher interest, particularly because of the high interest rates prevailing at the time in Britain, managed to attract funds to London, mainly from American multinationals present abroad, which they could then use in various national and international operations. The Interest Equalization Tax was a tax on foreign loans issued in the United States. This measure, intended to curb the export of American capital, increased the cost of foreign bond issues in the United States and made that of Eurobonds even more attractive.

44. The issue of Eurobonds increased from $258 million in 1963 to $6,490 million in 1972 and $136,543 million in 1985; that of foreign bonds from $1,804 million, $4,357 million, and $31,229 million during the same period (OEEC, *International Capital Markets Statistics, 1950–1995* (Paris, 1996)).

45. M. Baker and M. Collins, 'London as an International Banking Centre, 1950–1980', in Cassis and Bussière (eds.), *London and Paris as International Financial Centres*, 248–53; the gap narrowed in the following years, with 328 foreign banks in London and 234 in New York in 1979.

46. Consortium banks were institutions set up by groups of banks of different nationalities within the framework of strategic alliances. The Orion Bank, founded in 1970 (Chase Manhattan Bank, the National Westminster Bank, the Royal Bank of Canada, the Westdeutsche Landesbank Gironzentrale, the Credito Italiano, and the Mitsubishi Bank were its main shareholders), became the most important among them. Most disappeared in the 1980s, victims of their parent companies' diverging goals; see R. Roberts, *Take your Partners: Orion, the Consortium Banks and the Transformation of the Euromarkets* (Basingstoke, 2001).

47. Figures from Maddison, *Dynamic Forces in Capitalist Development*, 198–9.

48. S. Eken, 'Integration of Domestic and International Financial Markets: The Japanese Experience', *International Monetary Fund Staff Papers*, 33/3 (1984), 501–3.

49. K. M. Dominguez, 'The Role of the Yen', in M. Feldstein (ed.), *International Capital Flows* (Chicago, 1999), 145.

50. See K. Burk, 'Money and Power: The Shift from Great Britain to the United States', in Y. Cassis (ed.), *Finance and Financiers in European History, 1880–1960* (Cambridge, 1992), 359–69.

51. See D. R. Lessard, 'Singapore as an International Financial Centre' in R. Roberts (ed.), *Offshore Financial Centres* (Aldershot, 1994), 200–35.

52. These measures included abolishing the 40% withholding tax on income from investments by non-residents in 1968, the 20% liquidity ratio imposed on Asian currency units in 1972, which brought them into line with current practice on the European Eurocurrency markets, and, more generally, the controlled opening-up of borders to foreign banks and financial institutions.

53. The first issue of Asian dollar bonds took place in Singapore in 1971—$10 million on behalf of the Development Bank of Singapore, a publicly owned bank—followed in 1972 by an issue for $100 million on behalf of the Republic of Singapore.

54. Lessard, 'Singapore as an International Financial Centre'.

55. Y. S. Park, 'A Comparison of Hong Kong and Singapore as Asian Financial Centres', in P. D. Grub et al. (eds.), *East Asia Dimension of International Business* (Sydney, 1982), 21–8.

56. Y. C. Jao, 'Hong Kong as an International Financial Centre: Evolution and Prospects', in *The Asian NIEs: Success and Challenge* (Hong Kong, 1983), 39–82; R. Roberts, *Inside International Finance* (London, 1998).

57. See Roberts, *Inside International Finance*; Cassis, *Capitals of Capital*.

58. M. Obstfeld and A. M. Taylor, *Global Capital Markets: Integration, Crisis and Growth* (Cambridge, 2004), 53.

59. *Financial Times*.

60. World Bank, *World Development Indicators* (various years).

61. See N. Ferguson and M. Schularick, 'The End of Chimerica', Harvard Business School Working Paper 10-037 (2009).

62. For a discussion of this challenge, see M. Wolf, *Fixing Global Finance* (New Haven and London, 2009).